D0344437

A BRIEF HISTORY OF ENTREPRENEURSHIP

A BRIEF HISTORY OF ENTREPRENEURSHIP

The Pioneers,
Profiteers,
and Racketeers
Who Shaped
Our World

JOE CARLEN

Columbia University Press
Publishers Since 1893
New York   Chichester, West Sussex
cup.columbia.edu

Copyright © 2016 Joe Carlen
All rights reserved

Library of Congress Cataloging-in-Publication Data
Names: Carlen, Joe, author.
Title: A brief history of entrepreneurship : the pioneers, profiteers,
and racketeers who shaped our world / Joe Carlen.
Description: New York : Columbia University Press, [2016] |
Series: Columbia Business School Publishing | Includes bibliographical
references and index.
Identifiers: LCCN 2016014620 | ISBN 9780231173049 (cloth : alk. paper)
Subjects: LCSH: Commerce—History. | Entrepreneurship—History. |
Businesspeople—History.
Classification: LCC HF352 .C37 2016 | DDC 338/.0409—dc23
LC record available at https://lccn.loc.gov/2016014620

Columbia University Press books are printed on permanent
and durable acid-free paper.

Printed in the United States of America

c 10 9 8 7 6 5 4 3 2 1

Cover design: Faceout Studio/Kara Davidson
Cover image: © Shutterstock

CONTENTS

A BRIEF HISTORY OF ENTREPRENEURSHIP

Introduction

In 1985, Peter Drucker, the late management expert, defined entrepreneurship as "the act that endows resources with a new capacity to create wealth,"[1] among the most specific and meaningful definitions of the term. More literally, the words "entrepreneurship" and "enterprise" both derive from the Old French word for "an undertaking," *entrependre*. Yet even in French, the related word *entrepreneur* did not take on its current meaning until the economist Jean-Baptiste Say so imbued it in 1800.

In the English language, until the mid-nineteenth century, when the French term *entrepreneur* began to enjoy common usage outside France, the term *undertaker* (a literal translation of the French word) was sometimes used in its stead. More frequently, however, the more evocative term "adventurer" was preferred. In this vein, the American economist William Baumol once defined the entrepreneur as "the individual willing to embark on adventure in pursuit of economic goals."[2] These individuals and the often unintended impact of their adventures on the course of world history are the focus of this book.

Conducting research into this subject, I was particularly intrigued by such examples as Mesopotamian merchants' creation of the urban market economy, Chinese tea traders' ingenious invention of "flying" (i.e., paper) money, the central role of the entrepreneur in the onslaught of European colonization from the sixteenth through the nineteenth centuries, and the current "flattening" of the world's economic playing field—from Cameroon to Cambodia—a product of the modern entrepreneur's quest for cheaper labor and larger markets.

Throughout history, the entrepreneur's ceaseless quest to discover and/or develop new markets has been pursued through a variety of means, all of which have had an enormous impact on society. Among others, these methods have included overland and overseas trade, radical innovation of both products and processes, social engineering, territorial conquest, and most recently, interplanetary travel in the form of space tourism for the ultrarich. So while this book does not posit a moral argument for or against entrepreneurship, it does argue that it has been a "prime mover," an instigator of seminal transformations that have altered the course of history.

Often, these transformations have extended beyond the realm of commerce. Some, such as Phoenician merchants' colonization of the Mediterranean and the intercontinental Greek and Roman Empires that followed in Phoenicia's wake, were primarily geopolitical. Others, like the impact of the British inventor-entrepreneurs behind the Industrial Revolution, were more sociological. Others still, such as Mesopotamian merchants' invention of the shareholder-owned enterprise, developed further by Islamic civilization during the Middle Ages, or the commercialization of African American music, all generated an impact that extended across multiple facets of life.

It is also instructive to learn how entrepreneurship, often kindled by a streak of rebellion, interacted and even struggled with more entrenched aspects of society. Among other examples, this principle is illustrated by the array of entrepreneurial activities undertaken by slaves and recently freed men during the heyday of the Roman Empire and the impact of such enterprise on ancient Rome. Or, more recently, the increasingly Asian, Latin American, and African origins of many twenty-first-century entrepreneurs and their role in blurring, and in some instances even collapsing, the once stark contrasts between the "developing" and "developed" worlds. Indeed the spirit of entrepreneurship is often disruptive, even explosive.

Moreover, as entrepreneurs have helped spur momentous social, economic, technological, and other changes around them, the nature of entrepreneurship itself has been changing. Consequently, this book also discusses the evolving role of the entrepreneur throughout history. For example, as we see in the first chapter, in prehistoric and Mesopotamian times, almost all those seeking "new markets" were traders, while in the succeeding chapter about the Phoenicians, one learns of how entrepreneurial activities began to broaden into the production of finished goods and even a form of commercial colonization.

In the periods covered by subsequent chapters, entrepreneurs also became practitioners of "purposeful innovation," cross-pollinators, and evangelizers. One also sees how, over time, these once distinct functions have coalesced into the multifaceted and multidisciplinary role of the modern entrepreneur. So in the process of learning about the history of entrepreneurship and its role in shaping our world, one also gains a deeper understanding of each of its vital components. It is a timely era in which to examine this phenomenon; in our interconnected twenty-first-century global economy, the promise, perils, and impact of entrepreneurship have never been more pronounced.

1

"One Shekel of Your Private Silver"

Here's an excerpt from a letter to the editor titled "History Lesson," published in 2014 in *Entrepreneur* magazine: "I was stunned to read your editorial in which you stated: 'It is only within the last 20 years that entrepreneurship has become the aspirational journey and holy grail of . . . inspired and fearless youth.' I hope you meant the last *200* years. The railroads opened the West to thousands of entrepreneurs who made their fortunes with shops, restaurants and services they built."[1] The central point of that letter is valid, but entrepreneurship reaches back much further than the writer realizes. In fact, the "aspirational journey" of the entrepreneur is neither twenty nor two hundred years old. Rather, it is a voyage that began at least twenty *thousand* years ago.

Primitive Barter

Evidence exists of barter, in various forms, and even small-scale trade of luxury items as far back as twenty to thirty thousand years ago, well into prehistoric times. During this era, known as the Upper Paleolithic period and the end of the Stone Age, human life was brief, transient, and mostly carnivorous. The primary social unit, the tribe, organized most of its activities around the principal objective of hunting game. This often involved extended treks following the seasonal migrations of the tribe's prey. During this period, as the earth emerged from an ice age, some regions teemed with deer, mammoths, bison, and other game animals. The meat of these large mammals was the primary staple of the human diet.

Clearly, the advent of agriculture, let alone urban commerce, still lay thousands of years ahead. Nonetheless, despite these limitations, it seems that the entrepreneurial impulse still found expression among some of the more enterprising tribes. This is illustrated in a study of prehistoric south and southwest Asia, focusing primarily on the region that is present-day India, Pakistan, Bangladesh, and Sri Lanka. The study indicates that, in the Upper Paleolithic period, "the occurrence of marine shell and ostrich eggshell in the Tapti valley, far from the sea and the habitat of ostriches, indicates that exchange of luxury items from distant regions was initiated in some regional sub traditions."[2]

However, such exchanges were not limited to luxury items. In modern usage, the anthropological term "Stone Age" usually connotes savagery and backwardness. While there is plenty of evidence to support the first association, the same archaeological record actually reveals a time of technological progress, not stagnation. In fact, the Stone Age and the Upper Paleolithic period in particular, was when human ingenuity molded stone, wood, and other elemental materials into devices for hunting prey and waging war against rival tribes. To this end, spears, knives, chisels, and rudimentary fishing equipment were invented and continually improved upon.

In twenty-first-century global business, financial survival can depend upon a technological advantage, even a seemingly slight one, over a company's competitors. In the late Paleolithic era, the *physical* survival of one's tribe could hinge upon a technological edge in any of the vital tools and weapons of the time. So, among friendly tribes, such tools were bartered, alongside hunting dogs, luxury items, and a certain essential prized by the men of these tribes—women. There is evidence to suggest that men would sometimes barter their mates with other men, as deplorable as that may seem from a modern-day Western perspective.

For thousands of years, the scorecard for entrepreneurial performance has been money. Nonetheless, the historical record of the late Paleolithic era reveals that a primitive form of entrepreneurship preceded the advent of currency or even protocurrencies like unstamped gold and silver. After all, it is likely that the tribe with the highest quantity and quality of tools, weapons, hunting dogs, and ornamental items, and the most desirable women was more enterprising than a tribe that lacked one or more of those coveted "goods."

The Fertile Crescent

An expanse extending from the southwestern edge of modern Iran to Egypt's Nile valley, the Fertile Crescent was the scene of two critical developments: the agricultural revolution that enabled the first permanent human settlements and the advent of urban commerce that followed. Due to the arc of its course—extending northwest through much of modern-day Iraq, eastern Syria, and southern Turkey, then turning southwest through western Syria, Lebanon, Israel, and, finally, the Nile valley—the region is referred to as a "crescent." However, it is the first part of its name, "fertile," that speaks to its more significant attribute.

The region was home to abundant sources of fresh water, large grasslands and forests, and soil rich in silt from the frequent springtime flooding of the Tigris and Euphrates Rivers. Blessed with such plenty, it is not surprising that the Fertile Crescent was where sustained domestication of vital food sources, both plant and animal, first took place. Most likely beginning in modern-day Kurdistan/northern Iraq and then, over time, spreading to other parts of the Fertile Crescent, men began to domesticate the goats and sheep that grazed on the region's bountiful grasslands. Meanwhile, women of the same tribes, no longer compelled to accompany their men on long migratory hunting voyages, began domesticating plants.

The plants of choice were the wild, yet nourishing grains that grew tall in the fertile soil along the Tigris and Euphrates Rivers, in the ancient region of modern-day Iraq known as Mesopotamia. Soon, these hearty varieties of barley and wheat, along with lentils and other legumes, would be domesticated by the women of the region. Nourishing crops could now be grown successfully and more or less predictably. Over time, particularly in southern Mesopotamia, the agricultural yield improved considerably with the advent of irrigation and related processes, such as flood control.

Meanwhile, other nearby sources of food, domesticated animals, their by-products, and fish, were also being harvested. Consequently, a domestic human experience characterized by permanent agricultural settlements began to replace the nomadic hunting of previous generations. The profound implications of this more settled lifestyle would soon become apparent. No longer forced to hunt all day for subsistence, these more sedentary humans began developing the specialized skills that laid the basis for a more sophisticated society, including a larger and more diversified economy.

Regarding the latter, the archaeological evidence reveals that as early as the fifth millennium B.C.E., Mesopotamia was already importing goods from (and presumably exporting goods to) such distant regions as the Caucasus Mountains and modern-day Afghanistan. However, it was not until the latter half of the fourth millennium B.C.E. that Mesopotamia, beginning with the nation of Sumer, developed into an advanced civilization. Subsequently, for more than two thousand years, Mesopotamia was home to the dominant economic and military powers of the Middle East, rivaled only by another highly advanced civilization on the opposite edge of the region, ancient Egypt. A military and economic juggernaut and the site of unparalleled feats of engineering, during its heyday, the latter was one of the region's two great civilizations.

However, it was the other, older, civilization, Mesopotamia, where entrepreneurship evolved during this period of antiquity. This, in large part, is due to the distinction that it was the Sumerians, not the Egyptians, who developed the first cities. Moreover, while the economic activities of ancient Egypt were considerable, they were not only regulated but *directed* by a government that in modern terms would be described as totalitarian. The administration of the pharaoh controlled not only the means of production, but distribution and even consumption were tightly run bureaucratic operations as well. There was little tolerance, let alone incentive, for individual initiative in Egypt. Yet such initiative was encouraged and often rewarded handsomely in the more autonomous city-states of Mesopotamia.

Mesopotamia: Land of Sumer, Akkad, Babylonia, and Assyria

In the span of time addressed by this chapter, Mesopotamia was home to four successive, and in some instances overlapping, civilizations—Sumer, Akkad, Babylonia, and Assyria. Each had its moment as the leading power in the Fertile Crescent, with the latter two attaining dominance over the wider region as well. Emerging from the prehistoric period, early Mesopotamian history revolves around the Sumerians, a people distinguished by an unusual language and a highly sophisticated culture. Settled in lower Mesopotamia, this distinctive ethnic group established the land of Sumer and dominated the region for several hundred years until a Semitic people, the Akkadians, emerged from the west.

At its zenith under Sargon, Akkad vied with Sumer for supremacy over Mesopotamia. Nonetheless, a hybrid Mesopotamian culture developed, incorporating both Sumerian and Akkadian influences. Toward the end of the third millennium B.C.E., the Sumerians reclaimed their regional supremacy from their rivals, thereby ushering in the Neo-Sumerian period. Soon afterward, during the early stages of the second millennium, the Sumerians would blend in with the emerging civilization of lower Mesopotamia, Babylonia. Descendants of the Akkadians, the Babylonians established one of the most powerful civilizations in the region—one that preserved many aspects of the Sumerian culture they supplanted.

Meanwhile, the northern city-state of Ashur was expanding into the nation-state of Assyria. During the first half of the first millennium, both Babylon, as the Neo-Babylonian Empire, and the Assyrian Empire would reach their respective pinnacles of military and economic power. Within the various Mesopotamian realms, the city-states of these civilizations exercised varying degrees of autonomy and often conducted their affairs more in the manner of a confederacy than a unified nation-state. Nonetheless, there were definite ties of language, culture, religion (e.g., the Babylonian god of justice, Shamash), commerce, and during some periods, ties of common legal practices and military service that bound the peoples of these affiliated city-states together.

Another common thread of Mesopotamian civilization throughout its lengthy and ethnically varied heyday was inventiveness. The Mesopotamians pioneered a sophisticated system of measurements and weights, in part to accommodate their civilization's expanding level of commercial activity. Some aspects of this sexagesimal system have proved enduring, such as the 24-hour day, the division of an hour into sixty equal parts, and purchasing goods by the dozen.

However, it was the conception of the first system of writing that was, arguably, the most significant intellectual breakthrough of antiquity. There is evidence that some form of etched pictorial representation emerged in prehistoric Mesopotamia and Persia, albeit for a limited set of symbols, such as earth and water. Moreover, it is a later civilization, the Phoenicians, who are believed to have invented the first Western-style or "phonetic" alphabet, composed of symbols representing each letter that could then be combined to represent the full range of linguistic sounds.

Nonetheless, circa 3300 B.C.E., long before the Phoenicians even existed, it was the Mesopotamians who developed a set of syllable symbols.

This innovative leap, well beyond the bounds of mere pictorial art but not as efficient as letter symbols, is known as cuneiform ("wedge-shaped") script. The basis of the first viable writing system, cuneiform facilitated many of this ancient civilization's great advances in commerce and finance.

As well, the implementation of this ingenious new communication tool involved clever use of the region's abundant clay, molded into writing tablets, and marsh reeds, fashioned into writing styluses. A highly imaginative civilization, it is not surprising that Mesopotamia proceeded to elevate writing into the fine art of literature. Its literary classics include captivating legends that reveal much about its view of the universe, from its unique pantheon of deities, to the Mesopotamian creation story, to perhaps most intriguingly, the first written account of the Great Flood.

The Mesopotamian account is remarkably similar to the story of Noah's Ark in the book of Genesis, written several hundred years later. In fact, the *Epic of Gilgamesh* still stands as the best illustration of Mesopotamia's mastery of storytelling and its society's fascination with metaphysics:

> Anu granted him the totality of knowledge of all.
> He saw the Secret, discovered the Hidden,
> He brought information of (the time) before the Flood.[3]

With respect to the "hidden secrets" of life, Western astrology is deeply rooted in the works of this ancient civilization. In fact, hundreds of years after Mesopotamia's demise, the Romans would still refer to astrology as "Babylonian numbers." Mesopotamia's contributions to the less esoteric discipline of astronomy were just as significant; the seven-day week, with a day dedicated to each of the seven planets (including the sun and the moon) is a Mesopotamian invention that was adopted in Mediterranean Europe and then spread throughout the continent during the early first millennium C.E.

Mesopotamia was also the site of great advances in sculpture, masonry and carpentry, architecture, plaque engraving, gem cutting, leather working, textile production and garment design, basket making, glass working, and other crafts. Some of these were older occupations that the Mesopotamians merely refined, but others, such as brewing beer (another enduring Mesopotamian invention), were entirely novel. Weaponry and other forms of metalworking also grew far more sophisticated in the able hands of these inventive people.

In fact, bronze, the alloy of copper and tin for which this historical period is named, was the brainchild of Mesopotamian metallurgists, likely discovered around 2900 B.C.E. Roughly five hundred years earlier, Sumerian pottery makers revolutionized *their* craft with the potter's wheel, an invention with ramifications extending well beyond the realm of pottery making. Considering that the earliest evidence of the wheel being used for transportation purposes is from Mesopotamia circa 3200 B.C.E., it is likely that this more celebrated application of the invention is yet another enduring legacy of this extraordinarily creative civilization.

There are not many inventions as foundational to modern civilization as writing and the wheel, but the city, the primary setting of civilization's social, technological, and commercial development, is certainly one of them. Remarkably, Mesopotamia lays claim to the advent of urban life as well. It was in these ancient cities, now buried in the sands of southern Iraq, that the entrepreneur emerged as a leading, often *determining*, influence on the course of history.

A Bustling Metropolis

Toward the eastern edge of the Fertile Crescent, in what is now southeastern Iraq, the abandoned remnants of the "cradle of civilization" can be found. These are the ancient dwellings (royal and otherwise), cemeteries, temples, and other structures from the majestic city-states of ancient Mesopotamia. Although some of these communities did not develop into what we would describe as cities until the fourth millennium B.C.E., town-sized settlements in the vicinity of the future sites of the great cities of Uruk, Ur, and others date as far back as the later centuries of the sixth millennium B.C.E.

An impressively fertile society, Sumer required the implementation of increasingly productive agricultural methods to support its growing population. The most significant and lasting of these were irrigation and drainage. Given that a large and well-disciplined workforce was required to execute these methods effectively, this innovative society developed a more powerful regional government, a communal temple-centered religion, and a well-defined social hierarchy. These institutions ensured that this new "miracle" of regimented, large-scale food production would be adequately supplied, staffed, and supervised. In the process of organizing society to better harness the region's agriculture, an urban civilization was born. The transformation from rural agrarianism to urban commerce took place during the Uruk period of Sumerian history, an era that began almost 5,500 years ago.

Most importantly, during that period, small settlements steadily expanded into the urban centers of Uruk, Nippur, Kish, Lagash, Larsa, Adab, Isin, Eridu, and the most renowned Sumerian city of all, Ur. As the late Mesopotamian scholar Leo Oppenheim observed, "The center of urbanization lay in Southern Mesopotamia . . . there alone within the entire ancient Near East spontaneous urbanization took place."[4] A number of elements of Sumerian city life stood in stark contrast to previous forms of human settlement. Some of these were visual, like municipal planning and groundbreaking architectural achievements such as the *ziggurat* ("to build higher") and the Hanging Gardens of Babylon.

Others, though less immediately apparent, were equally momentous. Among the most significant of these was the new urban workplace, the setting of unprecedented economic mobility and occupational diversity. Of course, there was little of either in the agrarian settlements from which these cities sprang. In those communities, almost all residents were engaged in some form of subsistence farming—planting and harvesting crops or tending to livestock. However, cities like Kish and Ur were the sites of a remarkable degree of labor specialization as new industries emerged and older ones evolved into full-time occupations.

These new occupations included metalworking, ale brewing, boat-building, leather working/textile production, various forms of scientific research, a large civil service, stone masonry, pottery making, butchery, weaving, baking, gemology, weapons production, representational art, divinity, architecture, law, and writing. For the first time in human history,

Figure 1.1
Ur of Caldea, ziggurat. *Source:* Obtained (with Creative Commons permission to reuse) from Google Images, Wikipedia.

a varied labor pool became the norm. The Mesopotamian worker recognized that unlike the relative stability of subsistence farming, the dynamism of the new urban workplace meant that both the ceiling and the floor of potential income and wealth had been removed.

Regarding some excavated ancient texts, Oppenheim observed that with respect to Mesopotamian society, they reveal "a remarkable degree of economic mobility: poor people expect to become rich: the rich are afraid of becoming poor."[5] Many of these nouveaux riches envied by the poor and, in some instances, also feared by government administrators, were Mesopotamia's merchant-entrepreneurs. The twin pillars of economic mobility and labor specialization that characterized the ancient Sumerian workplace have since become two of the defining characteristics of urban capitalism.

Merchant-Entrepreneurs

Without the creative vigor and aggressive expansionism of Mesopotamia's entrepreneurial class, the new legions of artisans and craftspeople would have had neither sufficient supplies nor buyers for their wares. These were the enterprising tradesmen whom the renowned Near Eastern scholar Samuel Kramer referred to as "the venturesome merchant-entrepreneurs."[6] They traversed vast distances and, especially in the early stages, took on considerable risks to establish and widen the pipelines of trade between their native land and all regions of the known world. As with many of the crafts and professions discussed earlier, most of these merchant-entrepreneurs were part of a new phenomenon—the professional full-time trader.

Prior to Mesopotamia, there had been people, usually grouped in tribes, who had traded something that they had hunted or created in exchange for what was desired from another tribe. However, the concept of a professional intermediary who did not actually produce any portion of what he traded was both novel and highly entrepreneurial. Per Peter Drucker's definition of entrepreneurship, this new profession of the Mesopotamians was certainly "endowing resources with a new capacity to create wealth"[7] by identifying and cultivating new markets for Mesopotamia's resources. The middleman, a controversial fixture of Western commerce ever since, was born.

While personal wealth was the primary purpose of these endeavors, the primary *outcome*, as discussed later, was far more lasting and profound. Since Mesopotamia was the breadbasket of the known world, foreign peoples near and far were eager to trade with this unusual urban civilization. Due to its unique natural blessings, enhanced further by its technological ingenuity, Mesopotamia became recognized as the world's foremost source of grain, along with dates, sesame, and other forms of produce.

The well-irrigated land also yielded a number of other essential raw materials. These included rich mud and clay (often fashioned into building bricks and the region's famed pottery); reeds (an important component of furniture); writing styluses; bountiful harvests of fish and marsh fowl; and the sheep grazing on lush Mesopotamian pastures. Yet, other regions had blessings of their own, some of which were in short supply in the city-states of Mesopotamia. "Long-distance foreign trade, however, was essential to the Mesopotamian cities," Kramer observed. "For while they produced grain in surplus and their herds of sheep provided an overabundance of wool, the Mesopotamians had insufficient timber, stone or metal for building or for the luxuries craved by the temples, palaces, wealthy estates and by their citizens at large."[8]

Regarding such luxuries, much has been learned by the artifacts unearthed in the Sumerian city of Ur by the esteemed British archaeologist Sir Leonard Woolley. For example, among Woolley's findings was a statuette of a billy goat that featured various precious and semiprecious stones. Remarkably, archaeologists have traced the origins of the lapis lazuli on that Mesopotamian figurine to a mountain range located in modern-day northern Pakistan—more than 1,850 miles away. As noted earlier, Sumer is the first of the major Mesopotamian civilizations. So it is a remarkable testament to the pioneering spirit of the merchant-entrepreneur that Mesopotamia established the overland trade route between west and east Asia at least 2,700 years before China's Silk Road.

The merchant-entrepreneurs capitalized upon all aspects of their fellow citizens' needs with admirable resourcefulness and industry. From the sturdy timber found in the forests of modern-day Syria and Lebanon to the more luxurious items found farther abroad, they spared no effort in obtaining the wares that adorned the walls and persons of Mesopotamia. Moreover, recognizing that some foreign peoples had a wider variety of natural goods to trade, they proceeded to leverage Mesopotamia's advanced level of craftsmanship to develop high-value finished goods that could not be produced elsewhere.

This marked the advent of an important new form of entrepreneurship, the production and trade of added-value goods. In exchange for these manufactured goods, along with grain, wool, and in some instances,

Mesopotamian slaves, gold and silver were brought in from Egypt; wood from Persia and the Levant; ivory, spices, and other luxury materials from Nubia (a kingdom that extended across present-day northern Sudan and southern Egypt) and the Indus valley (modern-day India); and copper from Anatolia (modern-day Turkey). Given the wide variety of surrounding terrain and the different types of goods conveyed to and from those regions, Mesopotamia's merchants devised transportation methods for each pipeline of foreign trade.

For example, caravans of well-packed donkeys would transport gems of various sorts from Africa, while boats full of heavy grain were sent up the river and returned from Anatolia stocked with metals. In fact, the merchant-entrepreneurs' maritime trade in copper and other ores was so vast that, at the time, the Euphrates River was known as the "Urudu," the "Copper River." A Hebrew prophet described the Euphrates thus: "And by great waters the seed of Sihor, the harvest of the river, is her revenue; and she [Mesopotamia] is a mart of nations."[9]

Certainly, the trade undertaken by Mesopotamia's entrepreneurs was unprecedented in terms of geography, volume, and diversity. As the British archaeologist Jacquetta Hawkes noted with respect to the impact of this unprecedented volume of trade on other aspects of commercial life, "Foreign trade also served to stimulate the development of an astonishingly sophisticated financial system . . . that greatly encouraged the enterprise of merchants and traders."[10] Indeed, it was not only the extent but the *sophistication* of this trade that proceeded to reshape various aspects of commerce—including entrepreneurship—in ways that have endured ever since.

The following excerpt from a cuneiform tablet pertains to four aspects of commerce—the use of contracts, credit, and currency, and the establishment of merchant guilds:

> Thirty years ago, you left the city of Assur. You have never made a deposit since, and we have not recovered one shekel of silver from you, but we have never made you feel bad about this. Our tablets have been going to you with caravan after caravan, but no report from you has ever come here. We have addressed claims to your father but we have not been claiming one shekel of your private silver. Please, do come back right away; should you be too busy with your business, deposit the silver for us. (Remember) we have never made you feel bad about this matter but we are now forced to appear, in your eyes,

acting as gentlemen should not. If not, we will send you a notice from the local ruler and the police, and thus put you to shame in the assembly of merchants. You will also cease to be one of us.[11]

The Advent of Credit

The merchant-entrepreneurs played a pivotal role in the development, and possibly even the *advent*, of credit. Mesopotamia left a rich historical record of its financial past in the many cuneiform tablets that have been unearthed, giving us a glimpse into the civilization's commercial practices. Nonetheless, as the American anthropologist David Graeber observed, "The origins of interest [i.e., debt interest] will forever remain obscure, since they preceded the invention of writing."[12] That said, in the context of Mesopotamia's emergence as the first urban civilization, it remains likely that great culture was the point of origin for credit contracts and other financial innovations. Moreover, it is certain that its merchants were responsible for the refinement of these methods and their promulgation throughout the Bronze Age world.

The Merchant-Capitalists and the Development of New Financial Instruments

As Jacquetta Hawkes noted in *The First Great Civilizations*, "Much of the power that drove Mesopotamian trade so forcefully along the land and water thoroughfares was the institution of credit, and particularly credit at interest. It was in this way that the merchant capitalist financed the merchant adventurer."[13] During the Old Babylonian period, the former was known as the *tamkarun*, a man who tended to put his capital to work before engaging it himself. Often acting as a banker, the *tamkarun* would often finance the expeditions of other merchants.

Even when he decided to undertake a trading enterprise alone, the merchant-capitalist would employ *shamallu*, agents who were entrusted with most, if not all, of the legwork. In the context of intrigue involving a prominent Mesopotamian merchant, the employ of *shamallu* is referred to in the following excerpt from a clay tablet dated to the Old Assyrian period:

> We closely questioned Iddissin, the transport agent of the house of Enna-Sin, and he declared: "They keep the boss in seclusion." For this

reason, we have sent word to Belum-bani to take care of your affairs. You need not be worried about your consignment and that of the merchant.[14]

By the time of Hammurabi, the Babylonian king who united all of Mesopotamia under his reign during the eighteenth century B.C.E., the activities of the merchant-capitalist had become so pervasive that they were addressed explicitly in his renowned legal code. For example, the Code of Hammurabi's 102nd law stipulates that "if a merchant entrust money to an agent (broker) for some investment, and the broker suffer a loss in the place to which he goes, he shall make good the capital to the merchant."[15] Generally speaking, the failure of a Mesopotamian to "make good" on any kind of loan carried severe repercussions. For especially large unpaid debts, it was not uncommon to serve as a slave to one's creditor for up to three years.

I attended a presentation back in 2007 at which a prominent commercial real estate financier, pointing to several tables and figures on the board in front of him, affirmed that "the modern U.S. economy runs on credit"—a statement that, in light of the events of the following year, proved eerily prescient. The same could be said for the economy of ancient Mesopotamia. As in modern times, an entrepreneur's ambition often exceeded the bounds of his or her financial resources. In this manner, yet another form of entrepreneurship was birthed in "the cradle of civilization," as those with capital proceeded to, per Drucker's definition, endow those financial resources with "a new capacity to create wealth."[16]

This was accomplished by providing their surplus capital to the merchant-adventurers who, from the fruits of their trade and other ventures, could provide the merchant-capitalists with a healthy return on their capital. From a twenty-first-century perspective, both the variety and the complexity of the financial agreements and instruments that represented these transfers of capital are striking. Among these was an arrangement akin to what is known today as the "letter of credit" (LOC). Typically, the Mesopotamian LOC would operate as follows: With assigned agents, the *shamallu*, stationed along his route, a trader, typically carrying barley, wheat, and/or wool, would set forth to a particular city. Upon reaching his destination, he would unload part or all of his cargo in exchange for signed tablets indicating the value of the delivery, usually quantified in shekels of silver. The trader could then utilize the tablets in a number of ways. They could be exchanged directly for goods or for other tablets, ensuring the delivery of goods at a subsequent point of the trade route. Most importantly, should the trader elect to obtain the silver, the agents stationed along the route were obligated to cash out any or all of the trader's tablets.

In this respect, it is also worth noting that an early version of the forward contract, what Investopedia.com describes as "the foundation of all derivatives,"[17] also originated in Mesopotamia. This fact is particularly interesting from a twenty-first-century perspective, considering that the worldwide derivatives market is now estimated to exceed $1.2 quadrillion.[18] This figure is more than fifteen times larger than the current estimate of the world's aggregate gross output (GO),[19] a metric encompassing aggregate sales volume at, according to *Forbes*, "all stages of production."[20]

A contract stipulating that the seller must complete delivery of the item(s) in question to the buyer by a certain date and for a specified price, the forward contract effectively allows the buyer to place a bet on something's future value. If a particular commodity becomes more valuable a month from now due to shrinking supply, the buyer is liable to profit from the forward contract. Conversely, if the value of the commodity in question declines after the contract is sealed, it is the seller who has benefited from the contract.

Curiously, these contracts first appeared in the form of baked clay vessels enclosing clay tokens and various markings delineating all of the terms of the contract (e.g., the number of tokens represented the agreed-upon price), which were sealed by the mark of a witness. The terms would also be marked on the surface of the vessel, but if a dispute arose and there was any suspicion that the terms written on the surface had been altered, the baked vessel would be broken open and its contents would be consulted as the definitive tamper-proof record of the contract.

The level of sophistication, planning, and organization behind the creation of all of these innovative and enduring financial instruments is a remarkable testament to the creativity and resourcefulness of Mesopotamia's merchants. As well, it would have been almost impossible to implement and enforce such instruments without the advent of the contract itself, a development with immeasurable commercial ramifications. Although there are still a few holdouts in certain traditional societies, in the twenty-first century the contract is a standard tool of business transactions, no matter how large or small.

However, other capital-allocation mechanisms were fairly routine loans, for example, a notary-approved agreement that the borrower would repay the principal (along with total interest calculated by a fixed interest rate) to the lender within a clearly defined time frame. Moreover, particularly in the early stages of Mesopotamian civilization, some of these loans were granted by palace and temple bureaucrats. The decidedly clear-cut nature of such contracts reflected the suspicion with which these bureaucrats viewed the merchant class. Conversely, due to similarities of class and occupation, the higher level of trust and kinship between merchants allowed for more expansive and sophisticated financial arrangements.

The Merchant Guilds

Belanum sends the following message: May the god Shamash [the Babylonian god of the sun] keep you in good health. Make ready for me the myrtle and the sweet-smelling reeds of which I spoke to you, as well as a boat for (transporting) wine to the city of Sippar. Buy and bring along with you ten silver shekels' worth of wine and join me here in Babylon sometime tomorrow.[21]

Throughout the initial period of Sumerian dominance, until the emergence of Akkad in the twenty-third century B.C.E., both the government and the temple of the Sumerian city-states were often involved in the conduct of Mesopotamia's vast foreign trade. However, by the Old Babylonian period, such powers were now the domain of private entrepreneurs. As Mesopotamia outgrew the vestiges of its Sumerian origins, the *karu*, guilds organized by and for Mesopotamian merchants, began to assume powers that were once held by civil and religious officials. As long as palace officials received their custom dues and temple officials received their tithes, the *karu* were allowed to handle these affairs.

The relationship between Mesopotamia's governing powers and its ascendant merchant class evolved in a peculiar manner, one that would be repeated in subsequent entrepreneurial civilizations. As mentioned previously, Mesopotamian officials viewed the merchant-entrepreneurs with a mix of condescension and suspicion. However, over time the administrators recognized that despite the undignified manners of some of these upstart merchants, their well-established networks of trade supplied much of the revenue that both the palace and the temple had come to rely upon.

So, gradually and grudgingly, Mesopotamian officialdom loosened its grip on the organization of commercial activity as the power of these merchant assemblies expanded. Indeed, in many city-states, the *karu* became a kind of autonomous, if only semiofficial, governing body for the commercial affairs of society. Perhaps to underscore their independence and/or to ensure a higher degree of privacy than could be expected within the crowded confines of Mesopotamian cities, the guilds were often situated just outside the fortified walls of Ur and other large Mesopotamian city-states. In modern terms, the function of the *karu* could be described as a sort of combined chamber of commerce/commercial bank/venture capital firm.

Just as membership in a twenty-first-century chamber of commerce offers (or at least promises) business owners a certain level of respectability and regular networking opportunities, membership in one of Mesopotamia's "assembly of merchants" granted benefits to the merchant-entrepreneurs that were similar in some respects. However, the deep sense of kinship that is evident from the clay tablet excerpt quoted at the beginning of this section reveals that the interactions between *karu* members were probably somewhat more fraternal than the staid and aloof atmosphere of some modern chambers of commerce.

As well, the sense of prestige associated with guild membership was considerable, as reflected in the threat expressed in the concluding sentence of the clay tablet excerpt we looked at earlier: "If not, we will send you a notice from the local ruler and the police, and thus put you to shame in the assembly of merchants. You will also cease to be one of us."[22] Clearly, the writers believed that being ostracized from the *karu* was a threat compelling enough to give pause to their fugitive debtor.

The *Karu*: The Merchants' Combined Commercial Bank/Venture Capital Firm

With respect to banking, the *karu* was the usual setting of lending activity between merchant-capitalists and merchant-adventurers. Moreover, by the second millennium B.C.E., as the palace and temple loosened their once strict control over Mesopotamian trade, the merchant guilds effectively became the primary commercial banking option, with their resident *tamkarun* serving as both loan officers and bankers. It was at the *karu* where the various capital-provision schemes highlighted earlier were developed and executed.

The merchant assembly also witnessed the birth of other pillars of Western entrepreneurship: joint ventures and even a rudimentary form of passive venture capital. Regarding the former, it is important to clarify that Mesopotamian traders braved not only financial uncertainty but also significant physical dangers during their lengthy overland and maritime expeditions. Consequently, by joining with other merchant-adventurers, typically those trading similar goods in similar regions, they were able to form larger caravans. The imposing size of these traveling processions was more daunting to the roaming bandits of the era than a solitary merchant and his wares.

Moreover, by pooling their resources with others, the merchants found that not only were their travels safer, but their trade was also less risky and more profitable. As an unofficial conglomerate of sorts, these amalgamated trade expeditions had far more bargaining power and visibility in the marketplace. Both of which factors were, as they remain today, essential ingredients in generating a healthy profit from the exchange of goods in foreign lands. In this manner, a type of joint venture emerged involving multiple active partners, each serving a dual role as both merchant-capitalist and merchant-adventurer.

For example, the written record from Ur reveals that during the Old Babylonian period a large group of merchants who specialized in the import of copper and other ores from Anatolia established large expeditions as joint ventures. Under such an arrangement, all participating merchants would allocate a portion of the necessary resources *and* legwork. Then, at journey's end, all members of the joint venture would partake in the profits. Especially with respect to trading enterprises, this type of joint venture set the standard for the entrepreneurial class in prominent trading civilizations that would follow, including China of the Tang and Song dynasties and various European trading powers.

However, unlike the joint-venture participants, the *tamkarun* usually had little interest in sullying their fine robes with treks through swamps and mountains. They preferred to put their money to work instead. In this manner, the *tamkarun*'s quest for idle profit, coupled with the merchant-adventurer's quest for more resources, led to the central premise of modern finance— passive equity. In Mesopotamia, the merchant-capitalists and/or other parties would enter into agreements with the merchant-adventurers. These contracts would stipulate that the idle party would provide the capital required by the merchant who was undertaking the work and travel. Then, upon conclusion of the trade expedition, the profits would be split between the two parties.

As the classics scholar Stephen Bertman observed, "Their [Mesopotamian merchants'] commercial ventures were sometimes financed by loans from temple priesthoods or wealthy individuals who, in turn, were rewarded with interest on their financial investment or a share of the profits."[23] Such an arrangement is what would be described today as a kind of limited partnership involving both a passive and an active partner. It is particularly notable that in some ventures, the emergence of this phenomenon in Mesopotamia even involved the investment of multiple passive partners, such as a group of *tamkarun* or temple priests.

Passive equity's origin in Mesopotamia further underscores the lasting impact of the civilization's entrepreneurs. From a group of friends and family putting seed capital into a young entrepreneur's idea to a venture capital firm funding a new cancer diagnostic device, to the world's 120 stock exchanges, passive equity is the operating principle behind so many aspects of modern commercial activity. So it seems appropriate that the principle of profiting through an investment of capital (instead of effort) should have arisen from the original entrepreneurial society, Mesopotamia. Its merchant-capitalists had expanded the boundaries of commerce by discovering novel and profitable ways to put their dormant capital to productive use.

An Unofficial Currency

Mesopotamian merchants also led the way in another important facet of modern commercial life—the regular use and accumulation of money. The monetary term "shekel," mentioned frequently in the Bible, originated from the Mesopotamian monetary system. These shekel-weights (in modern terms, each shekel being roughly equivalent to 8 grams[24]) of barley were Mesopotamia's original medium of exchange and remained so for certain purposes, such as payment to agricultural workers.

Yet over time, particularly among merchants, shekels of silver became the preferred but unofficial currency. (Notably, during the latter periods of Mesopotamian civilization, there were efforts at setting official coinage with less expensive metals, one case of which is found in the following clay tablet inscription dated from 704–681 B.C.E.: "I built clay molds, poured bronze into each and made their figures perfect as in the casting of half-shekel pieces."[25]) However, for many Mesopotamians, actual payment could be made with barley, less expensive metals like tin or copper, or other items.

But the Mesopotamian merchant class preferred the hard currency of silver. In this manner, the merchant-entrepreneurs became the world's first monied class, hoarders of the world's most exchangeable and consequently most useful commodity. Unlike barley, figs, or copper, silver was welcome compensation to the Mesopotamian farmer, the Levantine wood seller, the Anatolian copper miner, and the Indus valley spice grower alike.

The First Commercial Colonies

The commercial life of the known world was, to a great degree, not only dominated but *shaped* by Mesopotamian merchant-entrepreneurs. Just as Latin, Arabic, and English would all in later periods become the international languages of commerce, Akkadian, the language of Babylonian and Assyrian traders, became the preferred means of communication among the merchants of the wider region. In modern times, a transaction between, for example, a Swedish company and a Brazilian company is likely to be transacted in English even though neither of the countries where the two companies operate is officially English speaking. Similarly, from the early third millennium to the early first millennium, a transaction between, for example, Persian and Hebrew traders would have been conducted in that era's lingua franca of commerce, Akkadian.

Certainly, the adoption of their language across the ancient world facilitated the activities of the traveling merchant-entrepreneurs. However, their drive to grow existing foreign markets while developing new ones farther afield called for more drastic initiatives. As early as the fourth millennium B.C.E., Mesopotamian merchants had decided to fortify their trade networks through much of the surrounding region with some strategically located trading outposts. Generally, these were established at or near the source of their most prized imports, such as the Levant, from which cedarwood was obtained, and Anatolia, the primary source of copper and other ores.

The latter was also the site of one of Mesopotamia's largest commercial outposts, Kanesh, in modern-day Kultepe, Turkey. Established around 1900 B.C.E. and situated at the juncture of several well-trafficked trade routes, this outpost grew into a sizable Mesopotamian trading colony and remained so for more than two hundred years. Like the guilds back home, the merchant colony was referred to as a *karum*, one established primarily for the export of Assyrian textiles and the import of Anatolian ores. The Kanesh *karum*, unearthed by Turkish archaeologists during the twentieth century C.E., featured fairly lavish quarters for its Mesopotamian residents. The luxury is not surprising in the context of the large volume of trade conducted at Kanesh and its environs, as recorded in the many cuneiform tablets discovered at the site.

As with the production of manufactured goods discussed earlier, the establishment of colonies such as Kanesh marked the advent of yet another form of entrepreneurship pioneered by the Mesopotamians—commercial colonization.

This particular variety of enterprise generated considerable added value through greater control of both resources and markets. However, the merchant-entrepreneurs did not extend these activities beyond the proliferation of foreign *karum*.

As will be discussed in later chapters, the commercial colonizers of subsequent civilizations employed this tactic far more aggressively. With their respective legions of entrepreneurs leading the charge, the Phoenicians, the Arabs, and the major European powers of the fifteenth to nineteenth centuries would all bring this particular form of enterprise to new heights or depths, depending on one's perspective. Notably, even during the Mesopotamian era, large-scale commercial forays into the lands of foreign peoples were often a source of controversy.

As recorded in the Bible, the Hebrew prophet Nahum, addressing the king of Assyria, proclaimed, "You have increased the number of your merchants till they are more numerous than the stars in the sky, but like locusts they strip the land and then fly away."[26] This would certainly not be the last time that the charge of exploitation would be leveled at foreign entrepreneurs, particularly those representing a large and dominant civilization. In some instances throughout history, the element of exploitation is indisputable.

However, with respect to the merchant-entrepreneurs, the situation is more complex. There is plenty of evidence that Mesopotamian imports were in high demand among many foreign peoples, and they were eager to expand their dealings with the merchant-entrepreneurs. Sir Leonard Woolley's observation regarding merchants from the distant Indian subcontinent is an apt illustration:

> By Sargon's time, if not before (as the seal from the tomb suggests), trade between Sumer and the Indus Valley had attained such proportions that Indian business firms at Mohenjo-daro or other towns there found it worthwhile to have their Indian agents in residence in the towns of the Euphrates Valley.[27]

On the other hand, there is some historical evidence behind Nahum's complaint that the merchant-entrepreneurs would "strip the land and then fly away." For example, the timber trade initiated and eventually controlled by the merchant-entrepreneurs grew to enormous proportions, largely to serve the vigorous demand for wood in Mesopotamia's expanding city-states. This was pursued with so little regard for sustainability that entire forests both west and east of Mesopotamia were cleared permanently.

It is now believed that this widespread logging instigated soil salinization and other environmental hazards in the region.[28]

A Fading Civilization

For better or worse, it is certain that the entrepreneurs of Mesopotamia were a major impetus behind a new way of living. Merchant-entrepreneurs helped instigate and shape the transitions from rural agrarianism to urban commerce and labor specialization and from isolation to international trade. Moreover, by innovating a wide assortment of capital attainment and repayment options, they were pioneers in commercial finance as well. Especially as the Babylonian and Assyrian Empires grew, this system would remake much of the wider region in the image of the Mesopotamian motherland. While neither empire lasted, the system they exported has proven to be remarkably enduring, particularly in the West.

By the sixth century B.C.E., the Assyrian Empire had been overcome by the civilization of the Medes with the eager assistance of Assyria's rival, Babylon. As for the latter, the Babylonian Empire was first conquered by Persia's Cyrus the Great during the fifth century B.C.E. Emblematic of the Persian emperor's deep reverence for Mesopotamian civilizations past and present, he proclaimed himself "king of Babylon, king of Sumer and Akkad, king of the four corners of the world."

The subjugated nation would limp along for another two centuries before its final demise at the hands of another ambitious foreign monarch. In 331 B.C.E., Alexander the Great captured Babylon, where just eight years later, the Macedonian emperor himself would die in the royal palace of Nebuchadnezzar. The sacking of Babylon by a European conqueror symbolized the momentous westward shift in geopolitical power that was already under way. However, with regard to *commercial* power, all of the Mesopotamian nations had long been eclipsed by the Phoenicians, a maritime nation of the eastern Mediterranean who had dominated regional commerce since the eight century B.C.E.

The transformations wrought by Mesopotamia's merchant-entrepreneurs were foundational to the course of human history. In terms of ambition, innovation, execution, and a lasting impact on subsequent civilizations, the merchant-entrepreneurs remain almost unmatched in all of antiquity. Curiously, this legacy would not be challenged by ancient Persia, Egypt, Greece, or even Rome, but by the audacious maritime-entrepreneurs of Phoenicia, the subject of the next chapter.

2

The Pirates of Phoenicia

When your merchandise went out on the seas, you [Phoenicia] satisfied many nations;

With your great wealth and your wares you enriched the kings of the earth.

"A LAMENT FOR TYRE," EZEKIEL 27:33

In the Bible, there are several passages in which the term "Canaanite" is employed interchangeably with the words for "trader" and "merchant." Evidently, among the writers of the Old Testament, the commercial skills of this rival Semitic nation were so impressive that a Canaanite was, by lineage, a cunning and effective merchant. This legendary flair for commerce was most apparent among the Canaanites who had settled north of the Hebrew kingdoms, on an unremarkable sliver of coastal land in modern-day Lebanon and Syria. From this inauspicious starting point, these northerly Canaanites, the Phoenicians, would remake the world of commerce and set the stage for the Greek and Roman intercontinental empires that would follow in their wake.

A Narrow Strip of Land

Necessity being, as Plato first observed, the mother of invention, critical needs of one sort or another have spurred important entrepreneurial developments. As we have seen in Mesopotamia, it was the scarcity of certain metals, timber, and other vital materials that spurred the initial wave of entrepreneurial activity within that society. In Phoenicia, the material shortcomings were even more acute, compelling its residents to take to the seas to obtain what was needed for their survival.

As was the case for Sumer and the Mesopotamian civilizations that succeeded it, Phoenicia operated more like a confederation of city-states than a well-defined nation-state. In fact, the Phoenicians themselves usually identified more with their city-states of origin as opposed to a larger sense of national identity. Nonetheless, they all shared a common tongue, religious heritage, and culture. The latter included a pronounced streak of resourcefulness that would often triumph over complicated logistical challenges.

Confined to a narrow strip of land between the Mediterranean Sea to the west and imposing mountain ranges to the east, the Phoenicians had very little arable land. However, they would discover that the apparent curse of the rocky terrain that kept them hemmed into what were essentially cramped beaches also represented the greatest blessing of their territory. The surrounding mountains were green with lush cedar and cypress forests. With sturdy lumber being in high demand in the rapidly developing Egyptian kingdom, Mesopotamia, and elsewhere, the Phoenicians came to rely on the export of cedar and cypress wood for their survival.

While lumber was often the primary export of the Phoenicians, there were other salable commodities they found and developed in their limited native territory. For example, *Murex* is a type of sea snail that prefers shallow and warm waters, such as those along the eastern Mediterranean coast. The Phoenicians discovered that a valuable purple dye could be extracted from these creatures by removing the sea snails from the water and placing them into large stacks on dry land. As they perished from the heat, each *Murex* would release its dye, which would then coalesce into a bright pool at the bottom of each stack.

This stunning dye and the premium, regal clothing it would be used to make elicited the admiration of other civilizations in the region. In later years, Greek civilization, for one, was so impressed that its writers named the strange sea people bearing these dazzling purple products after their wares. That is how the coastal Canaanite civilization became known as Phoenicia, ancient Greek for "the land of purple."

Another notable Phoenician export was wine. Making good use of the ample hillsides and sunshine that encircled their cities, the Phoenicians established many high-yield vineyards along their coastline. Later, as Phoenician settlements expanded across the wider region, these wine-making skills would help transform some of their new colonies into profit centers, particularly those situated in Greece and modern-day Italy and Spain.

However, from the early third millennium B.C.E., when the urban centers of Baalbek, Byblos, and Tyre were established, until around 1200 B.C.E., Phoenicia was not a colonizing power. Moreover, during that period its network of trade routes rarely extended beyond Egypt, the Hittite Empire to the north (in modern-day Turkey), Cyprus, and the kingdoms of the Hebrews, the Philistines, and other Semitic peoples living at the western edge of Asia Minor.

The Semitic peoples living to the south of Phoenicia were, by and large, farmers and shepherds. Like the merchants of Egypt, those of the Semitic kingdoms had foodstuffs and other products of interest to the Phoenicians. As for Cyprus, the primary attraction for the Phoenicians was the island's abundant copper. With respect to their primary destination, Egypt, Phoenician merchants would traverse a land route via oxcarts; over time, they began to prefer a sea route, crossing over the Mediterranean to Egypt on simple raft-like boats.

In exchange for their prized cedar and cypress wood, the first of Phoenicia's maritime-entrepreneurs obtained vital grains and other necessities from their Egyptian trading partners. This commercial arrangement with a much larger and almost neighboring economy was not particularly remarkable, except for the fact that it was during this period that the Phoenicians honed their legendary boat-building and seafaring skills. By the eleventh century B.C.E., it became evident that these had progressed well beyond the nautical achievements of any previous or contemporaneous civilization.

Nautical Engineers and Seaborne Profiteers

The Phoenician dominance of the sea and its trade stemmed from a combination of technical prowess and mercantile skill. Eager to expand the volume of their wood trade with Egypt and, more generally, to extend their network of business operations farther west, the Phoenicians grew frustrated with the limitations of simple raft-like boats. Particularly since they were transporting lumber, larger and more powerful vessels were needed. Fortunately, they were surrounded by cedarwood, a remarkably sturdy material well suited to the construction of Phoenicia's imposing cargo boats.

Moreover, boatbuilders in the ports of Sidon, Tyre, and Baalbek put their civilization's most renowned invention—the alphabet—to productive use. Each of the main parts of a ship bore the mark of a different letter. In order to spell a word correctly, each section had to be connected in the designated spot on the body of the vessel. This clever word-building exercise of the Phoenicians facilitated the quick and orderly assembly of their fleets. Moreover, these "masters of the sea," as the Greeks described them, devised a number of significant improvements to existing ship design. Collectively, these improvements rank among the most consequential engineering feats of antiquity.

Foremost among these nautical advances was the development of the keel, a large longitudinal plank or set of planks running from a boat's bow to its stern, forming a kind of spinal column for the vessel. With a stiff "backbone" in place, usually held firm with iron nails, these keeled boats could now carry much larger and heavier loads. It would be difficult to overestimate the significance of this seminal innovation. In his *The Phoenicians: The Purple Empire of the Ancient World*, the German documentary filmmaker Gerhard Herm declared that the invention of the keel "was equivalent to that of the wheel in land transport."[1]

Other notable nautical improvements generally credited to the Phoenicians include sharpened rams, the use of metals in ship construction, and watertight boats. Regarding the former, the rams were positioned strategically at the front of the hull to intimidate and, if necessary, thrust through enemy vessels. This technique was so effective that it would be adopted by other Mediterranean powers, including the Etruscans, Greeks, and Romans. In order to remain competitive on the high seas, these rival maritime nations were quick to observe and emulate the best of Phoenicia's nautical advances.

Of course, the Phoenicians were similarly willing to adopt the techniques of surrounding civilizations, but they often did so in innovative ways. Perhaps the best example of this was their use of iron and other metals in shipbuilding. From their trade with the Hittites, the Phoenicians learned of iron smelting and soon became highly proficient in the practice of "ore melting" themselves. It is believed that iron smelting was invented in Anatolia circa 1500 B.C.E., and the Iron Age, the epoch following the Bronze Age of the Mesopotamian era, began in the thirteenth century B.C.E. However, the first use of iron and other metals in shipbuilding is credited to the Phoenicians. Of course, such materials improved both the performance and *durability* of marine vessels, the latter being essential to the marathon seafaring expeditions of Phoenicia's entrepreneurs.

Over time, the Phoenicians fine-tuned these improvements. With respect to watertight boats, the Phoenicians came upon an ingenious caulking method: They would stop up gaps in their vessels with thick and sticky pitch extracted from their cedar and cypress trees. Once a primary impediment to lengthy uninterrupted sea excursions, the problem of water leakages had now been solved. Another noteworthy invention was the dry dock. A structure on which a vessel can be suspended or removed from the water and drained of moisture, a dry dock is an invaluable tool for extending the life of a ship.

The Phoenician-built docks were often situated around a promontory (an elevated ridge projecting over a body of water). This was another important nautical advancement, as it would expand the docking area by allowing ships to moor on each side of the promontory. This partly accounts for why the Phoenicians were known to have the largest shipyards and docking areas of antiquity. There was little of the Phoenicians' maritime infrastructure that was left to chance; their pursuit of nautical excellence was driven mostly by mercantile considerations, not merely a love of boats. For the Phoenicians, no effort was too great and no detail too small in the service of the merchant-sailor fleets.

These seminal advances in nautical engineering, among others, enabled these seafaring Canaanites to take their hereditary knack for profit making well beyond the confines of the eastern Mediterranean. In the early tenth century B.C.E., King Hiram of Tyre, the most powerful of Phoenicia's city-states, assisted King Solomon with the Hebrew monarch's quest for the "gold and silver, ivory, and apes and peacocks"[2] of east sub-Saharan Africa. This nautical journey through the Red Sea involved a fleet that was likely manned by sailors from Phoenicia, more accomplished in the nautical arts than Solomon's subjects. As Herm concluded, "The ships of the squadron were only nominally Israel's; their crews would have been exclusively recruited in Phoenicia."[3]

As with the later renowned sailors of Portugal, those of Phoenicia could be commissioned to undertake a nautical voyage on behalf of another power as long as ample compensation was provided. For example, more than three hundred years after their expedition on behalf of the Hebrew king, the Phoenicians were engaged by Pharaoh Necho to sail southward from Egypt and circumnavigate the African continent. The Phoenicians relished such an unprecedented challenge and proceeded to complete the voyage successfully. Moreover, aside from the Egyptian ruler's largesse, the circumnavigation afforded them the opportunity to scope out new commercial opportunities.

Staying Afloat: A Mercantile State

Unlike the Egyptians, Greeks, and Romans, the enterprising Phoenicians viewed all undertakings, especially maritime exploration, through the lens of commerce. All other ideals, from artistic beauty to military power, were regarded as secondary. Generally, such matters were only considered relevant to the extent that they might enhance or undermine mercantile operations. Perhaps the most striking example was how, in a particular instance of Punic-Hellenic hostilities, the (western) Phoenicians' primary preparatory strategy for war with Greece was the employ of battle-tested mercenaries from various other ethnicities surrounding Carthage, the largest Phoenician settlement in North Africa. Such an approach to war was, as Herm observed, "typical of a merchant race."[4]

Unlike any previous society and all but a few subsequent ones, the Phoenicians were a civilization governed, from top to bottom, *by merchants.* As discussed in the previous chapter, the merchant class of Mesopotamia was ever mindful of the temple and palace officials who, throughout most of that civilization's history, were the most influential political entities. Even during periods in which the merchants of Mesopotamia gained the upper hand in trade and other commercial matters, ultimate decision-making power on strategic/military, legal, and other matters rested with the palace and temple, not the merchants' *karum.*

As the Italian archaeologist Aldo Massa observed, "The true masters of the [Phoenician] cities were the heads of the leading families, or rather of the leading business houses." Aside from being "the custodians of the national wealth and the masters of huge business empires," collectively, these captains of family-run enterprises "used to form what really amounted to a senate, regardless of the name it was actually given."[5] Typically, these were the same families who profited the most from the jealously guarded network of Phoenician trade routes and, later, colonies. The latter were especially rewarding for this entrepreneurial elite who owned the largest tracts of colonized land, in some instances claiming title to entire Mediterranean islands.

Commercial and Territorial Expansion

In retrospect, with such avid entrepreneurs at the helm of Phoenician decision making, the civilization's onslaught of foreign commerce seems all but inevitable. The Phoenicians would expand their initially limited network of trade in all directions. To the east, they would establish profitable trading relationships with the Mesopotamians, Persians, and others who would transport their wares to Phoenician ports by land in large caravans. Yet it was the extraordinary nature of their *maritime* trade to the west that would define the Phoenician legacy.

Upon examining the available evidence, the British archaeologist Donald Harden concluded, "To start with, anyhow, the Phoenicians travelled westward not as true colonists but as traders."[6] To be sure, the initial purpose of establishing maritime trade outposts was not to establish a foothold from which land could be obtained. This is evident from the pattern of Phoenician outposts established in such locations as Egypt and the southern coast of Greece. While the Phoenician settlement in Memphis (the seat of the pharaohs) did not extend beyond a commercial district, the one in Sicily eventually spanned the western half of the island.

The territories of the great civilizations of Egypt and Greece, unlike those of less developed and less populous nations, were not viable targets for Phoenician conquest. Moreover, the maritime-entrepreneurs measured their success in profits, not acreage. To them, the acquisition of additional territory was only desirable to the extent that it facilitated an expansion of commerce. That is why, while the Greek conquests of the era tended to be large, expanding deep into the hinterland, the Phoenician colonies did not widen beyond a narrow strip of coastal land.

However, as the Phoenician trade network continued to expand, the locus of its activity moved well beyond the eastern Mediterranean. The Phoenicians needed to maintain some permanent settlements beyond the bounds of Phoenicia proper, and they soon recognized that trade was not the only form of commerce served by some of these more westerly islands and coastal territories. The island of Sicily, south of the Italian peninsula, serves as a strong example. Skilled in both the production and sale of wine, the Phoenicians recognized that the island was, like their home country, an ideal locale for wine making. This is how the enterprising spirit of Phoenicia converted part of a sparsely populated Sicilian island into the site of a thriving wine-making and trading industry.

They began their spree of Mediterranean conquests with a large section of the island of Cyprus and a slice of the southern coast of modern-day Turkey. Subsequently, the maritime-entrepreneurs progressed steadily westward and, by 900 B.C.E., the Phoenicians had permanent colonies established in the islands that are presently known as

Rhodes, Malta and Gozo (both constituent islands of the modern state of Malta), Sicily, and Sardinia.

While relations with the Greeks were still friendly, Lindos, situated in the southeastern section of Rhodes, was where the maritime-entrepreneurs would exchange their cedar and textiles for the gamut of Greece's renowned artistic output—from small pottery to life-size bronze statues. Regarding Sardinia, the maritime-entrepreneurs established ports on the southern coast of this copper-rich island with the cooperation of the natives. For more than three hundred years, the original inhabitants of Sardinia cohabited peacefully with the Phoenicians, due in large part to the exotic goods the maritime-entrepreneurs would offer in exchange for the locally mined copper.

The Phoenicians also established large ports and warehouses along the North African coast that evolved into permanent colonies over the next century. The region became a hub of settlement activity, culminating with the establishment of Carthage circa 800 B.C.E. "Qart-Hadasht," the Phoenician term for "new city," was established by Elisha, the Phoenician monarch

Figure 2.1
Engraving of an ancient Phoenician ship. *Source:* Obtained (with Creative Commons permission to reuse) from Google Images, Wikipedia.

immortalized in the works of the Roman poet Virgil as Queen Dido. The Phoenicians' North African coastal territory would eventually extend from modern-day Morocco all the way east to the western edge of Egypt. Carthage, in modern-day Tunisia, served as the commercial and military heart of Phoenician North Africa and the western Mediterranean region.

During the early eighth century B.C.E., the maritime-entrepreneurs, who demonstrated an exceptional aptitude for identifying strategic locations, began a series of impressive territorial acquisitions on the European shore of the Mediterranean. These colonies, situated primarily in modern-day Spain and France, included Gadir (present-day Cadiz), from which the Phoenicians could access the abundant silver deposits of southwestern Spain; Malacca (present-day Málaga); the Spanish island of Majorca; and perhaps most notably, Massilia, the city currently known as Marseille, France. The legendary French novelist Alexandre Dumas, in his classic *The Count of Monte Cristo*, described his country's third-largest city as "the younger sister of Tyre and Carthage, successor to the empire of the Mediterranean; Marseille, always getting younger as it grows older."[7]

Considering the mercantile background of the colonizers, perhaps it is not surprising that, of the foreign territories that had significant native populations, the Phoenicians preferred "conquest by commerce." In other words, through the establishment and ongoing development of commercial relationships and infrastructure, the maritime-entrepreneurs became the commercial lifeblood of the territory. Then, once the natives became their economic dependents, the territory could be claimed for Phoenicia. In this manner, the maritime-entrepreneurs could leverage their commercial acumen, unrivaled in the region, for territorial gain.

For example, once they were able to discern local tastes, the maritime-entrepreneurs would ply the natives generously with their luxuries of choice. Then, while these foreign peoples were enjoying Phoenician wine, Greek art, or any number of other exotic wares, the newcomers would negotiate the peaceful acquisition of territory. However, some of the prouder nations were offended by what they viewed as the Phoenicians' attempt to dispossess them of their ancestral lands with bribery. In such instances, the Phoenicians were not above using less congenial methods of persuasion. However, as noted earlier, even some of their early military conquests were conducted with a mercantile flair, involving the employ of large battalions of hired foreign mercenaries.

In most instances, the maritime-entrepreneurs were the first colonizers of these and other historic northern Mediterranean settlements. In fact, some locales were so sparsely populated that, effectively, the Phoenicians were the founders of new human settlements. Certainly, they were the first to build and maintain what could be described as an infrastructure in these colonies. That is why many historians and archaeologists describe Phoenicia as the first "civilizer" of these previously "backward" regions of Mediterranean Europe and North Africa.

With respect to the consequences of Phoenicia's westward expansion, as Thomas Noble and his colleagues write in *Western Civilization: Beyond Boundaries*, "The result, though unintended, was that Phoenician colonists exported the civilization of western Asia to the western Mediterranean."[8] As discussed in the preceding chapter, urban civilization began in the western Asian city-states of Sumer, the first great nation of Mesopotamia, the cradle of civilization. This was a pivot point in history—away from humanity's hunter-gatherer and agrarian past and toward the establishment of towns, cities, formalized trade, and diversified labor roles.

The city-states of Phoenicia were established long after the founding of Ur. Nonetheless, having traded with Mesopotamian merchants for millennia, the Phoenician city-states were permeated with Mesopotamian culture. For example, Baal and Ashtoret, the names of two popular Phoenician deities, are remarkably similar to those of the Mesopotamian deities Bel and Ishtar. Situated at the western edge of the Asian continent, the economically vibrant urban centers of Sidon, Tyre, and Baalbek stood as exemplars of western Asian civilization.

Particularly in the period preceding the emergence of the Greek and Etruscan civilizations in the eighth century B.C.E., the lands of North Africa and Mediterranean Europe were, with the notable exception of Egypt, settled by relatively primitive tribal societies. Thus the expansion of the Phoenician presence throughout the Mediterranean was certainly a civilizing influence to the extent that it helped spread the technological and social advances of the western Asians, the pioneers of urban civilization.

Over "the End of the World"

The Phoenicians provide us with the first of several notable historical examples of enterprising civilizations that in the pursuit of greater profits expanded the boundaries of the known world. Diodorus Siculus described this tendency as a skill in "making discoveries for their own profit."[9] While the Greek historian's description was certainly not intended as a compliment, discovery motivated primarily by financial gain is the engine of entrepreneurship. With very few exceptions, entrepreneurial pursuits are driven by self-interest, and even in its least glamorous forms, successful entrepreneurship usually involves some form of discovery. This may be as trivial as unearthing a new niche in a small local market or attaining a marginal improvement in manufacturing efficiency that allows for a slightly less expensive product.

However, the Phoenician story is among the most compelling in the history of entrepreneurship due to the momentous impact of many of their profit-seeking discoveries. Among the most notable examples is the maritime-entrepreneurs' daring voyage over what was then believed to be the end of the world. Various civilizations across the Mediterranean and Asia Minor stood in awe of the slender passage at the western edge of the "Great Sea," marked on either side by an imposing formation of rock. The one on the European side is currently known as the Rock of Gibraltar and, on the African side, there is a similarly high and rocky peak that the Moroccans refer to as Jebel Musa (Mount Moses).

In antiquity, these were referred to as the "Pillars of Heracles" (or, in Latin, "Hercules"), as they reminded the Greeks of the immense pillars to which, according to legend, the son of Zeus was once chained. The conventional wisdom held that beyond the western terminal of the Mediterranean, marked by the Pillars, was also the western terminal of what was still believed to be a flat earth. It was believed that any travel beyond that point was akin to sailing off the edge of a bottomless cliff.

To the Phoenicians, unlike any other Mediterranean or western Asian nation, the lure of rich untapped profits in parts unknown was so strong that it outweighed the perceived dangers of sailing past "the end of the world." Having already profited handsomely from expanding their commercial activities across the length and breadth of the known world, the maritime-entrepreneurs were intent on expanding their unprecedented network of trading outposts and colonies even farther. As they would demonstrate repeatedly, the Phoenicians were prepared to risk death in the service of this ambition.

Golden Shores and Celtic Tin

At some point in the sixth century B.C.E., likely led by the renowned Carthage-based navigator Hanno, the Phoenicians sailed around the Atlantic coast of northwest Africa, making a number of exploratory stops along the way. Some of these, in modern-day Morocco, were the sites of future coastal colonies. However, the most notable aspect of this expedition was the establishment of commercial ties with African tribes much farther south, in the coastal territory of modern-day Senegal. These ties would prove to be highly profitable, enduring, and in terms of both commercial and cultural exchange, transformational.

A contemporaneous Greek account of Phoenician trade with black Africa reveals just how well the maritime-entrepreneurs were rewarded for being the first entrepreneurs of the West to reach such rich shores:

> When they arrive, they unload their merchandise and, when they have set it in order on the shore, they return to their ships and make a great smoke, that the inhabitants, seeing the smoke, come down to the coast and, leaving gold in exchange for the goods, depart again to some distance from the place. The Carthaginians (or Phoenicians), then going shore, weigh the gold and, if the quantity seems sufficient for the goods, they take it up and sail away; but if it is not equivalent they return to their ships, never touching the gold until it is made adequate to the merchandise, nor the natives the merchandise before the other party has taken the gold.[10]

The passage above is from Herodotus, a prominent Greek historian of the fifth century B.C.E. Aside from Phoenician access to African gold, the quote reveals much about the particular form of barter devised by the maritime-entrepreneurs to help obtain trades on favorable terms. As with many successful entrepreneurs throughout history, the Phoenicians' profit-seeking innovations were not limited to the procurement, manufacture, and distribution of goods. The *sale* of said goods—the point at which wealth is transferred from seller to buyer—is an opportune time for innovative thinking as well, and one of which the maritime-entrepreneurs took full advantage.

With the shrewdness for which they were alternately admired and despised, the Phoenicians were quite adept at devising highly profitable transactions. Perhaps the most illuminating example in this regard is their exchange of inexpensive Greek pottery for the costly precious metals offered by the tribes of the modern-day African nation of Senegal. The people of these tribes were thrilled with the ornate Greek amphorae, vases, and bowls that the light-skinned traders laid on their beaches. However, the tribesmen remained ignorant of the value of the abundant yellow seams that they walked upon every day, and the maritime-entrepreneurs profited richly from their ignorance.

Aside from art obtained from trade with the Greeks, the Phoenician "merchandise" to which Herodotus refers also included an assortment of western Asian and southern European jewelry, all of which would have seemed quite exotic to people who had never had any contact with the West. It should also be noted that gold was Africa's primary attraction for the Phoenicians, while it is possible there were other goods obtained from these coastal tribes. For example, those who commissioned Hanno's African expedition had expressed an interest in both ivory and slaves, though it remains unclear whether either was obtained on this particular voyage.

Notably, black slaves had already made their way to the "civilized" world, albeit in limited numbers, as some were serving in the courts of high-ranking officials in Egypt. Especially since the Phoenicians had long been involved in the trade of Greek and other Mediterranean slaves, it is possible they played a role in obtaining these more exotic slaves for their longtime customers in Egypt. As such, the maritime-entrepreneurs may have the rather dubious distinction of being the first "Western" traders in black slaves.

Some hundred or so years later, they found another essentially remote society to trade with in exchange for another coveted metal—tin, an important alloy in the production of bronze and a useful metal in its own right. The maritime-entrepreneurs were eager to obtain large quantities of tin, both for their own purposes and to obtain yet another prized commodity that could be traded elsewhere. This is what motivated the Phoenicians to brave the treacherous waters of the north Atlantic to reach the land of the northern Celts. They traded with the Celts of Iron Age Ireland and the Britons, a Celtic tribe who were the dominant ethnicity in southern England at the time.

The islands south of Cornwall, presently known as the Scilly Islands, were named the "Tin Islands" by the Phoenicians. Due to the lucrative trade in tin that ensued, they ranked the islands and the northern Celtic world among their most significant seaborne discoveries. In fact, this new trade route was, according to George Rawlinson, a nineteenth-century Oxford professor of ancient history, "so highly prized that a Phoenician captain, finding his ship followed by a Roman vessel," would have "preferred running it upon the rocks to letting a rival nation learn the secret of how the tin-producing coast might be approached in safety."[11] Certainly, whether it was the gold trade with the West Africans, the art trade with the Greeks, or the tin trade with the northern Celts, the maritime-entrepreneurs guarded their routes jealously.

The Phoenicians had long known that the more varied and exotic their offerings were, the greater the opportunities for highly profitable trades. Moreover, they recognized that exoticism was to a large extent a function of distance. From the perspective of traders from western Asia, the Phoenician port city of Tyre, teeming with the most desirable goods from across the entire Mediterranean, was considered the warehouse of the Great Sea.

For such traders, Phoenician products themselves were often desirable but not particularly exotic. However, goods from trading outposts in the western Mediterranean certainly were, and the maritime-entrepreneurs were adept at procuring the highest possible price for items that only they, as "lords of the sea," were equipped to provide. Of course, this elaborate profit-making scheme was contingent upon the preservation of Phoenicia's maritime commercial supremacy, including its exclusive knowledge of certain trade routes.

It is believed by some scholars that Phoenician trade networks extended east from the British Isles to the Baltic Sea. There is evidence to suggest that the Phoenicians, whose necklaces were often made from amber, might have enjoyed access to the amber-rich Baltic region. However, it is also possible that the amber was obtained in southern Europe, where it was transported via overland trade from farther north. So the Phoenician Baltic trade theory remains unconfirmed, though compelling.

Less plausible are the more outlandish theories regarding the geographical reach of Phoenician trade, particularly those suggesting that it extended to the Polynesian islands, present-day Brazil, Newfoundland, or elsewhere in the New World. Moreover, in light of how the maritime-entrepreneurs' *proven* accomplishments still stand as marvels of nautical skill and daring, the wilder speculations are both poorly founded and unnecessary.

From an Iron Age Mediterranean perspective, black Africa and the British Isles were almost new worlds in their own right. With respect to Africa, this lack of familiarity with and understanding of black society is underscored in the most shocking terms in Hanno's candid travel diary. He recounts how he and his men tried, unsuccessfully, to capture some male creatures that Hanno alternately refers to as "gorillas" and "men." He then describes the capture of "three of the women." Hanno continues, "They bit and scratched those who carried them off, because they had no desire to come with us. So, we killed them and skinned them and brought the skins back to Carthage."[12]

It is unclear whether or not the captured females were human, but the confused language of his account indicates that the western Phoenician commander was at the very least perplexed by the appearance of some non-Caucasoid African tribes. Certainly, the possibility that the maritime-entrepreneurs brought human skins back to Carthage as an exotic import serves as a chilling reminder of just how limited contact was between the West and the southern portions of the "dark continent."

It is also a reminder of how historically significant these Phoenician expeditions were. Certainly, it would be difficult to overstate the impact of bringing that region and the land of the island Celts (as opposed to the continental Celtic peoples of modern-day Spain and France) into greater contact with the urban civilization of the Mediterranean. Both of these somewhat isolated regions were lagging technologically, economically, and otherwise in comparison with Phoenician civilization, of which Carthage had become the hub.

Carthage: Sea Power of the West

A Tyrian colony; the people made
Stout for the war, and studious of their trade:
Carthage the name; belov'd by Juno more
Than her own Argos, or the Samian shore.
——VIRGIL, *THE AENEID*

Elisha, the monarch who founded Carthage, was the granddaughter of King Mattan of Tyre. Her North African colony would prove to be the most consequential of the overseas territories claimed by the Phoenician race, destined to eclipse Tyre, Sidon, and the original city-states of Queen Elisha's ancestors. Indeed, the center of gravity in the Phoenician world would continue to shift westward from Tyre to Carthage. By the sixth century B.C.E., when the city-states of eastern Phoenicia had already fallen under the military jurisdiction of the Assyrian Empire, the Carthaginians had become the dominant power of the western Mediterranean.

Over the course of their storied seven-hundred-year history, the Carthaginians established a strong identity, independent in some respects from their forebears on the other side of the Mediterranean. Nonetheless, these western Phoenicians still maintained important ties to their motherland—the city-state of Tyre. For example, each year, as an expression of cultural and religious solidarity, a delegation of prominent Carthaginians would sail east to offer a sacrifice at Tyre's most sacred temple, Melqart.

Commercially, there was a strong sense of kinship between Carthaginian and Tyrian maritime-entrepreneurs. Although the business operations of one city were usually conducted independently of the other, the eastern and western Phoenicians would often work in tandem to counter competing commercial fleets, particularly those of Greece. Clearly, as a Mediterranean-wide naval and *territorial* presence, Greater Phoenicia had become better equipped to protect and expand its commercial interests, which is precisely why its leading merchants were such ardent colonialists. Although colonization was seen by the Phoenicians in primarily commercial terms, an important by-product of their westward expansion was the spread of the culture and technology of western Asia to the western Mediterranean and beyond.

The Phoenician Legacy: Pollinators, Producers, and Pirates

Pollinators

You are filled with heavy cargo in the heart of the sea.
Your oarsmen take you out to the high seas.
When your merchandise went out on the seas, you satisfied many nations;
with your great wealth and your wares you enriched the kings of the earth.
"LAMENT FOR TYRE," EZEKIEL 27:25, 26, 33

The biblical passages above are an expression of the curious mix of admiration and envy with which the Phoenicians were viewed by other nations. They also confirm the maritime-entrepreneurs' widely recognized role as the leading maritime adventurers and international traders of the era. The voyages to the Atlantic coast of Africa and to the British Isles are perhaps the most dramatic examples of how the maritime-entrepreneurs expanded the "known world" through their profit-driven discoveries of previously unknown or highly obscure regions. Their maritime exploits in the Indian Ocean and the Black Sea were less momentous but still stand as noteworthy examples of their nautical prowess.

However, aside from enlarging the map of the known world through commerce, the Phoenicians also pioneered a form of cultural and artistic exchange involving every corner of that map. Within their own region, the Phoenicians would often serve as intermediaries, exchanging one of their trading partner's goods for that of another. Jewelry from Greece, for example, would be traded for linen made in Egypt that, in turn, could be sold in Phoenicia. Similarly, the maritime-entrepreneurs were known to trade a wide variety of goods for Egypt's monkeys and crocodiles that would be sold to trading partners from western Asia. These merchants would then supply the Phoenicians with such exotic Eastern fare as carpets from Mesopotamia, spices from the Arabian Peninsula, pearls from Persia, and finely woven shawls from Kashmir.

Of course, these regional trading partners also partook in the more exotic imports that the Phoenicians brought back from Africa's Atlantic coast and the British Isles. Meanwhile, the peoples of those more remote regions marveled at the ornate art and jewelry that the maritime-entrepreneurs had transported from Phoenician settlements and trading partners. Although its activities were motivated entirely by the pursuit of profit, as a conduit between such distinct and distant societies, this peculiar race of maritime merchants broadened the cultural horizons of peoples across large swaths of Asia, Africa, and Europe.

Such archaeological findings as Iron Age African gold in Sardinia, a former Phoenician colony, stand as compelling artifacts of the maritime-entrepreneurs' role as the "pollinators" of their era. Just as bees do, by carrying and spreading pollen among different flowers, and in the process helping to create something new (i.e., a new generation of flowers), the Phoenicians created new combinations and connections as an incidental by-product of their intercontinental commercial activities. Many of these had entirely unforeseen and enduring impacts upon the course of human history.

The impact of the rich flow of novel goods and ideas that the maritime-entrepreneurs conveyed between distant regions was felt most strongly by their longtime trading partners across the Mediterranean and western Asia. Commenting on the influence of the maritime-entrepreneurs' African exploits, Harden concluded that, "There is no doubt that it was the Phoenicians and not the Greeks, whose African colonies were never powerful, nor the Egyptians, whose trade was confined to the Nile basin and its immediate hinterland, who passed on the products of this huge area . . . to the civilized Mediterranean World."[13]

Regarding the British Isles, despite the Phoenicians' best efforts to conceal their route to these remote tin-rich territories, it was uncovered by espionage conducted by the Romans—archrivals of the western Phoenicians of Carthage. Shortly thereafter, by following the course plotted by the maritime-entrepreneurs, the Romans commenced their own involvement with the land that would, by the middle of the first century c.e., become a Roman colony and would remain so for more than three hundred and fifty years. Britain became the site of large Roman settlements such as "Loudon," which became London. Of course, the fact that the English and Gaelic languages are written with the Latin alphabet is another lasting consequence, among many, of Roman contact with the British Isles. To some extent, these phenomena can be traced to Phoenicia, the first of the great Mediterranean civilizations to establish ongoing contact with the British Isles.

Producers

In his introduction to *The Innovators: The Essential Guide to Business Thinkers, Achievers and Entrepreneurs*, the British broadcaster/author William Davis described entrepreneurs as people who are "not content with reacting events; they want to control them."[14] This entrepreneurial drive for greater control is precisely why the activities of the Phoenicians, once relegated mostly to trade, gradually spread in several other directions. As discussed, among these were territorial acquisition and the development of colonial agricultural and related industries. However, another important branching out was the *manufacture* of goods, including some that the maritime-entrepreneurs had previously obtained from other civilizations.

From wine making to textiles and carpentry, industry was always a vital component of the economic life of the Phoenicians. Moreover, particularly as the colonial adventures of the maritime-entrepreneurs brought their civilization into contact with wider plots of cultivable land, they proved themselves to be excellent farmers and herders. The Phoenicians had long been admired for their superior shipbuilding skills and their dazzling purple-dyed textiles. However, over time, as their unrivaled skills in maritime trade and exploration enlarged their inventory of materials, their reputation for craftsmanship extended well beyond watercraft and fabrics.

It is telling that Ezekiel's writings on his people's northern neighbors, set down in the seventh century b.c.e., pertain primarily to their nautical and trading skills, with just one laudatory nod to Phoenician textile-making skills. Some three hundred years later, as recorded in the

Old Testament book of Chronicles, the Hebrews of *that* era were clearly awed by the breadth of Phoenician handiwork:

> His father was a man of Tyre, skillful to work in gold, and in silver, in brass, in iron, in stone, and in timber, in purple, in blue, and in fine linen, and in crimson, also to grave any manner of graving, and to devise any device; that there may be "a place" appointed unto him with thy skillful men...[15]

It is notable that gold is the first material mentioned. The Phoenicians had refined the art of shaping gold and other metals through the use of small molds, a skill that drew praise from other contemporary civilizations. Among these were the rival Greeks and Romans, generally considered to have been more advanced in the visual arts than the Phoenicians. Excavations at the site of the Phoenician colony in Sardinia uncovered a varied collection of necklaces, amulets, and ointment jars laden with this impressive metalwork.

Also found in these Sardinian excavations, alongside the metal-ornamented products, were remarkable examples of Phoenician glasswork. Regarding the latter, the Roman philosopher Pliny the Elder set down in writing what seemed to have been the consensus view in the Mediterranean world that a group of Phoenician maritime traders had accidentally "discovered" glass. "There were no stones to support their cooking-pots, so they placed lumps of soda from their ship under them. When these became hot and fused with the sand on the beach, streams of an unknown liquid flowed, and this was the origin of glass."[16]

Whether or not they were the originators of glass, there is no question that the Phoenicians were skilled makers and shapers of this important material. Phoenician colonies at Rhodes and Malta were the sites of thriving glass industries and, curiously, Malta is still a center of glass production, utilizing methods that are believed to be enduring relics of the island nation's Phoenician roots. Furthermore, archaeologists have unearthed shapely glass vessels of Phoenician origin, finely cut and molded, from the sites of the royal palaces of ancient Assyria and Israel. At the same sites, they also found Phoenician-made furniture fashioned from an impressive combination of ivory and glass. Sleek cushions and fine upholstery from Phoenicia (and later Carthage) were also highly regarded among the leading civilizations of antiquity.

Nonetheless, while the Phoenicians demonstrated great skill in shaping various materials, the aesthetic quality of their output does not always compare favorably with that of their contemporaries' artistic works. This accounts for why the maritime-entrepreneurs often had more success trading the artistic works of the Greeks and the Egyptians than those of their own civilization. However, as they were always on the lookout for higher yields, some grew discontented with mere middleman profits on such transactions. So, like the unscrupulous distributors of our own time who will slap a forged brand-name label on a purse held together by a rubber band, the Phoenicians entered and possibly originated the "knockoff" business.

Excavations at Carthage and elsewhere in the western Mediterranean indicate that, with respect to what Harden describes as "goods of the Egyptian type," a significant change seems to have taken place around the turn of the seventh century B.C.E. At that point, the origins of such goods shift from Egypt to Phoenician production facilities in Carthage and Phoenicia. One giveaway betraying the non-Egyptian manufacture of these products is their somewhat inferior quality relative to the Egyptian originals they were designed to replicate. In her *People of the First Cities*, the American archaeological journalist Ruth Goode observed that "the work of the Phoenician craftsmen has been found in all cities of the ancient world, from Mesopotamia to Italy and Spain," and "the Phoenician craftsmen cleverly imitated all the styles of the times."[17]

So, alongside more innovative ways of "endowing resources with a greater capacity to generate wealth," the Phoenicians helped pioneer the controversial yet enduring form of entrepreneurship commonly known as the knockoff business. In our globalized modern economy, the production of knockoff products has never been more prevalent. According to the Organisation for Economic Co-operation and Development, the annual production and sale of counterfeit products has reached a staggering $250 billion.[18]

Moreover, there is often a copycat element in businesses that are not knockoff operations per se. After all, there is just as much imitation as inventiveness behind some of the greatest innovation-oriented entrepreneurial successes of our own era—from JetBlue to Facebook, Chipotle to the Android smartphone. Unlike, for example, the St. Petersburg–Tampa Airboat Line or SixDegrees.com, the brands listed above did not define a new product/service category. Instead, they tweaked existing concepts and, perhaps more importantly, promoted their "new and improved" versions aggressively and effectively. These entrepreneurs, like the Phoenicians, recognized the value in building upon the ideas and designs of others instead of reinventing the wheel.

Pirates

"For indeed, among the barbarians there were in former times none who were seafarers, except the Etruscans and the Phoenicians, the one on account of trade, the other for the sake of piracy."[19] This quote from the great Roman orator Cicero, from his classic work *The Republic*, published in 54 B.C.E., is reflective of the violent hatred that many Romans still held for the memory of Carthage, the Phoenician rival that Rome had finally and permanently vanquished during the previous (second) century. As such, it can hardly be construed as a dispassionate analysis of the Phoenician character. In fact, Cicero derides the maritime civilization as a nation of seafaring barbarians, which in light of Phoenicia's great advances, is at best an outrageous oversimplification.

However, Cicero was certainly not the first foreign writer to accuse the maritime-entrepreneurs of piracy. Some four hundred years earlier, Herodotus described a harrowing instance of such piracy in considerable detail: "the Phoenicians arrived then at this land of Argos, and began to dispose of their ships' cargo." Subsequently, this cargo attracted the attention of a large group of women curious about what items might be available for purchase. Among these women was Io, whose father was the king of the Greek city-state of Argos. Herodotus continues, "all of a sudden the Phoenicians, passing the word from one to another, made a rush upon them; and the greater part of the women escaped by flight, but Io and certain others were carried off. So they put them on board their ship, and forthwith departed, sailing away to Egypt."[20]

Some three hundred and fifty years before Herodotus' time, Homer, writing in the voice of the fictional Greek hero Odysseus, offers a remarkably similar illustration of the deceit and avarice of the maritime-entrepreneurs in *The Odyssey*. Introducing a "man of Phoenicia," the Greek poet describes him as "well versed in guile, a greedy knave."[21] Then, as the narrative in the classic epic poem proceeds, this loathsome merchant-sailor attempts, unsuccessfully, to sell the Greek hero into slavery in Libya. Such a harsh depiction of the merchant-sailor from the pen of Greece's most renowned poet is certainly telling.

A similar tone of resentment, and even revulsion, can be found in some of the Hebrews' observations regarding the maritime-entrepreneurs with whom they often traded. One of many of Ezekiel's screeds against the supposed immorality of the Phoenicians reads as follows, "You corrupted your wisdom by reason of your splendor. I cast you to the ground."[22] Like the Greek critics of the Phoenicians, the Hebrew prophet also makes reference to "trading the persons of men."[23] Clearly, among at least two contemporaneous Mediterranean civilizations, the commercial practices of the maritime-entrepreneurs were seen as predatory. However, particularly with respect to the Greeks, who competed for maritime supremacy with Phoenicia and even warred with it at times, it is difficult to know how much of this criticism derived from legitimate grievances as opposed to a sense of competition and envy.

The evidence seems to suggest that the Phoenicians did, in fact, engage in piracy, particularly with respect to the smaller and more primitive Mediterranean societies. Where they were unlikely to face an effective resistance, some of the more rapacious maritime-entrepreneurs would abduct strong men, attractive women, and anyone else from the native population who might fetch a high price from a slave buyer. Then, at another port of call, they would proceed to sell this pirated "cargo."

However, antiquity's greatest maritime commercial empire was not administered by fools. The maritime-entrepreneurs were savvy enough to know that while piracy and other forms of theft might be profitable ways of preying on the weak, those practices would not sustain their far-flung network of trade and production centers. They recognized that each of the "nodes" on that network was predicated on some sort of business relationship with the natives of those territories. With some notable exceptions, such as their flagrant violation of a territorial understanding with the natives of Sardinia, the Phoenicians generally recognized that these relationships necessitated at least a modicum of trust and, if not affection, at least a sense of mutual respect.

Certainly, they managed to maintain mutually beneficial relations with some of their important trading partners. The strength and duration of some of their commercial relationships are striking, particularly a trading partnership with Egypt that spanned more than fifteen hundred years. That relationship, coupled with the fact that another Hebrew prophet, Isaiah, described the maritime-entrepreneurs as "traders the world honored,"[24] suggests that Phoenicia was a reliable trading partner. Nevertheless, there is no question that the legacy of its fabled seafaring entrepreneurs is tainted by a capacity for highly duplicitous dealings, particularly the scourge of piracy. In that regard, Phoenicia was the first but far from the last of the great entrepreneurial civilizations to engage in predatory practices.

Europa

Whether it was due to questionable business practices, competitive pressures, or some combination of both, the maritime-entrepreneurs were mostly reviled in the Greco-Roman world and the Greeks and Romans would ring the death knell, respectively, of the Phoenicians and the western Phoenicians of Carthage. Although there were long periods in which they traded with each other, the maritime-entrepreneurs of the original Phoenician city-states and the Greeks often coveted the same trade routes and territories.

Such competition intermittently exploded into hostilities, and as the Greeks became more powerful, their enmity would prove a considerable detriment to the survival of Phoenicia's original city-states. Over subsequent centuries, as the locus of the Phoenician world shifted to Carthage and the Romans overtook the Greeks, the rivalry between the two *western* Mediterranean powers descended into some of the most terrible carnage the world had yet seen.

After several hundred years of almost unfettered commercial expansion, Phoenicia's strategic position was gradually weakened by a succession of expansionary western Asian powers. Around 870 B.C.E., the conquests of the Assyrian King Assurnasirpal II brought him to the Phoenician coast. Wisely forgoing any armed resistance, the militarily inferior Phoenicians decided to welcome this powerful monarch with, as he noted to his court scribe, "gold, silver, tin, copper, copper vessels, linen robes with many colored borders, big and little apes, ebony, boxwood, ivory, and walrus tusks."[25] This colorful and varied display of their impressive wares was not only a form of tribute but also a reminder of Phoenician commercial prowess and how it might be of service to the Assyrian Empire.

As it happened, the Assyrians, like the Neo-Babylonians and Persians who followed, were generally content to be the dominant power of western Asia while allowing the Phoenicians to retain varying degrees of autonomy. Meanwhile, the power balance of maritime strength in the Mediterranean was tilting toward Greece, and by the seventh century B.C.E., the Phoenician character of some eastern Mediterranean islands was being challenged by more vigorous Greek trade and colonization. Nonetheless, the Phoenician trade was still brisk.

Although their golden age had passed and their territories were now satellite city-states of militarily superior western Asian powers, the Phoenicians were still more or less free to trade and preserve their way of life. Eventually even Tyre, as Massa noted, "Renounced the kind of grand ambitions which had long been abandoned by the other cities along the Syrian coast."[26] The maritime-entrepreneurs had resigned themselves to the new political realities because they "were content to be merchants, more knowledgeable, quicker to spot a good deal, more shifty and thrifty, and, therefore, richer than their enemies."[27]

Despite their wealth, the maritime-entrepreneurs' city-states were no longer truly independent. As such, they were expected to assist their overlords commercially and, where necessary, even militarily. In 539 B.C.E., when the territories held by the Neo-Babylonians were seized by the Persians, the latter enlisted the Phoenicians to help rebuild the commercial and civil infrastructure of Judaea. Sixty years later, faced with the military might of the Greeks, Persia converted the merchant-sailor fleet into its own Mediterranean navy. Of course, the vassal city-states of Phoenicia had no choice but to acquiesce. Two hundred years later, when the Hellenic world (comprising Greece and Macedonia) finally prevailed over Persia, Alexander the Great's army razed the city walls of Tyre, signaling the end of eastern Phoenician civilization.

However, the flame of Phoenician civilization was still alight in Carthage and its western Mediterranean colonies, which at the time included Sardinia, Corsica, the western half of Sicily, and several territories in Spain. The competitive pressures between Carthage and the decidedly noncommercial nation of Rome were minimal, and in fact, the two powers were allies for two and a half centuries before hostilities erupted over Sicily in 264 B.C.E. A formidable force by then, the Roman military evicted the Carthaginians from Sicily, Sardinia, and Corsica over the following thirty years.

In 218 B.C.E., the legendary Hannibal, intent on reclaiming Carthage's honor and territory, took the fight to the Italian peninsula itself. After Hannibal's series of stunning victories over Rome on its home territory, his enemies eventually regained their foothold, and by 211, Carthage was in retreat. Intent on quashing the "African" invaders once and for all, by 200, Rome's terms of peace had effectively outlawed the existence of a Carthaginian navy. Now, with all of its western Mediterranean colonies in the enemy's hands and without its primary line of defense, Carthage was left to wither for several decades before the Romans came in for the final blow around 148 B.C.E.

Those who had survived the extended siege and destruction of their city would be sold into slavery, and the Phoenicians on both sides of the Mediterranean had been permanently crushed by the European powers by 145 B.C.E.. The latter, having destroyed Phoenicia's civilization, persisted in undermining its reputation. As noted above, the Romans, even those writing long after 145 B.C.E., referred to the vanquished Carthaginians as barbarians. For their part, the ancient Greeks, would see to it that "the people of the Lebanon," as Herm wrote, "went down in history as a crowd of avaricious, thieving, deceitful traders."[28]

So, it is fitting that Europe, our word for the continent of the Greeks and Romans, stems from Europa, the Greek name for a beautiful Phoenician woman abducted by Zeus and carried off to Crete for an illicit affair. The European powers of the Mediterranean had, with some justification, accused the Phoenician merchants of piracy. Yet, like Zeus, these powers had practiced some piracy of their own upon this commercially brilliant maritime civilization, appropriating vital aspects of its enterprise, its seafaring technologies, its advanced western Asian urban civilization, and even its alphabet. So, although Phoenicia originated beyond the boundaries of Europe, the legacy of its maritime-entrepreneurs would endure within the same continent that had destroyed or, perhaps more aptly, *abducted* it.

3

The Reluctant Romans

"To those who are engaged in commercial dealings,
justice is indispensable to the conduct of business."
MARCUS TULLIUS CICERO

In the realm of entrepreneurship, the legacy of the ancient Romans stands in stark contrast to that of the enterprising Mesopotamians and Phoenicians. In fact, Rome bears the distinction of being among the least entrepreneurial civilizations not only of antiquity but of recorded history. This, of course, begs the question of why this civilization deserves a chapter in a book chronicling the history of entrepreneurship. Part of the answer is that the entrepreneurial experience in Rome is an insightful illustration of enterprise as practiced under unfavorable and at times even *hostile* conditions.

Some civilizations, past and present, have consciously fostered an environment conducive to entrepreneurship. These are societies where, provided that the end result is not illegal, the direction of one's creative impulse to a profit-making pursuit is actively encouraged. Conversely, from ancient Egypt to the Soviet Union and its satellites, history is replete with examples of political structures that actively discourage, even shun, such pursuits. Rome, in many respects, was structured in such a manner.

In fact, respectable Romans steered clear of entrepreneurship in a manner comparable with how most upstanding citizens in the modern West tend to avoid careers in the weaponry and pornography industries. While these are legal industries that are financially rewarding for some, many people still associate them with the less noble aspects of the human condition.

Similarly, the Romans associated entrepreneurship, and more broadly commerce, with instincts so coarse and indelicate that they were inappropriate for the Roman nobility.

Less respectable residents of Rome, from the semirespectable equestrian class down to slaves and former slaves (known as *liberti*, or freedmen), were another matter entirely. In the eyes of Roman nobility, such second- and third-class citizens had just the right moral and intellectual fiber for the "dirty work" of entrepreneurship. For a significant stretch of Roman history, these were the people who not only established and operated new businesses but, in some instances, even expanded them into something akin to chain stores. One can imagine the horror of an ancient nobleman time traveling to modern America and seeing how business dynasties like the Walton family (of Wal-Mart fame) are revered for engaging in activities that according to the mores of ancient Rome were best left to slaves.

There are a few other intriguing aspects of ancient Roman enterprise worthy of consideration. By and large, these are also illustrations of how entrepreneurship persists in unusual ways within the kind of restrictive environment exemplified by Rome during most of its extended reign as the military, cultural, and economic superpower of the known world. However, before delving into enterprise in the Roman world, it is important to highlight ancient Greece and the Hellenistic world—the "connective tissue" between the civilizations of Phoenicia and Rome.

Greece

In light of the spread of Phoenician mercantile practices throughout the Mediterranean, it is not entirely surprising that in some respects the commercial life of ancient Greece bore a strong resemblance to that of Phoenicia. Like that of its Mediterranean rival to the east, the economic health of Greece relied upon a continually expanding and diversifying base of trade. By the fourth century B.C.E., the Greeks were trading almost everything: manufactured goods and raw materials, luxury and everyday items, artistic works, metals, grains, fish, wine, olive oil, and even slaves.

While their trade network was not quite as far-reaching as that of the Phoenicians, it was impressive nonetheless, stretching from Persia to Gaul (modern-day France) and from the Baltic Sea to North Africa. With respect to nautical endeavors, the Greeks could not outshine the brilliance of the Phoenicians but they were certainly excellent seafarers in their own right. In a later period, when Rome had already supplanted Greece as the dominant power of the known world, it was the Greek sailor Hippalus who reached India and modern-day Sri Lanka by sea, an unprecedented feat of maritime travel.

As with Phoenicia's maritime-entrepreneurs, a class of domestic profit-seeking merchants rose to considerable wealth and prominence within Greece's lucrative trade and manufacturing sectors. However, unlike merchant-led Phoenicia, the civilization of Greece, like that of Rome, did not hold its merchants in high esteem. Although the Greek financial system—involving the widespread use of standardized coinage and the first appearance of formalized banking—was considerably more sophisticated than that of the Phoenicians, the ideals of the Greeks clashed with the notion of profit-seeking as an end in itself.

Greek farmers and shepherds, not entrepreneurs, were the exemplars of admirable work. Reflecting popular sentiment, the Greek scholar Xenophon declared that agriculture was "the most honored profession." In terms of more creative pursuits, the Greeks revered artistic beauty and philosophical profundity far more than commercial cunning. Despite the enormous wealth generated by the merchant class, the conduct of entrepreneurship—motivated by a quest for large profits—would always be suspect in the eyes of many Greeks. In the centuries that followed, as Greek civilization metamorphosed into what is referred to as the Hellenistic world, this somewhat disparaging attitude toward enterprise persisted.

Between the Greeks and Etruscans

After Philip of Macedonia conquered Athens, the civilization of the Greeks was usurped but largely preserved by the Macedonians. Due to the exploits of Philip's son Alexander the Great, this Hellenistic world would encompass the entirety of the former Persian Empire and was administered by Greeks, Macedonians, and an assortment of "client" rulers in semiautonomous colonies. Alexander's empire was carved up by three of his generals, and the unity of the Greek-speaking world of the eastern Mediterranean would be shaken continually by regional rivalries over the next three hundred years.

Commercially, the Hellenistic world monopolized the trade routes all the way from India to Gaul. One of this empire's possessions was the Magna Grecia, the southern portion of the Italian peninsula, or what some refer to as "the heel of the boot." However, in central Italy, a distinct and formidable nation was emerging between the Italian colonies of the Greeks to the south and the land of the Etruscans to the north—another prominent Mediterranean civilization of antiquity. Rome's origins trace back to the first half of the eighth century B.C.E. and until it fell under Etruscan rule more than one hundred years later, its economy was largely agricultural and trade was quite limited.

Like the Phoenicians, the Etruscans, believed by some to have originated in the eastern Mediterranean, were avid industrialists and traders. Accordingly, during the seventh and sixth centuries B.C.E., across the Italian peninsula a largely agrarian economy diversified into such industries as metallurgy, vase manufacturing, and the slave trade. During this time, three of the kings of the city-state of Rome were Etruscan. Despite this, Rome was deeply influenced by the Greek worldview and, once it emerged from the grasp of the Etruscans, the Greeks' more reluctant attitude toward entrepreneurship prevailed among the Romans.

The Roman Republic

Free of both the Etruscans and the institution of monarchy, the Roman Republic was born in 509 B.C.E. The constitution of this new republic remains a foundational document not only of Western civilization but of Western-style representative democracies throughout the world. Yet in practice, particularly in its early stages, the republic was an oligarchy wherein both political and economic power was concentrated in the hands of a small, allegedly well-bred aristocracy, the "well-fathered ones" known as the patricians. Entrenched in the corridors of power since the days of the kings, these were the men (there were no women in politics at the time) who were at the helm of the new republic. Ordinary citizens—that is, the overwhelming majority of Romans who were not born into patrician privilege—were known as the plebeians.

The tension between these two social classes, one tiny and powerful, the other large and often weak, would shape many aspects of life in the republic. Perhaps this is best illustrated by the fact that only one hundred families, all patricians, dominated Rome's political offices for more than four hundred years. Not surprisingly, in light of the considerable inherited land they held, the aristocracy leveraged their political power as an economic bulwark against the masses of commoners. The social historian Michael Grant observed that for the Roman patricians, "landed wealth was the only truly respectable asset and the best thing of all was to have inherited it."[1] Those holding political office, Grant goes on to say, "Must be able to live on [their] unearned income. This would naturally come from [their] estates, because trade was not quite reputable."[2]

That said, the political system of the republic did provide some form of representation for the plebeians, and it would be fair to state that the patricians were intent on maintaining a stable and harmonious society for *all* free Roman citizens. To a great extent, they succeeded. Although in a twenty-first-century Western context ancient Rome would not qualify as a just society, its legal system laid the foundation for our own. With respect to both a sophisticated legal system and a well-developed infrastructure, Rome was without peer among the civilizations of the known world.

Regarding the latter, the engineering feats of ancient Rome are still regarded as marvels of ingenuity and resourcefulness. Some, like the ramps built to access remote plateaus, served military objectives. Others, like the paved roads across much of Europe (many of which have been overlaid and are still in use as highways), served civil objectives. Of course, such roads facilitated the work of traders, retailers eager to keep their shelves well stocked, and other entrepreneurs. Similarly, a robust legal system enshrining the sanctity of property rights was and remains a critical pillar of a society in which entrepreneurship could flourish. Yet in Rome, it never did, at least not in a general sense.

Successful enterprise in ancient Rome was restricted to certain socioeconomic pockets and even then only during certain periods in Rome's history. These distortions resulted from ancient Rome's conflicted business culture and patronizing class structure. While the patricians held themselves atop the tower of wealth, they prided themselves on their allegedly benign supervision of the citizens of "lesser" birth living in the more modest dwellings around them. However, it was a tower surrounded by a moat. The plebeians were to enjoy a certain measure of freedom, particularly of the political and legal variety, but they were not to challenge the inherited economic supremacy of their patrician overlords.

Profits for Me, Not Thee

Entrepreneurship, often leading to the creation of new forms of wealth generation, was just the kind of "ladder to the tower" the patrician system sought to undermine. Meanwhile, the patricians were free to augment their inherited wealth in various ways, some of which even aroused the suspicion of fellow patricians. Pliny the Elder once remarked caustically that some military campaigns had been initiated so that aristocrats might have "a better choice of perfumes." Aside from various forms of war profiteering, there were those in public office who profited from large kickbacks when doling out large public building contracts.

As Juvenal remarked:

So farewell Rome, I leave you
To sanitary engineers and municipal architects, men
Who by swearing black is white land all the juicy contracts
Just like that—a new temple, swamp drainage, harbour-works,
River clearance, undertaking, the lot—then pocket the cash
And fraudulently file their petition in bankruptcy.[3]

The latter, of course, has proven to be a dubious yet enduring form of "entrepreneurship" still practiced by eager government officials throughout the world. Meanwhile other well-connected patricians put their capital to work in construction-related investment vehicles crafted by the "equestrians" (discussed further later in this chapter). These and other activities stand as proof that, as long as the "right" people and methods were involved, innovative ways of earning additional money were entirely acceptable. Curiously, trade, moneylending, and most other forms of commerce were frowned upon in Roman high society while real estate speculation was not.

Virtue and Vice

Cato the Elder, the staunchly conservative Roman politician of the second century B.C.E., was once asked about the comparative nobility of various professions. According to legend, he responded to "What about money-lending?" with the infamous rejoinder "What about murder?"[4] Considering Cato's role as a crusader against foreign influences in an increasingly cosmopolitan Rome, the contempt that he held for moneylending (a popular practice in other parts of the Mediterranean) can be viewed in that context. Nevertheless, there still seems to have been an odd disconnect between the aristocratic view of commerce and other forms of profit seeking.

At least part of the reason for this discrepancy is the fact that speculation, involving the use of inherited money and family connections, was largely passive. Conversely, trade, manufacturing, and other forms of commerce tended to involve a level of effort considered unbecoming to a Roman gentleman. Another important factor was the self-serving hypocrisy that typified the patrician attitude toward those of lower birth. Accordingly, those forms of commerce that did not require hereditary advantages were seen as greedy and unseemly, while those that did were unquestionably noble.

"Vulgar we must consider those also who buy from wholesale merchants to retail [resell] immediately," Cicero wrote, "for they would get no profits without a great deal of downright lying; and verily, there is no action that is meaner than misrepresentation."[5] Of course, Roman speculation, let alone outright corruption, often involved various forms of misrepresentation that were at least as egregious as those pertaining to trade. The Roman orator, mindful of his aristocratic patrons, was careful not to similarly disparage those commercial schemes that were popular among the nobility. These included entirely legal but somewhat questionable wheeling and dealing in plum administrative positions, such as Cicero's own tenure as governor of the Anatolian province of Cilicia, from which he made a considerable fortune.

Yet, reflective of the aristocratic milieu in which he operated, Cicero poured his scorn on almost every line of work that patricians generally did *not* engage in. "Tax gathering and usury," the occupations of "all hired workmen whom we pay for mere manual labor," and "mechanics" were all "vulgar." According to Cicero, "fishmongers, butchers, cooks, poulterers, and fishermen . . . perfumers and dancers" were even "less respectable," because they "cater to sensual pleasures."[6] Such a classification is baffling to the modern reader and underscores just how peculiar Roman attitudes appear when compared with those of today.

According to the patricians, the "place" of the plebeians was on the farm, working the land, tending to the livestock, and so on, and the humble workshop was the proper station for those plebeians who were producing their wares as artisans. Alternatively, according to the patricians, the plebeians also served a noble role as the "worker bees" of the republic's infrastructure-building projects, such as the construction of aqueducts and roads. Entrepreneurial activities, on the other hand, were not encouraged, at least not for the plebeian masses. Indeed, the socioeconomic divide of Roman society was, as Grant wrote, "bristling with barriers."[7]

Writing about the early years of the republic, the acclaimed Roman historian Livy illustrates just how formidable these barriers were. He describes how a representative of the plebeians "proposed a bill regarding the intermarriage of patricians and plebeians which the patricians looked upon as involving the debasement of their blood and the subversion of the principles inhering in the *genies*, or families."[8] The second half of that excerpt underscores how, despite the republic's impressive advances in political democracy, its two main social classes were kept both separate and explicitly *un*equal. Yet, establishing a pattern that would be emulated by others, a group of enthusiastic and able outsiders took advantage of patrician disdain for entrepreneurship to attain prominence, and in the process challenged Rome's rigid social hierarchy.

Equestrian Entrepreneurs

Once sandwiched between more powerful civilizations on both ends of the peninsula, by 272 B.C.E. the Romans had wrested control of the remainder from the Etruscans, Greeks, and others. Now having a firm hand on the entirety of Italy and a much larger population under its jurisdiction, Rome was becoming a regional military power of considerable strength. Battles with the Carthaginians ensued, as did conquests of territory in North Africa, Sicily, and Spain. The trade undertaken by the conquering Romans, often more akin to theft and plunder, catapulted Rome's merchant class to a level of power that would have been unthinkable in an earlier phase of the republic.

At the time, many of those who had established businesses pertaining to finance and trade hailed from the equestrian class, so named because its members were plebeians who met a threshold of property ownership to be granted their own horses and serve as legionaries in the Roman cavalry. Beginning at the turn of the third century B.C.E., with the conquest of Italy well under way, the Roman authorities needed more fighters than their own patrician class could provide. Compelled to open up such a prestigious military unit to the lowly plebeians, they did so in a way that would separate the wealthiest of the masses from the rest.

Nonetheless, the equestrians were still plebeians and ambitious ones at that. More concerned with advancement than appearances, many of them took advantage of the lucrative commercial opportunities that proliferated as Roman power expanded throughout the Mediterranean. They proceeded to establish businesses in trade and finance, some of them quite novel. Perhaps the most impactful of these innovative businesses was a kind of prototype of the initial public offering system.

As a spate of military conquests expanded Roman territory beyond Italy, particularly through the eastern provinces of Asia Minor, the large equestrian contractors behind these projects took the initiative to sell shares to Roman citizens, generally patricians and fellow equestrians, on the Wall Street of ancient Rome—the Via Sacra. Stock promoters, investment bankers, and ambitious international traders, the equestrians proved to be a highly entrepreneurial subset of Roman society.

The success of the equestrians, a group of outsiders reluctantly accepted into the higher circles of their society, is an early example of another oft-repeated pattern in the history of entrepreneurship. In many instances, some of society's most enterprising members are outsiders in terms of ethnicity or religion. Some examples in this regard include the prominence of Arabic- and Persian-speaking Zoroastrian, Christian, and Jewish merchants in the entrepreneurial surge of medieval Islamic civilization or the wildly disproportionate rate of business ownership among ethnic Chinese in twenty-first-century Vietnam, Thailand, and other countries in southeast Asia.

Similarly, there have been other instances, such as the sixteenth-century phenomenon of poor Spanish ex-convicts who made their fortunes in the Americas, where the entrepreneurial class has included a large contingent of socioeconomic outsiders. This pattern persists in our own time. Among the many revelations in their 1998 classic *The Millionaire Next Door* is authors Thomas Stanley and William Danko's observation that "eighty percent of America's millionaires are first-generation rich."[9] The overwhelming majority of these new rich are neither Fortune 500 executives nor movie stars but entrepreneurs: "Twenty percent of the affluent households in America are headed by retirees." However, "of the remaining 80 percent, more than two-thirds are headed by self-employed owners of businesses."[10]

The use of entrepreneurship as a socioeconomic ladder extends throughout the ages and transcends culture. Yet in all of history it is difficult to think of a more dramatic example of this phenomenon than the slaves of ancient Rome. The equestrians were disproportionately powerful in the "big business" of large building contracts and related investments, although patricians also played a prominent role in such endeavors. However, the smaller and even midlevel entrepreneurial work was dominated by slaves and the former slaves denoted by the Romans as *liberti*.

Slaves and the Spoils of War

Written evidence of Roman slavery extends back to the fifth century B.C.E., but it is likely that the institution existed in Rome even before the republican period. Slaves had been commonplace among the Greeks, including those who had been living in the south of Italy since the eighth century B.C.E. It is likely that these Italian Greeks were responsible for spreading the practice to the developing city-state of Rome. However, it really took on significant proportions as the republic began its steady expansion into the largest intercontinental empire the world had yet seen.

As highlighted in the previous chapter, upon their final defeat in 149 B.C.E., those Carthaginians who eluded death survived as slaves to their Roman masters. Over the next century, this same pattern of conquest and enslavement continued in Rome's victories over the diverse ethnicities inhabiting the Greek protectorates in western Asia and a number of other subject peoples, such as the Goths and the Gauls. Regarding the latter, it has been estimated that the Roman conquest of the land of modern-day France supplied Rome with no less than five hundred thousand additional slaves.

Remarkably, by the end of the first century C.E., slaves comprised between one-quarter and one-third of Rome's population, and it was not

Figure 3.1
Roman slaves at work. *Source:* Obtained (with Creative Commons permission to reuse) from Google Images, Wikipedia.

uncommon for a nobleman to own several hundred. By then, the republic had already fallen, replaced by an imperial system. Following a century of violent political strife prompted in large part by the unsettling economic impact of large-scale foreign conquest, Octavian became supreme leader of all Roman territory in 31 C.E. Four years later he became Emperor Augustus, and Rome was no longer a republic but an empire.

After the assassination of Julius Caesar in 44 C.E., Augustus Caesar ushered in the extended period of relative calm throughout Roman territory known as the *Pax Romana*, the Roman peace. This was attained through a combination of military might abroad and the preservation of some of the former republic's elected offices. The latter helped placate the home front while the empire kept expanding, reaching its apex under Emperor Trajan.

During Trajan's reign, Rome's territory extended from the south of Egypt as far north as modern-day Scotland and from the Atlantic coast of Iberia (modern-day Spain and Portugal) all the way east to Susa, in modern-day Iran. In his portrait of the empire during this magnificent period of 98 to 117, these are the territories designated by British historian Edward Gibbon as "the fairest part of the earth, and the most civilized portion of mankind."[11] From coastal North Africa, across much of Europe and Asia Minor, the "peaceful inhabitants," Gibbon continues, "abused the advantages of wealth and luxury."[12]

Certainly the proliferation of commercial opportunities from the empire's expansion, coupled with the growing cosmopolitanism of Rome itself, began to erode traditional Roman morality. In this manner, the traditional patrician hostility toward commerce began to diminish. "The smell of profit is good from whatever source," so wrote the Roman poet Juvenal in the late first century C.E. The phrase would become a maxim among some of the more enterprising segments of the Roman citizenry. However, while establishing businesses in certain industrial fields became more respectable, other aspects of commerce—particularly trade and moneylending—never lost their stigma entirely. Consequently, there was a role for slaves to play in these commercial activities.

By then, both the agriculture and the industry of the Italian peninsula had been dependent on slave labor for well over three hundred years. The growing militarism of the republic and then the empire exacerbated the prevalence of such labor by drawing large numbers of young men outside the Italian workforce to serve in foreign campaigns and then importing foreigners captured from these battles as slaves. Moreover, as the employment of large groups of slaves transformed traditional crop raising into plantation farming, many family farms became insolvent, and in some instances their owners' children were sold or forced into slavery.

So the burgeoning population of slaves from abroad was, albeit indirectly, creating more of the domestic variety as well. Alongside foreign conquest, the institution of slavery had become a mainstay of Roman commercial life. Consequently, as it transitioned from republic to empire, Rome's growing prosperity was not "balanced and wholesome," in the words of H. J. Haskell, but "a parasitic prosperity based on the consumption of the accumulated savings of the East and the explosion of slave labor in mines and on farms."[13]

Of course, the Roman aversion to entrepreneurship was intimately related to what Haskell describes as a "parasitic" form of prosperity. In an environment where, to paraphrase Peter Drucker yet again, endowing *existing* resources with the capacity to generate new wealth was discouraged, the profit motive was expressed through conquest and the subjugation of conquered people. However, consistent with patrician attitudes, this was often undertaken with little regard for industry. Carthage was one of several cities that the conquering Romans chose to raze to the ground. Some of these cities were the sites of important local industries that could have been salvaged had the Romans not been so fixated on the immediate gains of precious metals and slaves.

The French economist Paul Louis observed that in the service of Rome, humanity "labored" and "toiled in the mines." Moreover, "gangs of slaves," Louis wrote, "threshed grain in the plains of Palermo, upon the plateaus of Numidia, along the damp banks of the Nile."[14] Although Rome had developed a sophisticated legal system, captured slaves, as noncitizens, were generally treated like human cattle. Often malnourished and always subject to the whims—emotional, physical, and otherwise—of their masters, the life of a Roman slave was punitively harsh but mercifully brief. The average life expectancy of Roman slaves has been estimated at between nineteen and twenty-one years.

Battered into submission by unsympathetic masters, most slaves put up little resistance, but a number of violent slave rebellions challenged the institution. Many of these were relatively small and brief. However, the first large-scale incident of this kind occurred in 135 B.C.E. in Sicily. The historian Diodorus Siculus's summary of that rebellion is particularly insightful:

> For on account of the immense wealth of those exploiting this rich
> island, practically all of the very wealthy reveled in luxury, arrogance

and insolence. Consequently, as the slaves' hatred of their masters increased *pari passu* [proportionally] with the masters' cruelty toward their slaves, the hatred burst forth one day at an opportune moment. Then, without pre-arrangement, many thousands of slaves quickly gathered together to destroy their masters.[15]

This first mass slave rebellion inspired similar activity throughout other Roman territories in the Mediterranean, and within three years a slave army numbering almost seventy thousand threatened to destroy the patrician order. By 131 B.C.E., the rebellion was put down by the Roman military with bloody resolve. Nonetheless, two more mass rebellions ensued. The last, in 73 B.C.E., was led by Spartacus, the former gladiator known to many through the 1960 film starring Kirk Douglas.

With a slave army of ninety thousand men, Spartacus was able to wreak havoc throughout the Italian peninsula for almost three years before his rebellion was put down by Marcus Licinius Crassus, a Roman statesman and businessman who was close to Julius Caesar. Determined to ensure that a large-scale slave uprising would never happen again, Crassus not only subdued the rebellion, but as a forbidding example of what happens to disobedient slaves, he crucified six thousand of his rebel captives across the 120-mile stretch of Italy from Capua to Rome. Roman dependence on slave labor was such that collectively these rebellions had constituted, in the words of Michael Grant, "the most serious threat to Rome since Hannibal."[16]

Although Rome would not see another large-scale slave rebellion, the unresolved issues pertaining to such widespread use of slaves would continue to fester. Nonetheless, such humanitarian considerations were not especially interesting to Rome's patricians. As long as they were pliable and subservient, slaves fit in perfectly with the aristocratic view of Roman society. However, the patricians would soon learn that they had left the "back door" to their exclusive world of power and privilege open to entrepreneurship. As early as the late second century B.C.E., it was clear that some of the more talented slaves had slipped through that door to attain considerable wealth and even grudging respectability.

From Slave to Master

Even during the last century and a half of the republic, the supply of slaves had grown so large from conquest that many slaves were tasked both with the establishment of new businesses and the maintenance of existing ones. Since such labor, according to the republic's patricians, was mere grunt work, and thus beneath the dignity of their noble lineage, the slaves soon controlled much of the traffic in some of Rome's favorite foods—from basic foodstuffs like bread and salted fish, to delicacies like duck and sweets— along with clothes, sandals, and even art. In many instances, these transactions were conducted in shops financed by Roman citizens but founded and operated by slaves, many of whom were not Romans.

In light of Mesopotamia's and Phoenicia's extensive mercantile history, it is not entirely surprising that slaves from the Greek-speaking areas of Asia Minor recently acquired by Rome were best employed in shops rather than fields or factories. "The Syrian or Hellenized Oriental," R. H. Barrow wrote, "showed a capacity for business and figures and languages which few Italians showed."[17] Moreover, unlike the Romans and Greeks, who had moral qualms about such work, captives from Asia Minor preferred it to the backbreaking farm labor and potentially deadly mining work that was the lot of most slaves in Rome.

Many of the slave-merchants, foreign or domestic, were motivated by a more compelling objective than merely staying in the good graces of their masters—freedom. From a traditional humanitarian perspective, manumission, the freeing of slaves, was one of the few redeeming features of an otherwise ruthless system. In most instances, slaves became *liberti* upon the death of a master compassionate enough to include a provision in his will releasing some or all of his former slaves.

However, particularly among the more enterprising of Rome's slaves, another more immediate path to freedom was often pursued. Over time, the slave's allotted portion of a business's profits could accumulate into a sum sufficient to purchase freedom from his or her master. This was usually a mutually beneficial arrangement, as the masters would benefit from their slaves being offered the ultimate incentive for growing their assigned businesses. In many instances, the masters had grown reliant on their slaves for the maintenance, even survival, of businesses that the masters owned but neglected to manage. Extant records reveal that slaves even signed important business documents on their masters' behalf. "I, Vestalis, the slave of Popidia, declare in writing that I have received. . . ."[18]

Similarly, in the early imperial period, both slaves and freedmen comprised the *familia Caesaris*—a group entrusted with the lofty task of tracking and administering the empire's revenues. Remarkably, a group of slaves and former slaves had now made their way into the imperial equivalent of the Treasury Department. However, in many other instances, the former slave-merchants, as newly freed citizens of Rome, would apply their legendary commercial skills to businesses of their own. Some proved exceptionally talented in their own entrepreneurial activities.

This phenomenon is well illustrated by the bombastic words of a character representing a freedman-entrepreneur in the writings of Juvenal, "Oh, I know I'm foreign: Look here, at my pierced ears, no use denying it—born Out East, on the Euphrates. But my five shops bring in Four Hundred Thousand [sesterti], see?"[19] The Mesopotamian-born former slave continues: "What's in a senator's purple stripe, if true-blood nobles are reduced to herding sheep up-country, while I have more stashed away than any Imperial favorite."

Considering that even some of Rome's emperors had their private estates managed by commercially gifted freedmen, the privileged circumstances of Juvenal's character are not as far-fetched as they may seem. Here we have a former slave who was not only not a Roman but a despised "Asian," yet his wealth exceeded that of some Roman aristocrats. The latter were raised in an environment of prestige and comfort while the former did not even have his freedom for much of his life. This stark contrast points to another enduring aspect of entrepreneurship, the psychology of the underdog.

Jack Welch, the former chairman and CEO of General Electric, is widely regarded as one of modern America's greatest business managers. Along with his wife Suzy, he offered an important insight about this phenomenon in their 2008 book, Winning: "Most people instinctively hedge their bets even as they place them. The irony is that such hedging can doom a new venture to failure." However, as the Welches continue, "When launching something new, you have to go for it—'playing not to lose' can never be an option."[20]

But for Roman patricians eager to retain both their landed wealth and the respect of their peers, "playing not to lose" was a matter of habit. Consequently, even in such a class-conscious society as ancient Rome, the typical patrician was no match for an ambitious and commercially savvy freedman with little wealth and certainly no social standing to lose. As the Welches underscore, entrepreneurship is best undertaken by those who do not avoid but embrace risk. So the patricians' conservatism, coupled with their longstanding contempt for enterprise, paved the way for the entrepreneurial success of the freedmen.

This somewhat ironic turn of events would undermine Rome's ancient social hierarchy and provoke the hostility of its traditionalists. The latter is well encapsulated in the vitriol that Horace, one of Rome's greatest poets, aimed at the successful freedmen who through their superior wealth had humiliated the proud patricians. "Though thou struttest along proud of thy wealth," he wrote, "fortune does not change thy race."[21] Fortune may not have changed their "race," but to the great consternation of Horace and those of his well-born class, it certainly changed the nature of wealth and power in Rome.

For several hundred years, the patricians had maintained a rigid social hierarchy that to a great extent defined both the political and economic structure of Roman life. Then, as the classical historian Christoph Hocker observed, during the final stages of the republic, the unanticipated entrepreneurial success of some freedmen upset that hierarchy and effectively overturned its lower rungs. "The peasantry," Hocker wrote, "sank to the level of a proletariat, while the numerous urban *liberti* and even slaves themselves rose to wealth."[22]

By the early years of the empire, between 30 and 40 percent of the wealthiest men were freedmen. These are astonishing figures, considering how the patrician system had, with the exception of the equestrian subclass, managed to keep the plebeians in their "rightful place." Yet here were some of Rome's wealthiest men who, in the eyes of the nobility, were of inferior stock even when compared with the lowly plebeians. These were men who were once slaves, and as such were not even citizens of Rome for much of their lives. Worse yet, in some instances they were not even born in Europe, let alone Italy.

Although most of these affluent freedmen had earned their riches in trade, retail, crafts, and banking, much to the chagrin of the nobility, some of these detestable nouveaux riches were acquiring prized real estate and buying their way into the landed gentry. Moreover, during the early years of the empire, the freedmen came to dominate the imperial civil service, with many serving as provincial financial agents, the *procurators*. Perhaps the most revealing evidence in this regard was found in Pompeii, the resort town fossilized by the 79 C.E. eruption of nearby Mount Vesuvius. Rediscovered more than fifteen hundred years later, the unearthed Pompeii, frozen in the late first century C.E., has provided historians with something of a firsthand look at Roman life during that period.

Among the insights gleaned from Pompeii about the status of the *liberti* is the fact that freedmen and their descendants comprised roughly 40 percent of the town's governing aristocracy. For many patricians, such power and prestige in the hands of former slaves was a bridge too far.

After all, such a scenario would have been unthinkable before the onset of the growing pains of the empire. From a traditionalist Roman perspective, the socioeconomic and increasingly *political* prominence of foreign-born freedmen stood as the most humiliating and intolerable of these imperial consequences.

In time, as the empire consolidated, aristocratic pride eventually overtook economic expediency, and the ascendancy of the freedmen was brought to a swift close during the second century C.E. Discriminatory laws and practices arose to "reinforce the boundaries between the different [social] orders,"[23] as the historian Richard Alston observed. For example, during this period, under patrician direction, the more respectable equestrian class began taking the place of freedmen as agents in the civil service.

Nevertheless, by then a considerable number of freedmen and their descendants were already well ensconced in the highest echelons of Roman society. So, although the ascendancy of the freedmen-entrepreneurs was cut short, it had already irrevocably altered the social and even ethnic composition of Rome's elite. As such, it stands as one of the most impactful social changes wrought by entrepreneurship in antiquity.

A Peculiar Kind of Enterprise

The wealthiest Roman of recorded history is a real estate speculator, and a dubious one at that. During the period of Rome's transition from republic to empire, the aptly named Crassus grew a small fortune inherited from his father into an enormous one. He accomplished this primarily through the purchase of distressed properties. In modern parlance, that term describes properties experiencing financial difficulties. However, the properties Crassus sought out were distressed in the more literal sense of the word— they were on fire! At the time, many buildings in Rome were built from wood, and fires were certainly not uncommon in such wooden structures.

Crassus seemed to have an uncanny knack for appearing in the midst of a blazing inferno with money and an entourage of slaves. Then, in addition to the afflicted property, he would also purchase the surrounding properties for a fraction of their market price, convincing their owners that it was better to obtain *something* from him before the inferno spread and the whole neighborhood went up in smoke. Plutarch, the acclaimed Greek writer and Roman citizen, writing shortly after Crassus's death, characterized the late general's lopsided real estate speculations in pointed terms: "The making of contracts at the scene of a conflagration."[24] Despite Crassus's controversial methods, over time the better part of Rome fell into his hands.

In fact, his economic position was analogous to that of a modern-day businessperson owning more than half of modern-day Manhattan or Shanghai. Crassus also earned considerable income from mining, trade, and other businesses—all of which involved extensive and often specialized slave labor. Among his crew of more than five hundred slaves were silversmiths, scribes, accountants, and commercial agents, and for his real estate business, builders and even slave-architects. Crassus was the quintessential patrician entrepreneur—privileged, opportunistic, and heavily reliant on slave labor and knowledge for the operation of his businesses.

Moreover, he knew how to leverage his wealth to attain greater prominence as a politician, yet due in part to his commercial proclivities, Crassus never attained the respectability he sought. However, since money was always needed to feed and equip armies, his enormous wealth made him an attractive candidate for political alliance. As discussed earlier, Crassus was the general who put down Rome's largest slave rebellion. Subsequently, he formed a partnership of consuls with an ambitious politician known as Pompey the Great for several years. Then Crassus became part of the First Triumvirate, sharing power with both Pompey and the most celebrated figure of Roman history, Julius Caesar. Six years later, the wealthiest man in Roman history, serving as governor of Syria, was killed in battle in Asia Minor.

In our own era, the wealthiest individual in the world is Bill Gates, technology entrepreneur extraordinaire. Along with Steve Jobs and arguably a few others, the cofounder of Microsoft personifies American innovation-driven entrepreneurship. In this capacity, Gates certainly stands in stark contrast to Crassus. The exemplar of Roman entrepreneurship, which had little to do with innovation, Crassus made extensive use of patrician privilege and slave labor and no technological advances at all. The only innovation evident in his business career can be found in his unconventionally "fiery" negotiation tactics.

That said, the Roman world certainly had its share of innovators. Among the most renowned of these was Heron, a scientist, inventor, and lecturer who lived in Roman Egypt during the early first century C.E. His breakthroughs included a self-powered fountain, a wind-powered organ, and the world's first coin-operated vending machine. Most significantly, some seventeen hundred years before Britain's Industrial Revolution, Heron discovered the steam engine and even built a contraption that utilized steam to spin a glass ball.

Whereas the enterprising British, upon rediscovering the steam engine (building upon the work of a seventeenth-century Spanish inventor), recognized its revolutionary application to industrial production, Heron could not see a "practical use for his invention,"[25] in the words of classics scholar Stephen Bertman. Yet this failure to apply steam power to industry did not "diminish Heron's exhilaration when first his engine spun." Bertman continues, "The thrill he felt was no less than that experienced by Greek discus throwers whose striving served no higher purpose than to celebrate the pursuit of excellence and man's glorious triumph in attaining it."[26] Consistent with the Greek tradition in which most educated Romans were steeped, the primary objectives of innovation were the expansion of knowledge and the improvement of society.

Unlike that of most of the entrepreneurial civilizations that preceded and succeeded it, the ingenuity of Rome was seldom motivated by a quest for profit. In fact, from a modern perspective it is perplexing how such a powerful nation developed so few domestic industries, even as it was blessed with the natural resources of most of the known world and the most advanced engineering expertise of the era. Certainly, the Romans made profitable use of Spanish and Gallic mines, along with the production of various artistic and edible products from the empire's eastern provinces, but these were hardly domestic industries.

Even during imperial Rome's golden age (96 to 303 C.E.), when both the geographic and financial scope of Roman trade had peaked, Rome's exports were weak. Nevertheless, craftsmanship was encouraged, and some of the larger workshops, staffed by large numbers of slaves, did yield significant quantities of such household goods as tableware, inexpensive clothes, and oil lamps. Notably, workshop owners and other small and midsized entrepreneurs formed guild-like organizations known as *collegia* that began to wield considerable power in the third century C.E.

All Roads Lead Away from Rome

During the last two centuries of the empire, Rome staggered from one economic crisis to the next. Like that of ancient Greece, the currency of the Roman Empire was coinage. Beginning in the third century, severe monetary problems emerged as the empire's expenditures spiraled out of control. Wild fluctuations in the value, and even the supply, of various metal coins stifled healthy economic activity. However, alongside these monetary crises, a number of other systemic cracks in the edifice of Roman prosperity grew more apparent.

The social mobility that had, albeit to a limited extent, galvanized Roman entrepreneurship in the late years of the republic and the early years of the empire had all but vanished. In its place was a rigid and at times coercively regulated socioeconomic structure. A once vibrant middle class had been reduced to a relatively small cadre of merchants, often organized through their *collegia*. In order to support an increasingly untenable empire, taxes became ruinous for all but the wealthiest of Romans. As the plebeians and slaves coalesced into a large and discontented underclass, the Roman elite further tightened their monopoly on the imperial economy.

With dwindling employment and entrepreneurial opportunities in the city, many Romans left Rome for the countryside. If they had the means, they would farm their own land, but more commonly they would serve on their feudal landlords' estates as tenant farmers. The latter presaged the feudal system, which would dominate economic life and partially stifle western European entrepreneurship during the Middle Ages. "The estate," as the German sociologist and political economist Max Weber wrote, was "the nucleus of the feudal system, while the town was the birthplace of freedom."[27] Accordingly, as Rome's urban economy was fading, so did many of the entrepreneurial opportunities that its residents—including equestrian plebeians, former slaves, foreigners, *and* patricians—had once exploited.

Entrepreneurship Travels East

In 364 C.E., the empire permanently split between its western portion, administered from Rome, and its eastern or "Byzantine" portion, administered from Constantinople (modern-day Istanbul). Although the eastern empire's political institutions were modeled after Rome's, the largely Greek-speaking and Orthodox Christian Byzantine civilization was quite distinct from Roman culture. As the western Roman Empire entered its twilight, its eastern counterpart was faring much better economically and politically, so much so that Byzantium attracted some of Italy's best merchants. Remarkably, this eastern "Roman Empire" would endure until 1453. Ancient Rome, infiltrated by hostile barbarians from northern Europe, would not survive beyond the late fifth century.

Less than one hundred years later, back in western Asia, a boy by the name of Abū al-Qāsim Muḥammad was born into a relatively modest pagan Arabian family. A caravan export agent by trade, Muḥammad would spawn a new religion and, like Rome, a conquering empire. Islamic civilization, founded by a traveling merchant married to the widow of a much wealthier merchant, was unburdened by Roman (and Greek) disdain for entrepreneurship. So as Europe fell into its Dark Ages and the scope and variety of Western enterprise declined, the world of early Islam proved to be fertile ground for entrepreneurs of diverse ethnic and socioeconomic backgrounds.

4

An Enterprising Faith

An honest and trustworthy merchant will be raised with
the Prophets, the truthful and the martyrs.
—AT-TIRMDHI HADITH (ISLAMIC ORAL TRADITION)
COLLECTION

Nomads' Land

The region of Arabia, or the Arabian Peninsula, encompasses modern-day
Saudi Arabia, all of the smaller Persian Gulf States, Yemen, and to the east,
portions of Iraq and Jordan. Situated between the great western powers of
antiquity and the coveted spices and silk of the Indus valley, Arabia held
considerable strategic value. Not surprisingly, many of the nomadic Arabs
became involved in trade, and caravans of merchants were commonplace,
Arab or otherwise. Due to the vast commerce that passed through the
peninsula, at their respective peaks, the empires of Persia, Rome, and Byzantium all ensured a strong regional presence to secure their commercial
interests.

For several hundred years, the Arabs derived considerable profit from
the high volume of trade passing through their land. Moreover, the presence of more advanced societies led to a measure of urban development
in Arabia, facilitating a more stable and less nomadic existence for a sizable minority of its people. Nonetheless, trade was the dominant form of
commerce in the region, as the Arabs produced relatively few goods aside
from food and various other basic necessities. For example, they relied on
imports from Syria (which they had yet to conquer) for most of their clothing, and the Arabs' prized swords were usually imported from India.

Figure 4.1
Geography of the Arabian Peninsula. *Source:* Obtained with permission to reuse from Google Images (kids.brittanica).

Aside from supplying their own needs via trade, the Arabs served as vital intermediaries or transport agents for the Romans, Byzantines, Persians, Indians, and other prominent civilizations of the period. Notably, like the merchants of ancient Mesopotamia, those of the Arab caravan trade had, long before Islam, grown accustomed to financing their operations with venture capital. For these traders, it took the form of a contract known as the *mudaraba.*

As the Saudi Arabian writer and publisher Abdul Malik Mujahid explains, in a *mudaraba* contract, "Profits are shared by the two parties; the share of each party is determined by mutual agreement." Mujahid continues, "Losses, if any, are borne by the owner of the capital; the entrepreneur may not be compensated for his labor though."[1] In other words, it was a classic venture capital arrangement involving a passive investor and an active partner—a traveling trader more often than not. The need for such a mechanism, simple as it was, reflects the high volume of trade that passed through Arab hands.

Long before Muhammad's army conquered the region, Arab caravans were part of the landscape, from the western edge of modern-day Lebanon all the way east to India and all the way south to Abyssinia in modern-day Ethiopia. In terms of religious practice, most but not all of the Arab traders of that era were polytheists. Large Christian and Jewish communities were well established in the peninsula and, alongside the pagan Arabs, both of these monotheistic groups played a prominent role in the vigorous trade of the peninsula. However, during the period immediately preceding the advent of Islam, commercial activity waned as the region destabilized politically. Particularly in central and northern Arabia, the peninsula reverted to its ancient nomadism and Bedouin tribalism as various kingdoms disintegrated.

Both domestic food cultivation and urban trade declined to the point where several towns in the peninsula disappeared altogether. Nevertheless, some relatively large and advanced urban centers in Arabia would prove enduring. Among these was the city of Mecca, almost equidistant from the northern and southern limits of the peninsula but strategically located on its western edge, less than fifty miles from the Red Sea coast. Well situated along many trade routes and the site of a bustling marketplace, the city was dominated by a tribe of merchants known as the Quraysh.

The Intersection of Religion and Commerce

Aside from its marketplace, long before the birth of Muhammad, the city of Mecca's Ka-aba was one of Arabia's most popular pilgrimage sites. In one of history's great ironies, the cubical structure, now the center of Mecca's Great Mosque, was once a shrine for some of the most ardent polytheists in the Middle East. However, according to Islamic tradition, none other than the patriarch Abraham assisted Ishmael with laying the original edifice of the Ka-aba. Nonetheless, in pre-Islamic times, the primary feature of the site was its collection of more than three hundred sculpted clay deities. For the pagan Arabs, it was the Ka-aba's polytheistic splendor that was its primary attraction, not its link to Abraham and Ishmael. (Of course, the latter would become vitally important when the pilgrimage site became central to Muhammad's monotheistic faith.)

During the period preceding the advent of Islam, the Ka-aba attracted a wide and varied selection of pilgrims from all over Arabia, many of whom were traders with vast sums of money to spend. The presence of an important religious site was a boon to the Meccan economy, and among the primary beneficiaries of the resulting uptick in commerce were the members of a disciplined and ambitious tribe—the Quraysh. The tribe rose to prominence in Mecca through trade, livestock breeding, and various other endeavors, including the administration of the "holy city." "It is nothing new that there is a lot of money to be made in religion," the author Lesley Hazelton wrote, "the sixth century Quraysh knew this as well as any modern televangelist" and they "ran the city as a kind of oligarchy . . . access was always mediated, and always for a fee."[2]

Remarkably enterprising, the Quraysh devised collaborative methods for safeguarding and financing their operations. For example, eager to protect their lucrative Meccan trade, the Quraysh resolved to tighten the city's defenses and secure it from the roaming marauders who menaced the region. To this end, they engaged the local Bedouins, whose swordsmanship and camel-riding skills were legendary. However, it was the *structure* of this engagement that is most notable. In exchange for their services as the guardians of Mecca, the Bedouins received neither silver nor gold nor camels but shares in the Quraysh tribe's Meccan businesses. With the kind of maneuver preferred by modern start-up entrepreneurs, this ancient tribe had shrewdly enlisted their own security force with something akin to a "no cash, all stock" compensation and incentive plan.

The Quraysh comprised twelve clans. True to its tribal roots, the Banu Hashim, the Quraysh clan from which Muhammad sprang, was also known for intermingling its extensive commercial activities with religion. Custodians of the "Sacred Well of Zamzam," the Banu Hashim held a position of considerable significance in the spiritual life of Mecca. Gods of the sun and moon were two of the longtime favorite deities of Arabian polytheism. As such, the Well of Zamzam, where pilgrims could view the sun through the water's reflections, was hallowed ground for the region's many sun worshippers.

Alongside their religious activities, the Banu Hashim were also known for their commercial prowess. While there were many groups on the peninsula involved with trade, this particular clan not only participated in such activity, but often was its architect, having established the dominant pattern of Meccan trade with surrounding regions. During the summer, their caravans would bring dates, horses, harnesses, wool blankets, and various perfumes and spices to lands in the north (primarily Syria) and return to Mecca with various fruits, grains, weapons, olive oil, and manufactured textiles. During the colder months, the caravans of the Banu Hashin would transact a similar exchange with traders in the scorched deserts of Yemen.

As discussed in chapter 3, strategizing and profiting from new trade patterns was precisely the sort of entrepreneurial pursuit shunned by "polite society" in Roman culture. The elite of Mecca, on the other hand, generally admired and encouraged such activities. Moreover, whereas the Roman nobility would have been horrified to see their temples administered by entrepreneurs, the Meccans saw no inherent conflict between entrepreneurship and religion. To a great extent, this attitude would be preserved in the new Arabian religion that would soon be established, a legacy of Muhammad's tribe and clan.

An Enterprising Young Man

Despite the proud commercial lineage of his family, Muhammad's early childhood was marked by chaos rather than privilege due to a series of untimely deaths. Even prior to his birth, believed to have occurred in Mecca around 570 C.E., his story line was marked by the tragic loss of his father, Abdullah. His impoverished mother, Aminah, would follow her husband to the grave six years later, and the grandfather who became Muhammad's caretaker would die when the child was only eight. From that point forward, Muhammad would be in the care, and in many respects in the *employ*, of his uncle Abu Talib.

An accomplished and principled man, Talib was known as both a guardian of the sacred Ka-aba and in the words of the historian Washington Irving, "one of the most enterprising merchants of the tribe of Koreish [Quraysh]."[3] As Muhammad's father figure during the critical stage of adolescence and early adulthood, Talib, and his extensive commercial and religious undertakings, would leave his mark upon his nephew's character and ambitions. In fact, Muhammad's uncle would often take his nephew with him on lengthy trading expeditions throughout Arabia and beyond. From a very young age Muhammad earned his keep as an assistant on Meccan merchant caravans, many of which traveled beyond the Peninsula. A few years later, another uncle, Zobier, would benefit from Muhammad's assistance with a trade expedition to Yemen.

Regarding the entrepreneurial type, Craig Hall, a contemporary American real estate entrepreneur, observed, "You can't teach somebody who has no desire or lacks an innate, risk-taking mind-set to be entrepreneurial."[4] While this is often true, the sway of experiences and coaching during one's formative years should not be dismissed. Whether it is a frightening brush with poverty during one's childhood or the mentorship of an elder during adolescence, there are circumstances that help shape desire, risk tolerance, and the other essential ingredients of successful entrepreneurship. In Muhammad's case, both his lineage and his early experiences of hardship, caravan work, and mentorship by older family members all but ensured that entrepreneurship would play a prominent role in his later life.

By the time he turned twenty, Muhammad had learned a lot about travel, trade routes, and dealing with competitors—negotiating with them and, when necessary, battling them to the death. Some twenty years later, he would draw upon all of these skills as he promulgated the new faith. Until then, aside from spells working as a sheep herder, Muhammad spent his adolescence and young adulthood in the world of commerce. As he "advanced in years," Irving writes, Muhammad "was employed by different persons as commercial agent or factor in caravans . . . all of which tended to enlarge the sphere of his observation."[5] The young Muhammad's encounters with the many Christian and Jewish traders who were prominent in the region would also inform many of the monotheistic ideas that would later be expressed in the Koran.

Muhammad bin Abdullah, Chief Executive Officer

By the time Muhammad turned twenty-five, his reputation as a reliable and experienced caravan agent had won him a measure of recognition within Mecca's business community. However, while his patrons entrusted him with great responsibility and decision-making power for their caravans, Muhammad was still operating as an agent, not as an owner or even a manager. Despite his expertise, Muhammad had not amassed significant wealth. That would all change soon after he encountered his next client, Khadijah bint (daughter of) Khuwaylid.

Khadijah was the widow of one of Mecca's wealthiest merchants, who had been one of the largest caravan operators in the peninsula. Hearing of Muhammad's longtime expertise in the caravan industry, she was eager to retain his services for an imminent caravan expedition to Syria. He gladly accepted, and upon his return to Mecca, his client was so impressed by both his work and, according to some sources, his youthful good looks that she paid him twice the sum they had originally agreed upon. Although she was fifteen years Muhammad's senior, Khadijah had already decided that she would like to marry the young caravan agent.

Aside from genuine romantic feelings, there were also practical considerations behind the marriage proposal that she would tactfully impart through her slave. Khadijah had been left with the administration of a sizable commercial empire—in an industry for which she had neither the requisite expertise nor interest. She believed that Muhammad, already a veteran of Meccan trade, would be able to take the reins of the family business into his competent and ambitious hands. He recognized this as well and did not hesitate to accept his wealthy patroness's offer.

Catapulted to a position that his fellow caravan agents could only dream of, Muhammad leveraged his extensive industry experience to become one of Mecca's most revered caravan tycoons. Caravans operated by Muhammad were so dependable that, among some merchants, he was referred to as "Al Amin," "the trustworthy one." Aside from reliability and professionalism, the young trade mogul also demonstrated his abilities as a consummate promoter. "The CEO," according to the Indus Entrepreneurs, a nonprofit networking organization for entrepreneurs, is "the leader of the organization . . . the storyteller and evangelizer, the voice to market."[6] As the owner of a large business, Muhammad proved highly adept at such storytelling and evangelizing.

Although the most common modern usage of the term "evangelism" denotes the promotion of the Christian faith, the word is rooted more generally in the (Koine) Greek verb *euangelzomai*, meaning "to proclaim" or "to bring good news." Spreading a positive word about a product or service is certainly a vital aspect of commerce, as reflected in such recent book titles as *Evangelist Marketing: What Apple, Amazon, and Netflix Understand About Their Customers* (Benbella, 2011) and *The Product Evangelist Primer* (Amazon Digital Services, 2014).[7] Of course, it is also a vital aspect of proselytization. So perhaps it is not surprising that Islam, the second largest of the proselytizing faiths, was founded by someone with a natural talent for evangelizing.

An Entrepreneurial Evangelist

For fifteen years, Muhammad enjoyed his life as a prosperous Meccan merchant and family man. However, as the years wore on, he grew more reflective and spiritual, a change encouraged by his wife. Prior to her death at age sixty-three, Khadijah would be Muhammad's first convert, remaining loyal to him even as his monotheistic message roused the anger of Meccan traditionalists. According to Islamic tradition, the founder of the faith experienced his first divine revelations in 610 C.E. Over the next three years, more revelations ensued, and the basis for a distinctly Arabian monotheistic faith was formed.

By 613 C.E., Muhammad began preaching this controversial message publicly. Muhammad's own tribe, the Quraysh, as the dominant power in Mecca and the administrators of its primary religious sites, were concerned about certain aspects of the new faith. With the advantage of historical hindsight, there is some irony in the fact that the Quraysh feared that this Arabian form of monotheism would diminish the importance of Mecca as a pilgrimage site. However, their fears concerning the new prophet's apparent ambition to overturn the existing religious order and create a new one with him at the helm proved to be well justified. Moreover, while Muhammad's emphasis on charity and his thinly veiled barbs against the behavior of the privileged appealed to some on the lower rungs of Meccan society, such a message did not sit well with the Quraysh.

However, it is important to clarify that, as reflected in the contents of the Koran and the Hadith, Muhammad's primary message was monotheism, not wealth redistribution. The Koran is a posthumous compilation of what, according to the Caliph Umar, was every utterance of the Prophet, "whether inscribed on date-leaves, shreds of leather . . . or the hearts of man."[8] The Hadith is believed to comprise something akin to Islam's oral tradition, a "record of the traditions or sayings of the Prophet Muhammad," in the words of the *Encyclopedia Britannica*, "revered and received as a major source of religious law and moral guidance."[9]

Sura 81 of the Koran states that for someone whose longing for wealth supersedes spiritual pursuits and whose greed prevents charity, "wealth shall not avail" on the Day of Judgment. Apparently, such a message was sufficiently radical to strike fear into the hearts of a Meccan elite comprised of wealthy merchants. Nonetheless, it is a far cry from New Testament passages such as "it is easier for a camel to go through the eye of a needle, than for a rich man to enter the kingdom of God,"[10] wherein the possession of great wealth, regardless of one's attitude to charity, is deemed sufficient to keep one from entering heaven.

Despite his disgust with the behavior of some of the wealthy Meccans, Muhammad's words always bore a certain respect for commerce, provided that it was undertaken in the "right" manner. In fact, the Koran bears the mark of a businessman, characterized by, in the words of the historian Bernard Lewis, "the frequent use of commercial metaphors and turns of phrase."[11] Furthermore, according to the Hadith, when asked about the most honorable ways of earning a livelihood, the Prophet replied, "A man's work with his hands, and every legitimate sale."[12] In this respect, Islamic civilization, founded by an Arab caravan operator, was quite distinct from ancient Rome and its elite's disdain for commerce.

To be clear, alongside the more business-friendly passages cited earlier, Muhammad is also reported to have disparaged such practices as bribery, price gouging, and usury. Regarding the latter, it was the charging of interest on loans that he found objectionable. However, the Islamic Empire would circumvent this prohibition by borrowing from non-Muslims (Christians and Jews in particular) and even, when the interest rate was considered to be "appropriate," from fellow Muslims. When it came to financial matters, pragmatism tended to trump puritanism for Muhammad and his converts.

For example, in 623, when the early Muslims were exiled in Medina, as Marilyn Tower Oliver writes, almost any means of financial gain—including outright piracy—was employed when deemed necessary: "Because the Muslims from Mecca were businessmen who found it difficult to adapt to the farming economy of Medina, finding another source of income had become an urgent need. Attacking the rich caravans that travelled to and from Mecca became a lucrative and alluring solution to their problems."[13] Moreover, the former caravan operator devised clever ways of incentivizing and rewarding his cohorts in this predatory form of commerce. The spoils from a raid of the "rich Jewish colony" of Khaybar, Robert Payne writes, were apportioned according to "a complicated system of shares" that accounted for seniority, performance, and other factors. Such a system provided ample motivation for the conquerors, and soon "more spoils and more treasure came from the Jewish colonies in Fadak, Wadi al-Qura and Tayma."[14] Furthermore, subjugated peoples who refused to convert were compelled to pay a poll tax, or *jizya*, to their new Muslim masters. The *jizya* proved to be an important recurring source of income for the new empire and its many collectors and agents.

These dynamics underscore the fact that along with piety, charity, and the like, territorial and financial gains in the name of *jihad* (holy war) were also encouraged among believers of the new faith. To be sure, the religious fervor of the Prophet of Islam and his followers was sincere.

Yet as a seasoned businessman and someone who had engaged in violent battle on the caravan trails, Muhammad saw both commerce and combat as essential tools for the dissemination of his message. "Unlike feudal Latin Christendom," the encyclopedia of *Medieval Islamic Civilization* elucidates, "Islamic society held commerce in high esteem."[15] This helps explain why, as enterprise in much of Europe lay somewhat dormant during this period, it would flourish not only in the Middle East but in the growing expanse of territory that would fall under Islamic rule.

Commerce and Converts

The founder of Islam passed away in 632, less than twenty years after he began preaching. During that relatively brief period, Muhammad's *ummah* (Islamic community) had grown from a ragtag collection of Meccan outcasts to the largest faith community of the Arabian Peninsula. This rapid growth continued as a series of aggressive successors to Muhammad, or "caliphs," took on the mantle of leadership of a rapidly expanding Islamic world: In 633, less than a year into his reign, forces under the command of Caliph Abu Bakr had conquered eastern Arabia. One year later, Abu Bakr's forces, fighting for the first time as a unified Arab army, defeated the Byzantine army at a battle near Gaza.

Within a decade of that critical victory, the emerging Arab-Islamic Empire had conquered all of Iraq, most of Iran, the entirety of the Levant (modern-day Lebanon, Syria, Israel, and the Palestinian Authority), Egypt, and even portions of modern-day Libya. Over the next hundred years, the empire would consolidate its initial conquests and expand much farther. To the west, Muslim conquests reached all the way to modern-day Morocco and Spain, to the east, all the way to India's Indus River. The empire reached as far north as modern-day Armenia, to Yemen in the south, and to parts of the Sudan in Africa.

For the world's new conquering army, Islam was "its battle cry," as Robin Winks observed in his *History of Civilization*. Yet, "its motives included the age-old ones of conquest for living space and booty."[16] Certainly, many young soldiers in the service of the caliph were motivated by faith in Islam and reverence for its Prophet. Concurrently, many Muslims, including recent converts, also had their eye on more material considerations when they joined the new colonizers. This aspect of Islamic expansion is captured well by the story of Ubayd Allah.

The Wages of War

The son of an Arab woman and a black slave who had converted to Islam, he was named Ubayd Allah, "the slave of Allah," by his father out of dedication to the new faith. During the late seventh century, Ubayd made his name as a great conqueror by leading an Islamic military force known as the "Army of Destruction" in several far-flung military expeditions. Perhaps the most legendary of these was the toppling of the kingdom of Bukhara in modern-day Uzbekistan in 680. However, he made his fortune by moving out to an area of southern Iraq, not long after the territory fell under Muslim rule, and starting a large contracting business.

Not surprisingly, the company established by the triumphant Muslim general was awarded large contracts, mainly for the construction of large public baths in the new city of Basra. Later, as the faithful captured the western Iranian province of Fars, Ubayd made a second fortune in a somewhat less scrupulous manner by pillaging the lavish remnants of the region's pagan "fire temples." Collectively, his conquest-related enterprises were sufficiently lucrative to support a remarkably lavish lifestyle. Ubayd's estate included an enormous house and a collection of eight hundred water buffaloes grazing on his marshlands in southern Iraq.

Such fortunes were not uncommon, particularly among those who were so well connected with the leaders of the new empire. At the time, the caliphate was in the hands of the Umayyads, a prominent mercantile family from Mecca's Quraysh tribe whose commercial prowess was legendary. It is telling that such a business-oriented family, appointed to high administrative posts by Muhammad himself shortly before his death, had become the directing minds of the Islamic Empire.

Crossroads of the World

Especially during the early phase of Islamic expansion, financial opportunities, such as those exploited by Ubayd, revolved around the spoils of war. Toward the end of the seventh century, the Berber queen Kahina, whose territory extended along the Mediterranean coast of modern-day Algeria and portions of Tunisia, was challenged and ultimately defeated by the westward march of the Muslim Arabs. As recounted by the British historian Edward Gibbon, Kahina's condemnation of her enemies was revealing. "Our cities and the gold and the silver which they contain," she said, "perpetually attract the arms of the Arabs. These vile metals are not the objects of our ambition; we content ourselves with the simple productions of the earth."[17]

Evidently, some of the conquered believed that these religious ambassadors from Arabia were driven by desires that were more earthly than celestial. From their own correspondence, it is clear that at least some of the conquerors saw their work in strikingly material terms. When asked to describe the Egyptian city of Alexandria that he had just absorbed into the caliphate, the Arab general `Amr ibn al-`As wrote to his superiors back in the peninsula: "I have captured the city, but I shall forbear describing it. Suffice to say that I have taken therein four thousand villas, four thousand baths, forty thousand Jews liable to poll tax, and four hundred pleasure palaces fit for kings."[18]

Slavery

Plunder—both material and human—cronyism, and the administration of taxes levied on subject nations were the well-worn paths to riches during this early phase of Islamic history, as they were during the expansion of the Roman Empire. So, perhaps it is not surprising that the caliphate also shared the patricians' enthusiasm for slavery. However, the mostly African origin of slaves in the Islamic world bore little resemblance to slavery in ancient Rome. Relative to the large number of European and western Asian (Syrians, Mesopotamians, Carthaginian Phoenicians, etc.) slaves in their employ, the Romans actually had very few black slaves. The Islamic Arabs, on the other hand, were the first of several non-black civilizations to systematically enslave large numbers of black Africans.

Certainly both the Phoenicians and the ancient Egyptians had some experience with black slavery, as did the pre-Islamic Arabs. Yet during antiquity, the trade in black slaves was like that of any other "exotic good" in the sense that the supply was limited and the customer base was generally restricted to the wealthiest segments of society. In antiquity, as inhuman as it seems from a twenty-first-century perspective, black slaves were often sold as expensive curios to people like the Egyptian pharaohs or the viceroys of Persia. Consequently, the slave trade during that period never extended beyond a very select market.

As Muslim conquests and trade routes penetrated ever deeper into Africa from the continent's north and east, Arab merchants gained more extensive and direct access to black African tribes than any preceding foreign civilization. A sizable number of enterprising Muslim Arabs capitalized upon this access by procuring slaves for their own use or, more commonly, for sale to other Arabs. Slaves would be obtained through a variety of deceptive methods, including such trickery as luring the young boys of a tribe with sweet Arabian dates. However, in other instances, the less scrupulous members of these African tribes would voluntarily sell their neighbors' children to the foreign slave traders.

It is important to clarify that some subject peoples of the Muslim conquests were treated with a measure of mercy, particularly if they were "People of the Book," a term in the Koran denoting Christians, Jews, and "Sabeans," members of another Abrahamic faith of that era. As long as these people paid the poll tax, they were allowed to live and practice the religion in which they were raised. In fact, there are some instances in which Arabic-speaking Christians, Jews, and Zoroastrians lived reasonably well and even prospered under Islamic rule. However, non-Muslims like the natives of black Africa, whose religions were considered "primitive," were disparaged for their backwardness. As it happened, their pitch-black hue did not engender much respect either.

In fairness, one would be hard-pressed to find distinctions between races in Islamic theology. In that regard, the Islamic texts are quite egalitarian. Nonetheless, like the Phoenicians before them and the Europeans who would trade in slaves in centuries to come, some Arab Muslims, particularly those engaged in the slave trade, had trouble seeing darker people as their equals. "The children of a stinking Nubian black God," a seventh-century Muslim Arab poet wrote, "[who] put no light in their complexions."[19] Many of the traders believed that taking a free person from one of these tribes and enslaving him or her in the Muslim world was a way of civilizing that person, and hence a godly act.

What is certain is that due to high demand for slaves, it was often a *profitable* act. The political and military elites of Islamic civilization, like those of the great civilizations of antiquity, certainly made ample use of slave labor. For example, the slave holdings of an early tenth-century Muslim ruler are astonishing. The Caliph al-Muqtadir, who reigned over the empire from 908 to 932, was served by eleven thousand male slaves—both Sudanese and Greek—in his immense palace in Baghdad.

More generally, although slaves in the Islamic world were not the default source of labor they had been in ancient Rome, they were commonly put to work in mines, on marsh drainage projects, and as deckhands on Muslim fleets. Moreover, Arab Muslim merchants, most of whom were upper-middle class, would often acquire black slaves to tend to agricultural work on their privately owned estates. For the first time, the supply of slaves was so large that men from a relatively wide swath of society, many of whom had no royal or aristocratic connections, were able to afford slaves.

In many respects, it was this Arab Muslim form of black slavery that would serve as the model several hundred years later, when ambitious men from various western European powers would employ black slaves on their estates throughout the New World. (Yet unlike those Europeans, Arab slave masters tended to castrate their black slaves.) The Arab slave traders' immediate objective was profit, alloyed, perhaps, with a sort of paternalistic piety. However, the long-term impact of their work would extend well beyond what they could have imagined and influenced the course of world history, particularly *Western* history, in profoundly controversial ways.

Of course, it also altered the composition of Africa itself. The dogged determination of Arab merchants to find new sources of human cargo, along with gold and other prized African goods, is certainly one of the reasons why, while over 95 percent of what is now Arab North Africa is Muslim, so is almost 40 percent of black Africa. In fact, the relentless quest of Arab merchants to seek out and develop new markets left its mark throughout the world.

Certainly, the heart of the Islamic Empire—the Middle East, North Africa/Spain, and even parts of central Asia—were all obtained through military conquest, much of which was at least partly motivated by mercantile concerns. For example, some of the conquests in formerly Buddhist central Asia (e.g., modern-day Afghanistan, Tajikistan, etc.) were undertaken to gain access to lucrative overland routes to countries farther east.

While many of the conversions in the Indian subcontinent can be traced to Muslim conquests—modern-day Bangladesh, India, and Pakistan—those in east Asia resulted primarily from the prominence of Middle Eastern merchants seeking new markets and trade goods. Today, southeast Asia is home to the most populous Muslim country in the world, Indonesia. Even in Buddhist/Communist China, where Muslim Arab merchants had established business operations almost five centuries before the arrival of Marco Polo, there is a sizable ethnically Chinese Muslim community numbering almost twenty-five million.

A Commercial Empire

Arab caravans had been part of the connective tissue of international trade for many centuries prior to the spread of their new faith. However, as Islamic armies conquered much of the territory that was once part of the Roman, Persian, and Byzantine Empires, the Arabs had elevated their role in international commerce from transport agents to directors. Unlike the Romans, the Arabs had long been unashamedly entrepreneurial, seeking financial opportunity from wherever it might be gained.

Notably, during the Umayyad dynasty and much of the succeeding Abbasid dynasty (750–1258 C.E.), the caliphate was often administered like a modern multinational company. Many decisions, even military ones, were predicated solely on profit maximization. Within such a political environment, entrepreneurship was encouraged to develop. Since the bulk of territorial gains had already occurred, the locus of opportunity for ambitious Arabs had shifted somewhat from the spoils of conquest toward more durable forms of commerce. By the ninth century, with almost the entire known world in a trade network for which their civilization was the central node, the Arabs were now at the helm of the greatest commercial power the world had yet seen.

Founded by Arabs, the Islamic Empire was naturally conducive to trade. However, as Islamic civilization solidified within the conquered, originally non-Arab territories of Syria, Iraq, North Africa, etc., the entrepreneurial proclivities of its Arab originators grew more varied and sophisticated and diversified into other areas. So, alongside traditional trade wherein Arabs served as intermediaries between the end buyers and sellers, a more multifaceted form of commerce emerged. Not unlike the Phoenicians of antiquity, as their sphere of influence grew, some Arab entrepreneurs branched out of conventional trade and became pollinators, producers, and to a far greater extent than the Phoenicians, financiers.

Pollinators: Coffee and Writing Paper

"This," the author Jon Littman observed, "is where cultures, industries and ideas cross in a fertile breeding ground."[20] Mr. Littman, speaking to *Forbes* in 2013, was referring to the San Francisco Bay Area and, more specifically, an early twenty-first-century technology environment dominated by the likes of Facebook, Google, and other Silicon Valley behemoths. However, his observation applies just as well to Baghdad, Damascus, or a number of other cities that served as the Islamic Empire's commercial hubs from the eighth to the thirteenth centuries.

It was almost inevitable that Islamic civilization would become an influential pollinator. After all, this was the civilization that conquered Spain to the west, and to the east controlled the Silk Road, the fabled central Asian overland trade route to China. To the north, significant amounts of Muslim coinage dating from the seventh to the eleventh centuries have been found in Sweden and elsewhere in Scandinavia—remarkable findings that affirm the economic power and reach of the Muslim world during its commercial peak. To the south, the volume of Islamic trade with sub-Saharan Africa was unprecedented, not only for slaves but also for gold, coconuts, and other goods.

The Islamic world's close interaction with civilizations at the farthest ends of the known world yielded some remarkable "pollinations." Through its extensive contact with the Greek-speaking Byzantine Empire, the Muslim world not only helped disseminate the scientific knowledge of classical Greek civilization but also, in some instances, advanced them further. For example, with respect to medicine, the Muslims "developed [medical knowledge] beyond the standard works of the Greek masters," the historian Robin Winks concludes. "They wrote textbooks, for instance, on diseases of the eye, on smallpox, and on measles, which remained the best authorities on those subjects until the eighteenth century."[21]

There were other notable pollinations in science and mathematics, such as the Arabic numeral system, since adopted throughout the world, which actually originated in India but was brought west by Arab merchants. However, the Arabs made important contributions of their own to mathematics. Among these were major advances in what we now refer to as algebra, a Latinized version of *al-jabr*, an Arabic term for "the reintegration of broken parts." The pollinations of the Islamic Empire also included a number of products from which large global industries developed, some of which are still major economic forces today. Among these, writing paper and coffee stand out as two of the most impactful and enduring legacies of early Islamic commerce.

Paper

Writing paper was in use in ancient China as early as the second century C.E. In 751, Arab forces defeated a Chinese contingent in the central Asian region of modern-day Kazakhstan and Kyrgyzstan. The surviving Chinese were taken captive and brought to Samarkand, a nearby region in modern-day Uzbekistan that was already under Muslim rule. As it happened, there were several experienced papermakers among the prisoners, and their skill aroused great interest among their Arab captors. "Paper," the eleventh-century Arab writer Tha'ālibī observed, "looks better and is more supple, more easily handled, and more convenient for writing than papyrus and parchment,"[22] which is precisely why the Muslim world was eager to embrace this skill and develop its own paper manufacturing industry.

So under the guidance of these foreign experts, a Muslim paper manufacturing industry emerged in mid-eighth-century Samarkand. The "new" industry then made its way to Baghdad, the seat of the caliphate and the nerve center of the Muslim world. By the end of the eighth century, the city would boast its first paper mill, a timely development considering that the caliphate and other administrative bodies had been running low on parchment for government documents. From Baghdad, both paper and papermaking expertise would be disseminated throughout the Muslim world and beyond. "By facilitating and indeed encouraging correspondence and record-keeping," Lewis writes, "[paper] brought a new sophistication and complexity on the one hand to commerce and banking, on the other to bureaucratic administration."[23]

By the end of the tenth century, aside from Samarkand and Baghdad, paper mills were also operating in Damascus, Tiberias, Hama, Tripoli (Syria), Cairo, Fez, and even Valencia in Spain. In fact, it was through Islamic Spain that papermaking seeped into Christian Europe during the twelfth century. Although the practice originated in China, Islamic civilization would prove a worthy pollinator and embellished upon the art of papermaking with admirable panache. For example, Muslims in Persia used a variety of colorful dyes, traditionally used for fabrics, to heighten the contrast with the text. Of course, with the invention of movable type in the fifteenth century, the Christian world would also help spread the Chinese invention and enhance its value further.

Coffee

"Coffee," the seventeenth-century British merchant and author Thomas Tryon wrote, "is the drunkard's settle-brain, the fool's pastime, who admires it for being the production of Asia, and is ravished with delight when he hears the berries grow in the deserts in the Arabia."[24] For almost one thousand years, coffee berries have grown in Arabia. Yet, like the invention of writing paper, the advent of coffee as a rejuvenating beverage took place in one of the outlying regions with which the Islamic world traded.

According to legend, around the eighth century c.e., an East African goatherd by the name of Kaldi noticed that his animals grew more energetic and animated after grazing on certain red berries. These berries were growing wild in Kaffa, located in the southwestern region of present-day Ethiopia, an area from which the beverage probably obtained its name. Once Kaldi discovered that the berries had the same effect on humans, the word gradually spread about coffee. By the tenth century, the berries had become a popular stimulant among Ethiopian tribesmen, who would consume them mainly by wrapping the berries in balls of animal fat that they would chew on as they traveled. Alternatively, they would make a sort of coffee-infused tea by leaving the berries to soak in and flavor cold water.

Toward the end of that century, coffee is believed to have made its way to the Arabian Peninsula. Well acquainted with the pollination process by then, having established a trade channel that brought a steady supply of the foreign-grown crop to their homeland, the Arabs soon began tinkering with it to enhance its appeal. Most notably, unlike the East Africans, the Arabs began crushing raw coffee beans into boiling water; over time, they advanced to roasting the beans, grinding them, and brewing something very similar to the hot coffee beverage that is so ubiquitous today.

Since Islam prohibits both the consumption and the sale of alcohol, there was considerable interest in such a tasty and mildly "mind-altering" beverage in the Islamic Empire—both by the masses who thirsted for it and, more specifically, by Arab merchants who were eager to profit from its sale. Considered a religiously acceptable substitute for alcohol, coffee became known as the "wine of Araby" to the many Muslim pilgrims, Arab or otherwise, who were introduced to the invigorating drink during their stay in Mecca. The merchants behind the early coffee industry in the peninsula jealously guarded all aspects of coffee production, from sourcing the crop to roasting, in an attempt to maintain monopolistic profits on this new trade.

By the mid-thirteenth century, *qahveh kaneh*, or "coffeehouses," were found throughout Arabia and elsewhere in the Muslim world. Soon thereafter, the Arabs grew less reliant on East African growers as they began cultivating the crop on the Arabian side of the Red Sea, in modern-day Yemen. In 1453, when Ottoman Muslims seized Constantinople and permanently dissolved the Byzantine Empire, coffee became popular throughout the Ottoman Empire, not only in Turkey but also throughout the Christian Balkan territories that would fall under Ottoman rule.

Meanwhile, the beverage was making steady inroads throughout Italy as Venetian traders imported the exotic bean from Arab traders in North Africa and the Middle East. Coffee had become a highly lucrative cash crop for Arab traders, as it remains today for a number of developing countries throughout the world. The export alone of coffee is estimated to be a $20 billion industry, while the full range of coffee-related industries, including retail, now exceeds $100 billion in annual sales.[25]

Producers

Just as enterprising Phoenician merchants branched out into manufacturing in the quest for an additional layer of profit, so did Muslim merchants during Islam's golden age, generally considered to correspond to the period from the ninth century until the sacking of Baghdad in the mid-thirteenth century. After all, the Islamic Empire enjoyed greater access to a wider array of raw materials than any preceding civilization. Territories controlled by Muslims were significant sources of prized raw materials, including copper, gold, rubies, marble, sulfur, lead, pitch, tar, salt, rice, and various types of produce—citrus, sugarcane, dates, various berries. For those goods that could not be procured within the empire, Arab and Persian Muslim traders controlled the trade routes to the sources of such foreign luxuries as Indian spices and Baltic furs.

So it was an opportune time for the Arabs, the founders and masters of the empire, to augment their traditional role as intermediaries between producer nations and manufacture more of their own products to improve the balance of trade in their favor. Arab merchants, in concert with artisans and other laborers, proceeded to develop several domestic industries, the most successful and enduring of which was the textile industry. Beginning in the eighth century and expanding further over the next three hundred years, it became the largest Islamic industry in terms of both output and overall employment.

From almost all manner and fabric of clothes to upholstery, cushions, and, of course, carpets, no other civilization could compete. Both small-scale and larger-scale textile enterprises flourished to serve both enormous internal demand and a considerable export trade in these products.

The industry marshaled the resources of almost the entire Muslim world. Silk came from modern-day Iran, the best carpets from central Asia, cotton from locales as varied as Iran and Islamic Spain, and linens from Egypt.

Aside from textiles, other finished products manufactured within the Muslim world included furniture, soap, kitchen utensils, refined sugar, pottery, perfumes, jewelry, glassware, weaponry, and other forms of metalwork. The advanced level of Islamic industry and its lasting impact is well illustrated by Lewis's account of the diverse industries found in the towns of Islamic Spain:

> Wool and silk were manufactured in Cordoba, Malaga, and Almeria, pottery in Malaga and Valencia, arms in Cordoba and Toledo, leather in Cordoba, carpets in Beza and Calcena, paper . . . in Jativa and Valencia. As elsewhere in the lands of Islam, textiles were the chief industry.[26]

Finance

The growth in Islamic commerce, not only from an unprecedented volume of both trade and production but also an attendant enlargement of the services sector, called for a more sophisticated financial system. This in turn created a new realm of opportunity for financially savvy entrepreneurs—banking. Beginning in the ninth century, merchant banking established its foothold in the Islamic Empire. The Islamic world had long circumvented the Koranic prohibition against usury by engaging both Christian and Jewish moneylenders. So when the time came to build an Islamic banking system, non-Muslims, primarily Christians but also Jews, were its primary architects.

A network of merchant banks emerged that provided an impressively varied and well-coordinated range of services. Perhaps the most common of these was money changing, a necessary function in light of the lack of uniformity in the empire's monetary system, where coins of different compositions were minted in different locations. However, banking also encompassed various forms of capital provision, including merchant loans and various credit instruments such as the *hawala*, comparable to a bill of exchange; the *sakka*, comparable to a payment note; and the *suftaja*, comparable to a modern cashier's check.

Aside from providing an additional avenue of entrepreneurial opportunities, particularly for non-Muslims, a robust banking system facilitated the overall conduct of entrepreneurship across the empire. For example, a *suftaja* drawn in Basra could be redeemed at its face value at a bank in Algiers or almost anywhere else in the empire. Such a streamlined international banking system facilitated the operation of any enterprise, trading or otherwise, that involved long-distance delivery. Perhaps most importantly, the availability of credit to approved merchants was the same vital lubricant of entrepreneurial activity that it remains today.

Crescent Eclipsed

While entrepreneurship flourished during Islam's golden age, there were some problematic aspects of its commercial laws and traditions—shortcomings that would become more apparent as Europe leaped ahead of Islamic civilization during the coming centuries. For example, although the Arabs and other Muslims utilized the *mudaraba*, these passive-equity partnerships tended to involve small investments and usually lasted for only a few months, the duration of the typical trading expedition.

The concept of a corporation was largely absent from Islamic law and, as Timur Kuran argues in *The Long Divergence: How Islamic Law Held Back the Middle East*, the lack of such a structure hampered the kind of large-scale entrepreneurship that Europe and its New World progeny would master. Moreover, despite the significant scientific contributions of the Islamic world, its entrepreneurial activities were somewhat less innovative than those of the Phoenicians, the medieval Chinese, and some later civilizations such as the British at the time of the Industrial Revolution. Nonetheless, Islamic enterprise, woven into the founding of the new faith, was notably expansive, multifaceted, opportunistic, and a primary factor behind the unprecedented size and influence of the Islamic Empire during its golden age.

Most scholars date the end of the Islamic golden age to 1258, when Baghdad was seized and destroyed by the invading Mongols. Although notable territorial gains, such as the Muslim conquest of Constantinople, were yet to occur, so too were significant defeats, such as the loss of Islamic Spain to a reinvigorated Christendom. In fact, over the coming centuries, Christian Europe would continue on its ascendancy, military, commercially, and technologically, while Islamic civilization weakened and fractured.

However, those subsequent developments do not detract from the remarkable breadth and reach of Islamic entrepreneurship during its heyday. Certainly, from Islam's seventh-century inception through its empire's golden age of the ninth to the mid-thirteenth centuries, the strength and diversity of its enterprise was unmatched throughout Europe, Africa, and western Asia. Farther east, however, there was a contemporaneous civilization whose entrepreneurial vigor was comparable. That civilization, Tang and Song dynasty China, is the next stop on our journey.

5

Flying Money and Capitalist Monks

"...lend money to those who have no capital and let
them engage in cultivation."

YESHUIXUN

The Middle East and Mediterranean Europe were the settings of most of the significant developments in the early history of entrepreneurship. However, by the medieval era, Chinese civilization had not only caught up with those regions commercially but in some respects surpassed both the Islamic world and Christian Europe. The diary entries of Marco Polo, the celebrated Venetian trader and explorer, express his breathless astonishment as he took in the sights of Hangzhou, capital of the Southern Song dynasty in medieval China.

"The number and wealth of the merchants," Polo wrote, "and the amount of goods that passed through their hands, was so enormous that no man could form a just estimate thereof." He continues, "Everything appertaining to this city is on so vast a scale, and the Great Kaan's [sic] yearly revenues therefrom are so immense, that it is not easy even to put it in writing, and it seems past belief to one who merely hears it told."[1] Officially, the Song dynasty, spanning the period of 960 to 1279, had ended just a few years prior to Polo's arrival. Nonetheless, he was privileged to witness the Song-era splendor of China's fabled medieval "City of Heaven" before its erosion under the new era of Mongol rule.

The period of the Song, along with the latter half of the Tang dynasty that preceded it, witnessed a level of commercial development and prosperity that was not only without precedent in Chinese history but without parallel in the rest of the world. Marco Polo had already seen much of Europe and Byzantium long before his well-chronicled eastward journey in the late thirteenth century. On his way to Hangzhou, he had passed through much of the Islamic world, including the Levant, Persia, and central Asia.

Polo, a world traveler and possibly the first European to visit China, was uniquely qualified to assess the relative mercantile vigor of the Song capital. So his awestruck reaction to the scale and speed of commerce in Hangzhou is telling. Certainly, Song-era China stands as one of the most remarkable examples of an entrepreneur-driven society. Not since ancient Phoenicia had a civilization's resources, both physical and human, been so effectively marshaled toward entrepreneurship. That is why the Song dynasty is the primary focus of this chapter. However, since some of the pillars of enterprise during that dynasty grew from seeds planted during the preceding dynasty, the Tang, that dynasty, particularly its later years, will also be examined.

China Reunited

At the outset of the Tang dynasty, as they had for many centuries prior, most Chinese lived a rural agricultural existence. Not unlike much of seventh-century Europe, peasant farmers comprised the bulk of the China's workforce during this period. However, particularly in the country's towns and cities, some Chinese found work as artisans, merchants, and professional scholars. At the top of this social pyramid sat the emperor and an aristocratic class of landowners. Such incidents as forced labor projects reveal that royal and aristocratic power was not always exercised benignly. Nonetheless, for its time, the Chinese legal system was relatively humane. Moreover, in terms of ethnic and religious tolerance, Tang-era China, already twenty-seven hundred years old, was among the most pluralistic societies in the world.

At the inauguration of the first Tang emperor in 618 C.E., China already boasted silk, porcelain, tea, paper, and the labor-saving wheelbarrow among its transformational innovations. The country was a coveted destination for international traders from the late second-century B.C.E., when the eastward expansion of Rome and the westward expansion of Han dynasty China progressed to the point that a set of overland trade routes, known collectively as the Silk Road, became practicable. In later centuries, these overland routes would serve as China's primary portal to the West.

In 220 C.E., the Han dynasty fragmented into three kingdoms, and China would remain divided until the late sixth century, when it would be reunited under the Sui dynasty. However, the Sui proved to be a brief two-emperor line lasting only thirty-six years. Accordingly, the dynasty did not last long enough to build upon its historic territorial reunification. That task would be left to the Tang, a dynasty spanning twenty-two emperors that would endure for almost three hundred years. The transformations that took place during this seminal dynasty would elevate China from a regional to a global commercial power and set the stage for the splendor of the Song era.

The Early Tang

Established by a rebel military general, the early Tang dynasty strengthened China's defenses by constructing new military bases. In time, this network of bases reached as far west as modern-day Afghanistan. This was a tactic intended to expand China's sphere of influence, deter invaders, and cultivate further trade along the Silk Road. During the early Tang, the dynasty's leadership was successful on all three counts. To preserve security and maintain cohesion in a country that was still adjusting to its recent reunification, dynasty officials imposed greater internal order within China proper. This emphasis on order, often draconian, would constrict commercial activity to some degree. For example, during this period a decree was issued that limited all transactions but the sale of food, beverages, and entertainment to assigned spaces.

Nonetheless, despite a tendency toward both authoritarianism and, as will be discussed further, nepotism, the early Tang rulers grappled energetically with the formidable task of facilitating a livelihood for their many subjects. Presiding over a population of almost fifty million (accounting for almost a quarter of humanity at the time), Tang rulers faced a formidable task. To this end, the early Tang rulers pursued significant reforms, targeted at almost all facets of Chinese economic life, designed to encourage more economic activity among the great masses of farmers, craftspeople, and merchants.

According to historians Roger Des Forges and John Major, Tang land reform, for example, "stimulated investors to put money and labor toward creating additional rice fields in the Yangzi River valley," and "city workers also benefited from Tang policies, as increased trade created more jobs for merchants and craft workers."[2] Indeed, the economic expansion of the early Tang was remarkably broad. Agriculture, handicrafts/manufacturing, and trade—the three pillars of medieval Chinese commerce—all thrived.

Much of this upsurge was propelled by private enterprise. Aside from greater private investment in agriculture, an increasing share of the production of such Chinese exports as silk, paper, and porcelain was claimed by privately owned manufacturers. Moreover, due in part to the Tang's improved geopolitical position, the volume of Chinese trade had increased from multiple directions. Aside from the Silk Road to the west, a significant volume of trade passed between Tang-era China and other regions of Asia, most notably Burma and the Indian subcontinent.

In an opportunistic frenzy analogous to the California gold rush, a massive influx of entrepreneurs hurried in to carve out their particular product and trade route niches. Especially for westbound Silk Road trade, many of these opportunists were foreign, generally originating from the Islamic Empire. The latter is a major reason why "Chang'an [the dynasty's capital, located in north central China] in Tang times," as the historian Charles Hucker notes, was "unquestionably the most populous, most cosmopolitan, and most brilliant city in the world."[3]

However, the foreign origins of some of China's most prominent merchants did not always sit well with the natives. For example, several historical sources, including an account by an Arab traveler to China, recount an 879 massacre of foreign traders in southwestern China. The traveler, Aboul Zeyd al Hassan, described the victims as "120,000 Muslims, Jews, Christians and Parsees [Zoroastrians]."[4] The scale of the atrocity also underscores just how large the foreign contingent was among the merchant class of the late Tang.

Still, there were many enterprising Chinese eager to claim a piece of the lucrative trade to and from their home country. Moreover, like their counterparts in Arabia, even those Tang dynasty entrepreneurs who lacked capital were often able to obtain it from passive investors. During the early Tang, these capital-raising arrangements usually took the form of a two-person joint-stock business organization. In fact, the roots of the *ho-pen*, "joint-stock company," extend as far back as the third century c.e., and the *chiu-ho huo-pan*, "association of partners" (i.e., two managers who had invested their own money into the enterprise), had long been a mainstay of Chinese commerce, as the investors of preceding dynasties tended to play some sort of active managerial role in the invested business.

However, during the later period of the Tang dynasty and especially during the Song era, the focus shifted to passive investment. Moreover, it was during this period that Chinese entrepreneurs grew impatient with such conventions as the two-investor limit. So the Chinese conception of joint-stock arrangements had to expand accordingly, becoming far more sophisticated and sizable enough to capitalize some large-scale enterprises. Clearly the expansion of entrepreneurial capital commonly associated with the Song dynasty has its roots in the Tang.

"Flying Money"

Tea merchants were among the most active Chinese entrepreneurs during the Tang era. Tea had been a popular drink in the south of China, its region of origin, since the fourth century. By the eighth century, the custom of drinking the hot beverage had become something of a national pastime. Moreover, through Chinese influence it was spreading to other east Asian countries, including Japan and Korea. Consequently, the demand for tea leaves, native to the southwest of China, was growing so rapidly that the tea trade had expanded from a regional to an international industry.

Business was so brisk that tea traders grew tired of carrying large bags of coin *guan*, as Chinese currency was known at the time, to purchase product from growers only to carry even more of these coins back home after a trading expedition. Happily, at the turn of the ninth century, some of the more innovative tea traders in China's Sichuan region came up with some more efficient methods for transferring wealth. The Tang's "tea merchants," as the historian Jacques Gernet observed, "played a considerable part in the invention of new methods of transferring credit."[5]

Living in the land where paper had been invented several centuries earlier, these Chinese entrepreneurs began using paper bills of credit representing and exchangeable for a certain sum of *guan*. Upon selling their shipments of tea in the city, usually the dynasty capital Chang'an, they would receive paper IOUs. Then, upon the merchants' return to the south, the paper statement would be exchanged for the stated amount of coin *guan* at any provincial depository. The lightness of paper money, especially in comparison with copper coinage, inspired the name *fei-qian*, "flying money."

This remarkable innovation facilitated economic activity within the burgeoning tea trade and by the end of the ninth century had spread to various other industries in the Sichuan region. Moreover, in some instances, the flying money evolved from an IOU to something comparable to a certificate of deposit. But it would be over a century before paper money became official legal tender in China. As such, both the advantages and the perils of fiduciary paper money would only become apparent during the Song era. It was then that Chinese officials built a statewide monetary system around the principle of paper bills of exchange.

The Late Tang

The nobility and the high officials of the Tang dynasty were not only well compensated by the royal treasury but exempt from all taxes. Moreover, the Tang taxation system tended to favor larger landholders. Such glaring inequities stoked discontent among smaller landholders and to some extent even discouraged agricultural entrepreneurship among the masses of ordinary farmers. Yet it took a violent upheaval to force dynasty officials to revisit these controversial policies.

From 755 until 763, China was gripped by a bloody civil war spurred by An Lu-shan, a charismatic general who led many disaffected Chinese in an attempt to establish a rival dynasty to the Tang. Ultimately, the Tang prevailed, but in the wake of the violence, dynasty officials enacted a number of reforms, including some designed to ease the tax burden on smaller farmers. Under the impact of these reforms, coupled with growing domestic and foreign demand for Chinese produce during the later Tang, the agricultural sector became more entrepreneurial.

Most significantly, landowners focused their efforts on cultivating just a few top-selling crops that were best suited to the land's climate. In our modern world of conglomerated agribusiness, such a strategy seems like standard practice, but prior to the ninth century, most Chinese farmers saw themselves less as businesspeople and more as custodians of a piece of land that would nourish them and their families, not make them rich. In fact, agriculture became such a lucrative enterprise in the Tang dynasty that Chinese entrepreneurs literally let no crop go to waste. In *China's Cosmopolitan Empire*, his book about the Tang dynasty, the American historian Mark Edward Lewis observes that even human manure became "an important business in this period, as entrepreneurs began to specialize in collecting human excrement in cities for sale in the countryside."[6]

The changes in the agricultural industry during the late Tang were part and parcel of the dynasty's overall policy of commercial liberalization. This was especially evident in Chang'an, the Tang capital and the commercial heart of the dynasty. Whereas strict zoning laws were enforced during the early Tang, by 830, regulations concerning the location of stores had been relaxed in order to facilitate more commercial activity. Consequently, opportunities for retail entrepreneurship proliferated throughout the city, particularly in specialized commercial precincts such as the jewelry district, fabric district, musical instrument district, and so on. However, the unregulated growth of retail outlets, some of which were even spilling out into the street and impeding traffic, had its detractors among the residents of Chang'an.

Meanwhile, during the latter years of the Tang dynasty, as the emphasis of Chinese trade shifted from luxury goods to more basic items and as investment capital became more accessible, the socioeconomic makeup of successful trade entrepreneurs reflected a wider cross section of Chinese society. Through entrepreneurship, ambitious Chinese of "low birth" would achieve unprecedented levels of social mobility within a society that in many ways was still resistant to such change.

Certainly, despite some significant reforms, the Tang dynasty was still plagued by a measure of nepotism, bureaucratic corruption, and other systemic problems. In the late ninth century, the resentments generated by these issues would find their expression in peasant rebellions that would extend from 874 until 884 when the Emperor Tang Xizong finally regained power. Although order had been restored, the Tang would never recover from the shock of a lengthy and violent rebellion in which millions of people perished. The dynasty's foundations were cracking, and in 907, when the last Tang emperor died from poison administered by an advisor, they crumbled.

The death knell of the Tang ushered in the chaos of "the Five Dynasties and Ten Kingdoms," described by Ann Paludan, author of *Chronicle of the Chinese Emperors*, as "one of the darkest periods in Chinese history."[7] It would be fifty-three tumultuous years before the onset of the Song dynasty, when China would continue on the trajectory set by the Tang dynasty. Particularly with respect to entrepreneurship, Mark Edward Lewis has aptly characterized this trajectory as "the rise of a meritocratic ethos."[8]

The Song Dynasty

The Song dynasty commenced with the military coup of 960 C.E. that would replace Chai Zongxun, a seven-year-old child emperor, with a seasoned military general by the name of Zhao Kuangyin. There is a measure of irony in the martial underpinnings of the new dynasty considering that, in modern China, the Song era is hailed as a golden age of almost all aspects of society *except* national defense. In fact, the consensus view is that the general neglect of this vital aspect of governance was the ultimate undoing of both the Northern and Southern Song dynasties.

Established in 1126, the Southern Song dynasty began when the Northern Song, headquartered in the city of Kaifeng, fell to invaders from a rival Chinese dynasty. The relocation of the Song capital to the southern city of Hangzhou marks the dividing line between these two periods. Both are relevant to this discussion, as they share the common features of vibrant commercial activity and an astonishing level of innovation across multiple spheres of endeavor, including commerce.

An Inventive Society

Peter Drucker once extolled the virtues of an "entrepreneurial society in which innovation and entrepreneurship are normal, steady, and continual."[9] In the medieval era, Song dynasty China exemplified such a society to a greater degree than even the contemporaneous Islamic Empire. With respect to innovation, the technological advances of the Song dynasty were a significant factor in China's emergence as a global commercial power during this period. Among the most notable of these advances were the advent of the compass, estimated to have occurred in 1044, and a number of significant improvements in ship design.

The product of considerable experimentation and admirable engineering, the enormous sailing ships of the Song dynasty boasted an unprecedented load capacity of more than one thousand tons. The size and speed of these ships, coupled with the first maritime applications of the compass, elevated the seafaring Chinese trader from relative obscurity to high visibility across southeast Asia, the Indian subcontinent, and even the ports of east Africa. In fact, like ancient Phoenicia at its zenith, Song dynasty China became the world's leading maritime power.

Moreover, during this time, the Silk Road, the fabled network of overland trade routes through which silk and other exotic Chinese goods were transported to western Asia and Europe, was intermittently obstructed due to tensions between China and an Islamic Empire that was expanding eastward. So the Song dynasty's newfound naval strength proved an invaluable strategic asset when its traditional overland trade channels were challenged. Due to its improvements in nautical technology, China, once a largely agrarian economy, was now in possession of a commercial fleet superior to that of any nation in the Islamic world and Europe.

Other notable Song dynasty inventions include canal locks, invented in 984; gunpowder, 1044; movable type, 1045; mechanical clocks, 1092; and playing cards, 1122. Regarding movable type, Song-era China was the first civilization in the world to enjoy the benefits of printed books, an appropriate match considering its high intellectual plane. Nonetheless, true to China's agrarian origins, farming was still a fundamental pillar of society that, like most others, would be revolutionized by Song-era innovation. By the late tenth century, China's agricultural technology had advanced so far that the Song dynasty's per-unit grain yield was the highest in the world. The advent of the high-yield rice field led to an explosion of China's population, which reached the one hundred million mark by 1020.

It is not coincidental that the Song dynasty marked a high point in Chinese history for both innovation and entrepreneurship. As discussed previously, entrepreneurship can occur without great innovation and vice versa. However, in some instances, they can feed each other, thereby generating more of both. Unlike many other social roles, that of the entrepreneur lends itself naturally to the experimental thinking and brash risk taking that under the best of circumstances lead to notable innovations. These can range from brand-new products, processes, and services to mere improvements, albeit significant and measurable ones, upon existing things.

Of course, the entrepreneur's creative inclination finds its fullest expression in societies characterized by inventiveness. The ingenuity of the Song dynasty, at least until the onset of the European Renaissance several hundred years later, was arguably without parallel in world history. This phenomenon, coupled with its robust level of international trade, made Song-era China fertile ground for the intertwined growth of innovation and entrepreneurship. The unprecedented inventiveness of the Song reshaped China into a civilization that was more prosperous than it had ever been during its lengthy history. However, the nautical improvements that spurred a higher volume of trade led to a number of unanticipated growing pains. Among the most significant of these was a severe shortage of currency.

Flying Money Revisited

The swelling ranks of seafaring merchants, shipping brokers, and others involved in the provision of supplies and capital to the dynasty's burgeoning maritime trade often found themselves running out of metal coinage. In 1024, this shortage finally compelled Song officials to apply the monetary innovations of the previous dynasty's tea merchants on a national and official level. Soon thereafter, the dynasty's paper banknotes became known as *jiao-zi*, which among other meanings, can mean "folded paper." Notably, it is also the term for "dumpling," which aside from being a staple of Chinese cuisine, signifies prosperity.

Coins were still being minted, but as with our modern currency system, more money was issued as paper than metal. As the historian Kevin Reilly observed, "Song-dynasty China created many of the elements of modern commercial society that we take for granted. [Official] paper money is perhaps the most notable."[10] Remarkably, it was not until 1661, when the Stockholm Banco issued banknotes for Swedish currency, that official paper money made its first appearance in Europe—more than six centuries after its adoption in eleventh-century China.

The world's first official paper currency proved to be yet another structural boon to the commercial vigor of the Song dynasty. The "special paper made from mulberry trees," as David Wolman, the author of *The End of Money*, describes the world's first official paper currency, had the effect of "enriching the kingdom and turbo-boosting commerce." After all, as Wolman continues, "when people far and wide readily accept the same medium of exchange, opportunities for trade expand exponentially."[11]

The new medium seemed like little more than officially stamped mulberry bark to many Chinese. Nonetheless, it was accepted widely—as one might expect, considering that its refusal was punishable by death. Due to paper money, many residents of the dynasty enjoyed both unprecedented purchasing power and a widening array of appealing goods and services on which to spend it. (Less positively, due to its adoption of paper currency, by the second half of the twelfth century, China suffered through the world's first incidence of hyperinflation.)

Merchant Ambition

Aside from rapidly expanding international demand for Chinese silk, cotton, porcelain, ceramics, tea, salt, iron, copper, and other goods, in the Song era, the domestic consumer market—one hundred million strong—had never been larger or more prosperous. Moreover, many of these newly moneyed Chinese consumers would develop a taste for an ever-widening range of goods and services, many of them imports from such exotic locales as Sri Lanka and Abyssinia. An ascendant class of entrepreneurial merchants went to work, recognizing these ideal business conditions for what they were. In the process, they would complete the transformation that began during the previous dynasty: the conversion of China from a semifeudal agrarian civilization to one dominated by urban nouveaux riches.

One example of the effect of this shift from agrarianism to urbanism is found in the changing composition of tax revenue before and after the onset of the Song dynasty. During both periods, taxes were drawn from two primary sources—land tax and product tax. The former was paid in agricultural produce, silk, and other tangible goods, while the latter was paid in currency (i.e., coins and, after 1024, paper money as well). In eighth-century pre-Song China, 96 percent of tax was paid in tangible goods with only 4 percent paid in money. Conversely, by the mid-eleventh century, more than half of the taxes were paid in money.

A passage from "The Merchant's Joy" (1187), a Chinese poem penned by the acclaimed Song-era writer Lu Yu, encapsulated the ascendancy of the urban entrepreneur:

> The great ship, tall-towered, far off no bigger than a bean;
> my wondering eyes have not come to rest when it's here before me . . .
> Rumble rumble of oxcarts to haul the priceless cargo;
> heaps, hordes to dazzle the market—men race with the news.
> In singing-girl towers to play at dice, a million on one throw;
> by flag-flown pavilions calling for wine, ten thousand a cask;
> the Mayor? the Governor? we don't even know their names;
> what's it to us who wields power in the palace?
> Confucian scholar, hard up, dreaming of one square meal . . .
> Now I know that merchants are the happiest of men.[12]

Evidently even the social position of learned scholars and high-ranking government officials paled in comparison to the opulent glamour of the urban merchant during the Song era.

The entrepreneurs of this dynasty proceeded to transform the nature of Chinese commerce itself. They shifted the center of economic gravity from China's rice fields to its bustling cities. This in turn led to mass urban development, now the norm in much of the modern world. Yet as evidenced by

Marco Polo's astonishment in Hangzhou, even in the thirteenth century, the extent of the city's development was fantastically novel to a European merchant who had seen so much of the known world. Song-era entrepreneurs not only served as the catalysts for this momentous shift, but they shrewdly positioned themselves to be its primary beneficiaries. From home and garden renovation services to exotic east African wares, the dynasty's merchant class adapted eagerly to the evolving tastes of China's well-heeled urban consumer.

As Polo observed in the Southern Song's capital city just a few years after the dynasty's conclusion, "In each of the squares is held a market three days in the week, frequented by 40,000 or 50,000 persons, who bring thither for sale every possible necessary of life."[13] With opportunities proliferating among an expanding array of goods and services, Chinese entrepreneurs grew increasingly specialized, in some instances even developing new niches. Moreover, they began organizing themselves into guilds established along specialized lines. These organizations wielded considerable power, and when the government needed to obtain large quantities of particular goods, dynasty administrators were compelled to call on guild leaders to procure them.

Entrepreneurial Power

The status of the merchant class vis-à-vis the governing class had been elevated considerably. As the historian Arthur Cotterel observed: "Bewildered as they were by these business developments and the vast profits they made, officials turned to merchants for assistance in running government monopolies and enterprises."[14] Among other factors, this change was reflective of a new Chinese society in which the urban merchant, not the rural farmer, supplied the bulk of government revenue.

Meanwhile, the Song-era entrepreneurs assumed control of a growing segment of this urbanized economy, including the dynasty's employment opportunities. For example, in his 1970 analysis of commerce and society in Song dynasty China, Yoshinobu Shiba, a Japanese academic who specialized in Chinese history, discussed "the circumstances under which the boatmen had left farming, and their dependence upon the merchants and brokers for a living."[15] Consequently, by the late eleventh century, there were already five Chinese cities with populations of more than one million. To put that figure in perspective, barely twenty thousand people lived in London at the turn of the twelfth century, and it was not until the thirteenth century that the population of Marco Polo's hometown of Venice reached the one hundred thousand mark.

Not unlike modern China, with its large numbers of rural citizens eager to take part in the country's burgeoning urban commerce, the Song dynasty saw millions of former agricultural workers migrate to the cities for more lucrative employment. Instead of feudal landowners, their new employers were urban entrepreneurs. As the historian Miyazaki Ichisada observed, "It was true that there were overwhelmingly more farmers; however, capital was concentrated in the hands of the merchant class. In this aspect as well, the essence of the Song dynasty was remarkably capitalistic."[16] From tax revenue to workers' salaries, the entrepreneurial class was paying the freight for the dynasty.

Capitalism and Confucianism

As with certain comparable periods in other civilizations, the great entrepreneurial success of the dynasty's merchant class elicited a volatile mix of admiration and resentment. Regarding the former, the following passage from the Song-era political scholar Yeshuixun encapsulates the sentiment well: "Capital accumulation by the rich is eventually good for the society, and considering their mental stress, their labor was not easy as physical laborers, so we shouldn't envy capital accumulation (concentration) of the rich."[17]

The fact that "capital accumulation" was lauded in a contemporaneous publication is significant because such a laissez-faire attitude toward the expansion of private capital was uncommon in a Confucian society. By the Song era, the Chinese philosophical and spiritual outlook was a blend of Daoism, Buddhism, and Confucianism. However, the latter was dominant among many Chinese citizens, including many scholars and government officials. Among the most prominent Song-era Confucian scholars was Zhu Xi, a man who detested any form of corruption.

"For every person," Xi reflected, "the most important thing is the cultivation of himself as an ethical being."[18] Confucians traditionally viewed the pursuit of large profits as inherently contradictory to an ethical life. As such, they tended to hold a rather dim view of entrepreneurs. The opinions of Confucian scholars had little direct effect upon the merchant class, but government officials schooled in Confucianism were another matter entirely. So it is not entirely surprising that the imperial government did its best to limit the participation of private entrepreneurs in salt mining, grain cultivation, cloth manufacturing, and other vital industries.[19]

However, the government, eager to maximize its tax base, often found itself reversing course from its Confucian policies and hiring successful entrepreneurs to help manage these government monopolies. By the time that the capital of the dynasty moved from Kaifeng to the Southern Song capital and longtime commercial hub of Hangzhou, it was evident that the political influence of the ascendant merchant class was irreversible. Certainly, the pace of change was unsettling to some officials. Yet not surprisingly, those Confucians at the highest echelons of dynastic power, who watched with glee as tax revenues grew, believed that the net impact of the entrepreneurial surge was positive.

A More Orderly Commerce

Even beyond the urban centers of the Song dynasty, such vital industries as metals mining, salt extraction, and porcelain artistry were transformed by more methodical and efficient divisions of specialized labor. This change proved to be yet another productive surge for Song-era commerce. This is illustrated by the following contemporaneous account of improvements in grain transport recorded by Song-era writer Wu Tzu-mu:

> There are, moreover, Labor Hirers who provide men to unload the sacks. The carriers and porters likewise have bosses who control them; and each boat has its Receiver of Cargo. Although the arrangements for transport at the rice markets are complicated, there is never any squabbling. Therefore the shopkeepers do not waste any unnecessary energy and the rice comes directly to their shops.[20]

During the dynasty, the efficiency of several vital aspects of commerce grew curiously close to our modern standards. For example, as the expanding foreign trade swelled the ranks of the *ching-chi*, that is, the professional brokers and middlemen, it soon became apparent that sound guidelines were needed to minimize the legal complications that would result from multiparty transactions. As indicated by a summary of these guidelines recorded by Song-era writer Li Yuan Pi, the rules devised for this purpose were impressively sophisticated:

The broker is not (willfully) to force up prices; nor when goods have
been sold to him on credit is he to delay the
merchant concerned (by withholding payment);
and if, according to regulations, goods are sold on credit with a
time-limit set for payment, then an explicit contract must be made
out and numerous reliable guarantors called in, so that, whatever
happens, no lawsuit is provoked.[21]

Moreover, symptomatic of the growth of enterprises from small to large,
the entrepreneurial functions became increasingly distinct from the
managerial ones. From production to long-distance trade, the founders
of enterprises that had grown beyond a certain point were increasingly
hiring professional long-term managers.

Capitalist Monks

Buddhism, a faith of northern Indian origins that had made its way to
China during the second century C.E., was continuing to make inroads
into Chinese civilization. By the Song dynasty, its popularity was evident
in the great number of Buddhist monasteries and temples across China
and the many seekers of enlightenment who populated those institutions.
Of course, for such institutions to survive, the growing ranks of Buddhist
monks needed to develop methods to finance their religious activities—
and they would do so with gusto.

Considering the current preconceptions and stereotypes about loan
sharks compared with the modern Western image of the antimaterialistic,
even otherworldly, Buddhist monk, it would be difficult to think of a more
bizarre pairing than the one we find in the term "capitalist monk." Yet in
the Song dynasty, China's half-million Buddhist monks and their institutions were among the most prevalent and creative sources of loan capital
and investment opportunities. In fact, as far back as the eighth century,
during the mid-Tang, monks had already established themselves as providers of such services. Describing Chang'an in the mid-eighth century, Mark
Edward Lewis reveals that "some shops" in the Tang capital, "especially businesses that made secured loans," were "owned by Buddhist monasteries."[22]

The monks were so adept at the loan business that they amassed
enough wealth to arouse the envy of dynasty rulers, a sure sign of great
success. The intense persecution of the Buddhist faith that occurred during

Figure 5.1
Buddhist monk on the Silk Road. *Source:* Obtained with permission to reuse from Google Images (khanaacademy.org).

the mercifully brief reign of Tang emperor Wu-Tsung was "motivated primarily by financial considerations," Witold Rodzinski writes, because "the immense wealth of the Buddhist establishment appeared irresistible."[23] During the Song era, Buddhism merged with both Daoism and Confucianism to become a syncretized and officially sanctioned national religion. So although the old-school Confucians in the dynasty maintained a certain suspicion of the "foreign" religion, Buddhist institutions were generally left alone as they expanded their lucrative financial services operations and innovations.

Perhaps the best example of the remarkable ingenuity of these monk-entrepreneurs is the "long-life treasury" investment, an innovative financial instrument that became popular during the Southern Song dynasty. It is a form of what was known as *dou-niu*, "collecting and tying." The latter is a term denoting the pooling or collecting of resources from multiple investors and then allocating them according to terms that applied to all the pooled capital—in other words, tying everyone's capital to the same set of rules. Yet unlike some forms of *dou-niu*, the long-life treasury had elements of both a loan and a stock (i.e., an equity) investment.

The earliest documentation of this curious innovation, wherein pooled capital was invested in pawnshops managed by the monk-entrepreneurs operating through tax-exempt Buddhist institutions, is found in the early thirteenth century. An article in a 1201 edition of the *Song Digest*, a periodical that was published by the government, reveals some of the more intriguing elements of the investment. Drawing from that article and later sources, the following is a step-by-step summary of one of the most well-documented examples of sophisticated Song-era financial instruments devised by China's monk-entrepreneurs.

1. Monastery officials would identify and assemble a group of merchants seeking investment in monastery-owned pawnshops. Since it was known that these pawnshops were operated conservatively, wealthy merchants considered these investments to be relatively safe. Often, the investing group would be limited to a certain number, for example, a twenty-person limit. On occasion, multiple groups would be permitted, but the number of these groups would be limited to a certain number, for example, a ten-group limit. In the parlance of the time, this step was the "collecting."

2. The officials proceeded to establish a universal set of rules that would "tie" together all groups and all members of each group of provisional shareholders. Hence, this step was known as the "tying." The applicable guidelines would encompass such vital issues as the responsibilities of management (i.e., the monastery officials) and the rights of shareholders. Regarding the latter, these included the length of the "investment" or, more accurately, loan period, often set at ten years; the size of the investment unit from each group (e.g., 5,000 *guan* per group) and/or from each shareholder (e.g., 500 *guan* per investor); and the timing, calculation, and method of annual profit sharing.

3. This system would proceed accordingly for the duration of the term of investment. Upon its conclusion, these provisional shareholders would effectively rescind their "shares" in exchange for a return of principal. Or put another way, their profit-sharing loan would reach its maturity. A boat-building company, a teahouse, or a number of other prominent categories of businesses in the Song dynasty would employ the *dou-niu* arrangement to sell shares representing real business ownership. However, the pawnshop at the heart of the long-life treasury was the permanent property of the local monastery and could not be sold during or even after the stated term.

Creative Capital

Buddhist monks were certainly not the only entrepreneurs who were creating new forms of capital during the Song era. In fact, as documented in *The Continuation of the Comprehensive Mirror for Aid in Government*, throughout the dynasty's merchant class, some of the most significant entrepreneurial innovations occurred in the realm of investment finance. The work of prominent Chinese historians commissioned by Song emperor Yingzong, *The Continuation of the Comprehensive Mirror* was intended to be the most comprehensive and far-reaching account of Chinese history that had ever been attempted. However, the 294-volume book, written over a nineteen-year period (1065–1084), is also rich with insight into the setting of its creation—the Song dynasty during the eleventh century.

Regarding investment finance, *The Continuation of the Comprehensive Mirror* includes a revealing statement ascribed to the acclaimed Song dynasty statesman and writer Ou-yang Hsiu. Several hundred years before the writings of Adam Smith, Hsiu seemed to have been a champion of the social benefits of private capital investment. He wrote: "What reason can there be for storing it [money] in strong-boxes rather than taking advantage of it as a source of profit and benefitting everyone?"[24] Judging from the historical record, it seems that a good number of Song-era entrepreneurs heeded Ou-yang Hsiu's advice.

The Tang dynasty witnessed a significant uptick in investment activity, much of it in the context of the structure known as *ho-pen*, a joint-stock company with one active partner and one or two passive investors. By the Song, as evidenced by the popularity of *dou-niu*, the original concept of passive investment had expanded to accommodate a much larger number of investors. A particular class of merchants known as the *ching-shang*, "agent merchants" or merchants who employed external capital in the operation of their businesses, enjoyed great prominence during the Song era. These merchants, like modern officers and directors of many modern companies, benefited enormously from the passive-equity shareholder system.

The initial impetus behind this expansion of passive equity was provided by the dynasty's growing ranks of seafaring merchants. As profitable maritime trade opportunities continued to multiply, Song-era entrepreneurs began crafting new financing options, many of them revolving around investor compensation on a profit-sharing basis. So aside from relieving the burden of regular interest payments entailed by traditional loan arrangements, these new financial instruments enabled a larger number of merchants to pursue their ventures without bearing the full financial risk.[25]

Most importantly, entrepreneurs now enjoyed greater access to resources with which they could expand their current operations and/or establish additional businesses, thereby generating new investment opportunities. As for investors, most of whom were also merchants, passive-equity investment permitted them to put their capital to productive use without demanding a significant expenditure of their time and effort. Yet it still carried the cachet of a business owner's return on capital that was potentially much higher than that offered by a traditional fixed-rate loan arrangement. Of course, shares in a venture that does not succeed as planned are usually far *less* lucrative than an interest-bearing loan. Nonetheless, the large upside potential of equity ownership proved to be just as enticing to the dynasty's ultra-ambitious merchant class as it is to modern investors.

In 1958, the Japanese historians Kaisaburo Hino and Yasushi Kusano, both specialists in the socioeconomic dynamics of China's Song dynasty, provided some excellent insight in this regard. (For several decades, due in part to political sensitivities regarding the study of Song-era capitalism in the People's Republic of China, Japan has been the locus of modern scholarship regarding the commercial aspects of the Song dynasty.) Regarding the Song dynasty specifically, Kaisaburo Hino and Yasushi Kusano observed in a study entitled "Ho-pen in the Tang-Song Period": "The aggressiveness of merchants who had enough business ability but lacked capital elicited passive millionaires' capital skillfully, added them to the group of co-investors, expanded sales and generated additional profits."[26]

In the same study, the authors described how, in their quest for the additional capital offered by this system, the primary obstacle faced by the dynasty's merchant class was psychological:

This way of investor participation (only by capital, no management efforts) was enabled so that the increase in both the number of investors and the amount of invested capital could continue. However, as a condition of such a development, absolute trust by the investors in management is necessary. Clearly, the company's strength and management's character and capability are the basic essences of trust, but the rules and arrangement to reinforce and guarantee the trust became necessary.[27]

The dynasty's famously inventive entrepreneurs proceeded to develop such rules, and like the monk-entrepreneurs behind the long-life treasury, they did so with impressive thoroughness and foresight.

Indeed, many of the essential features of "collecting and tying" practiced by Song-era entrepreneurs, particularly in those instances in which full ownership rights were conferred, bear a striking resemblance to common features of modern equity investing. Among these are the accommodation of a large number of shareholders into a single investment, the establishment of a set of comprehensive guidelines applicable to all shareholders, the proportional distribution of dividends, and perhaps most significantly, the clear separation of active management and passive investment. In other words, we have not only the contours but some fairly intricate details of the core elements of the contemporary Western shareholder system, set down on paper in China more eight hundred years ago.

The "joint-stock arrangement," the late historian Shepard B. Clough observed, was "one of the most important inventions in business organization of all time. Its greatest advantage was that it could tap the savings of very large numbers who had liquid capital at their disposal and thus could bring together the sums that were needed for large enterprise."[28] Clough was writing in the context of seventeenth-century Britain, not Song dynasty China, and the "very large numbers" of investors that London's public stock exchange enabled mark an important distinction from the Song dynasty. Nonetheless, the fundamental benefits that he outlined still apply to Song-era Chinese advances in corporate structure that facilitated a much larger scale of enterprise investment than had previously been available.

Mongol Victory and Chinese Stagnation

By the time of Polo's visit to Hangzhou, he was already in the employ of Kublai Khan, the Mongol ruler who drove the final nail into the coffin of the

Southern Song dynasty. With its economic dynamism and military vulnerability, the prosperous Chinese dynasty was irresistible prey for the Mongol
conqueror. It was a target made all the more attractive by the timbre of its later
leaders, described by some historians as "mediocrities" and "weaklings."[29]

Kublai Khan's notoriously ruthless army, long dominant in the border-
ing territory that was once ruled by the Northern Song dynasty, descended
upon the Southern Song dynasty in 1275. By 1279, the "barbarians," as Song
emperor Wen Tianxiang called them, had uncontested dominion of the
former Southern Song dynasty. Four years later, Emperor Wen was executed and the entirety of China was under Mongol rule. Subject to ongoing
military siege, along with its attendant famine and disease, by the onset of
the fourteenth century China's population had contracted by 30 percent
(roughly thirty million people).

Under such harsh conditions, it is hardly surprising that the former commercial splendor of the dynasty paled beyond recognition. As the (anony-
mous) contributors to *What Life Was Like in the Land of the Dragon* wrote,

> When Kubilai died in 1294, he left behind a crumbling empire. Neither
> he nor his Yuan successors ever mastered the art of governing those
> they conquered. In effect, they were still ruling from horseback and
> trampling those whose labor and talents the future of their dynasty
> depended on.[30]

With their "labor and talents" and much of their property "trampled" upon,
China's merchant class would lose a great amount of their Song-era prosperity and influence. As the subsequent seven centuries of Chinese history
would demonstrate, the wider Chinese economy would struggle, with only
partial success, to regain its Song-era strength. "The Song," the historian
Craig Lockhard observed, "marked the high point for Chinese commerce
and foreign trade." Given the Communist affiliation of modern China's
leadership, it is perhaps ironic that China's commercial and entrepreneurial
vigor has enjoyed one of its most significant revivals in recent decades (the
dynamics of which are discussed in chapter 9).

Entrepreneurship Returns West

To some, both the extent and the sophistication of Song-era entrepreneurship, particularly with respect to currency, corporate structure, and other

forms of financial ingenuity, are surprising. For example, the fact that the advent of official paper currency is traced to Chinese tea traders seems strange, even counterintuitive, to some. After all, Europe, not Asia, is often assumed to be the source of great commercial advances. Yet as demonstrated in this and the preceding chapters, Europe was not the locus of innovation and development during the early history of entrepreneurship.

Moreover, with the exception of ancient Rome, European dominance of global commerce only began to emerge toward the end of the medieval era. However, as the next two chapters will make evident, not long after the demise of the Song, some Europeans proved to be remarkably adept at large-scale entrepreneurship. In fact, they were so proficient in that regard that not only their continent but the entire world would be permanently transformed by Europe's innovative, adventurous, and, highly controversial entrepreneurial class.

6

Western Europe and a "New World" of Profit

Well I know who'll take the credit—all the clever chaps that followed—

Came, a dozen men together—never knew my desert-fears;

Tracked me by the camps I'd quitted, used the water-holes I'd hollowed.

They'll go back and do the talking. *They'll* be called the Pioneers!

—RUDYARD KIPLING, *THE EXPLORER*

From Dark to Light

Relative to the vigorous economic activity that would follow, it is fair to characterize most of the Middle Ages, the period from the fall of Rome to the thirteenth century, as an era of economic inertia. It wasn't until the later or High Middle Ages that a number of dynamic commercial trends began emerging, many pertinent to the development of enterprise. Until then, entrepreneurship had generally not flourished in western Europe. Since the fall of Rome, western Europe had been beset by invasions from both north and south that often disrupted important trade routes and stifled commerce.

However, there were also significant internal factors behind the lengthy European stagnation. As highlighted in the previous chapter, the urbanization of Europe lagged far behind that of China during the Middle Ages. Consequently, economic power in this primarily agrarian region was largely measured by landownership, which was in turn determined by a highly regimented socioeconomic system known as feudalism. Feudalism operated as a hierarchy, with royalty at the top, followed by noble lords, knights, and skilled craftsmen. Finally, the great masses of peasants toiled at the bottom; these were the serfs, lowly tenant-farmers who worked on a fiefdom, an estate owned by those of higher birth.

Agrarian, class-oriented, and tightly regimented, the feudal system fell far short of the kind of environment that allowed for, let alone *encouraged*, private enterprise. Moreover, the Church, possessed of enormous political and economic influence, condoned the feudal system and generally viewed entrepreneurship as ungodly. But during the transition period between the Middle Ages and the Renaissance, the power of these institutions began to weaken in the face of factors like the weakening of the nobility, the expansion of regional trade, and in England, the Crown's rejection of papal authority.

Meanwhile, industrial production benefited from a series of technological innovations, such as the spinning wheel, which greatly enhanced textile production. Certainly these advances were not as momentous as those of the Industrial Revolution, which would transform Europe and its colonies several centuries later. Nonetheless, they were significant enough to begin the economic shift from agricultural fiefdoms toward the urban centers where the textile, metalworking, papermaking, printing, and clock-making industries were expanding.

With both trade and industry reinvigorated, urban entrepreneurship, long dormant in much of western Europe, was gradually awakening. This in turn led to important developments in commercial law, such as merchant courts for adjudicating commercial disputes. New business structures emerged, ranging from sophisticated partnership arrangements to a structure that the historians Edwin Hunt and James Murray describe as a "super-company." Hunt and Murray write that such an entity was "unusually large and qualitatively different" and "engaged in an exceptional range of activity—general trading, commodity trading, banking, and manufacturing—over a wide geographical area for an extended period."[1]

By the second half of the fifteenth century, the Renaissance, which had originated in the Italian city-states (Italy was not a national entity at the time) some two hundred years earlier, was enjoying some of its greatest triumphs. Many of these occurred in a uniquely Italian milieu in which "people in all walks of life," a biographer of Luca Pacioli observed, "were eager to improve their present and to leave something of substance to the future."[2] Just as his personal friend and erstwhile housemate Leonardo da

Vinci is credited with being the father of architecture (alongside many other artistic and scientific feats), Pacioli is considered to be the father of bookkeeping and accounting.

Certainly, some of Pacioli's work built upon that of earlier mathematicians, including those from the civilizations of medieval Islam and ancient Greece. Nonetheless, he was able to synthesize previous knowledge in a highly practical manner. Most relevantly, Pacioli's *Summa de Arithmetica, Geometria, Proportioni et Proportionalita* included a treatise on double-entry bookkeeping that helped facilitate the operation of the larger and more sophisticated business structures for which European entrepreneurs were becoming known.

This highly creative period in European history was also marked by significant innovations in armaments, including the advent of powder-fired weapons for individual soldiers and maritime mobile canonry. In fact, by the end of the medieval era and for the first time since the days of the western Roman Empire, western Europe once again led the world in science, technology, industry, and military strength. The latter would ensure that Europe's explorer-entrepreneurs held a lethal advantage over the indigenous peoples of Africa, the Americas, and even large swaths of Asia.

River of Gold

With Christendom's "Reconquista" of Muslim territory in Iberia still under way up until the fall of Granada in 1492, the global commercial ambitions of Spain and Portugal were thwarted to some extent by their Muslim enemies' domination of both Mediterranean and African trade. Portugal, much smaller than Spain and somewhat isolated on the southwestern edge of Europe, was especially vulnerable in this regard. In response, the Portuguese turned to improving their maritime capabilities. As early as 1330, the Portuguese had discovered the Madeira Islands, and their discovery of the mid-Atlantic Azores Islands followed roughly two decades later.

However, it was not until the early fifteenth century that an organized effort commenced to bypass Muslim North Africa through maritime expansion. Though the initiative involved several ambitious independent explorers, it was largely financed and organized by the Portuguese Crown. Portugal established a school of navigation that leveraged the best of recent European nautical advances, some of which were adopted from Arab and Chinese innovations, to enhance the seafaring capabilities of its explorers.

In order to facilitate more southerly maritime exploration of the Atlantic coast of Africa, the Crown seized Ceuta on the northern coast of Morocco and converted it into a Portuguese naval base.

The most compelling goal of this particular group of Portuguese explorers was to make their fortune on the *rio d'oro* ("river of gold") near the western coast of Africa, a portion of which would be shared with their royal sponsors in Lisbon. Some two thousand years earlier, the Phoenicians had conducted some trade there, but no Western power had ever conducted as extensive a maritime exploration of that coast as the Portuguese did during the early to mid-fifteenth century. Even the Muslim Arabs and Berbers of Africa, dominant in much of the continent and monopolists of an overland route from Morocco to gold-rich areas of western Africa, generally eschewed the western coast farther south along their continent. This was partly due to rumors of deadly coastal waters and flesh-eating marine life that had gained currency in the Muslim world.

However, a series of Portuguese expeditions to this area brought back enough gold and black slaves for those fears to be outweighed by the desire for great riches. In fact, as well as launching the great era of European exploration and colonization, those early Portuguese adventurers also pioneered the practice of large-scale European enslavement of black Africans. The latter commenced around 1440, when sugar was introduced to Madeira, and black slaves were transported there to work the plantations—a practice that would be replicated on a gargantuan scale during the Portuguese colonization of Brazil that began in 1501. By 1888, when Brazilian slavery was banned, roughly five million black slaves had been brought to that country.

In 1457, Portugal claimed the uninhabited Cape Verde Islands off the coast of modern-day Senegal and Mauritania. However, the Crown soon lost interest in investing further in these efforts and proceeded to sell off the African exploration charter to a group of private Portuguese merchants. For fourteen years, this group exploited a wide range of mercantile opportunities, including slaves, gold, and ivory, and operated without government intervention or oversight.

At the request of King Alfonso V, the African charter was returned to the Crown in 1471. This was the first time that a European colonial charter would pass back and forth between private and government entities, but it would not be the last. However, some of the largest colonial commercial concerns were wholly privately owned. Moreover, even when the companies were royally sponsored, the European monarch in question usually served only as a passive-equity partner. Leadership was the responsibility of the *active*-equity partners, the explorer-entrepreneurs who risked their lives to make their fortunes on the high seas.

In 1487, one of these explorer-entrepreneurs, Bartolomeu Dias, sailed down and around the southern tip of Africa—most likely for the first time since the Phoenicians undertook the same voyage in ancient times. There was now no question that Portugal was a dominant naval power, able to reach any point on the African coast, and both the royal treasury and more than a few private bank accounts had grown larger as a result. These early successes whetted the Portuguese appetite for greater overseas spoils. As traders and other settlers further consolidated Portugal's African presence, a new crop of explorer-entrepreneurs shifted their gaze farther east, all the way to India.

The Spice Trail

Traders from the Italian city-state of Venice had controlled the European supply of Indian spices through their exclusive relationships with inter-mediaries in the Muslim world. Marco Polo was one of many Venetians who traveled throughout the Middle East and other Muslim regions. This Venetian monopoly on the spice supply to Europe, a highly lucrative trade, generated considerable resentment among other European powers. The Portuguese, working their way down and around the coast of Africa, soon saw an opportunity to best the Venetians: They sought to establish a mari-time route, thus gaining *direct* access to India.

Portuguese explorer Vasco da Gama accomplished just that at the close of the fifteenth century. But his voyage to India is a cautionary tale of great profits intertwined with great peril. In 1497, he set forth from Portugal with one hundred and seventy men and four ships. With this crew, he reached Calicut, the "city of spices," known today as Kozhikode. The following year, he returned with only one ship and a decimated crew; he had lost most of his men, including his brother, to illness or turbulent weather. However, within the single ship that returned was a cargo of spices that fetched such a high price in Europe that it paid for the entire expedition sixty times over.

A Seafaring Entrepreneur from Genoa

The Portuguese bounty from its maritime adventures aroused great inter-est throughout Mediterranean Europe, including the Italian city-state of Genoa. The seafaring merchants of that city were known to be quite skilled at maritime trade. (In fact, it was Genoese merchants returning from the Black Sea who unknowingly carried the Black Death contagion to their hometown, leading to outbreaks that claimed roughly 30 percent of Europe's population during the fourteenth century.) During the late fifteenth century, one Genoese merchant in particular, born Cristoforo Colombo, surpassed the impact of any preceding explorer. Columbus's all-consuming desire for wealth and recognition personified a new generation of European explorer-entrepreneurs and the many thousands of settlers and pioneers who would follow in his wake.

Meanwhile, in Spain, Queen Isabella and King Ferdinand were busy crushing the few remaining Muslim, or "Moorish," strongholds. Finally, in 1492, Granada fell to the Christian army. With the Reconquista now complete, the Spanish royal couple turned their attention to other matters. Alarmed by their Iberian neighbor's expansion of trade routes and the steadily growing number of overseas territories flying the Portuguese flag, the Spanish king and queen were eager to claim their "fair share" of overseas treasures. Isabella, in particular, was willing to back these ambitions with a financial investment, albeit a limited one.

By this time, the forty-one-year-old Christopher Columbus had more than twenty years of commercial sailing and charting experience. During the first fifteen years of his maritime career, he had accompanied Genoese merchants on expeditions throughout Mediterranean Europe and North Africa, sailed north to Ireland and Iceland with Portugal's "merchant marine" (the country's nonmilitary commercial fleet), and procured sugar from Madeira on behalf of Genoese traders. By the mid-1480s, Columbus operated as an independent seafaring entrepreneur, trading in gold and other wares obtained in West Africa. However, despite attaining a measure of the wealth he craved, Columbus was growing restless.

With Portuguese explorers reaching farther and farther down the African coast, the discovery of an eastward maritime route to India was imminent. Columbus was more interested in the pursuit of a new *westward* route to east Asia across the Atlantic, which would allow him to establish a trade monopoly. Although Columbus was not the first person to conceive of such a route, he was the first to attempt it. The Genoese sailor lacked the means to realize such a grand vision, so he turned to the Portuguese Crown. Not only did the king and queen possess the requisite means, they had already declared themselves in favor of such expeditions.

Considerable funds would be needed for the vessels, sailors, and provisions that such a bold undertaking would necessitate. "Just like any modern-day entrepreneur with a brilliant idea," the biographer Emma Carlson Berne observed, "Columbus needed someone to invest money in his idea in return for a share of the profits."[3] The Crown was asked to supply three fully staffed and stocked caravels (the caravel being the forerunner of the galleon ship). Moreover, for his efforts, Columbus requested 10 percent of all precious metals and other revenues originating from any territories that he might "discover" and the right to sail an eighth of all private vessels conducting trade with those newly discovered lands. Additionally, he insisted upon a permanent appointment as viceroy of those territories, a title that would grant him considerable power and elevate him to the nobility.

Columbus's terms are revealing. Much has been made of the explorer's piety and desire to "civilize" and Christianize foreigners. It is likely that Columbus was sincerely devout in his Catholic faith and that its spread was an important consideration for him. However, it is evident from his conduct that it was a secondary one. For example, to make up for a disappointing haul of gold on one of his voyages, Columbus, recalling how the Portuguese had made a profitable trade out of West African slaves, suggested selling some of the indigenous island (as opposed to mainland) Caribs that had been taken captive. In this case (and many others), he seemed more concerned about monetizing the "savages" than "civilizing" them.

That said, especially from the Crown's perspective, expanding the power and reach of the Church was an important consideration. As European colonization continued, the clergy would play a significant role in westernizing natives and helping European settlers—particularly those from the Catholic powers of Spain, Portugal, and France—forcibly transplant elements of the Old World onto the New. Still, due to the entrepreneurial bent of those like Columbus, the primary thrust of New World colonization was material.

The Portuguese Crown was unable to agree to Columbus's aggressive terms and rejected his proposal. Dejected but undeterred, Columbus relocated to Spain and took his pitch to the Spanish Crown. After years of relentless lobbying, Columbus finally convinced Ferdinand and Isabella to hitch their hopes of Spanish expansion to his fleet. It is notable that Columbus persisted through seven years of frustrating rejection without compromising on his initial terms.

In his 2010 book, *New Strategies for Social Innovation*, Steven G. Anderson reviewed multiple studies that have helped identify and clarify the personality traits of entrepreneurs. He noted that persistence, passion, and a propensity for calculated risk taking were among the more common traits.[4] Clearly Columbus did not lack for persistence or passion, and considering the lack of any definite certainty about what lay ahead on the westward Atlantic journey, it is apparent that he had an ample appetite for risk too.

Although he never actually reached Asia during the four expeditions he undertook from 1492 to 1502, he maintained his belief that the Caribbean islands he visited were just to the east of Japan, within reach of his original goal of India. Nevertheless, the gold-rich islands that would be known as the West *Indies* would bring him much of the wealth that he had yearned for. "Without doubt," Columbus's journal entry of November 12, 1492, reads, "there is in these lands a vast quantity of gold."[5] His 10 percent stake in this "quantity" amounted to a considerable fortune.

As for great renown, that would not materialize until several decades after his passing, when the enormity of his accomplishment became more evident. It is important to underscore that the "Enterprise of the Indies," as Columbus's voyages would be known, was not a Spanish project per se, but a *Columbian* one.[6] After all, had his first pitch been successful, it would have occurred under the aegis of the Portuguese instead of the Spanish Crown.

A New Platform for Entrepreneurship

Several years ago, I was working on a project pertaining to mobile applications for Apple and Google. As I learned more about what at that time was still a new world of opportunity, I was fascinated by the potential these platforms had opened up to technology entrepreneurs around the world. Ian Chaston, professor of entrepreneurship and marketing at Britain's Plymouth University, put forth an insightful axiom in this regard. He observed that "entrepreneurial discoveries stimulate the identification of new opportunities."[7]

Like Apple and Google in our day, Columbus's entrepreneurial "discovery" of the New World opened up a fresh vista of opportunities for the entrepreneurs of *his* day (at least, from an exclusively European perspective). Beyond spurring on Spanish, Portuguese, and later, French, British, and Dutch adventurers to explore and settle the Americas, these entrepreneurs developed new methods and systems for the development and, in some instances, the exploitation of these vast new territories. Some of these inadvertently led to other avenues of opportunity, and then others still.

More controversially, Columbus's platform of opportunity often felt more like a platform of exploitation for non-Europeans. Columbus himself set an unfortunate example in this regard by taking indigenous island inhabitants as prisoners and, in 1503, exporting black Africans to the West Indies as slaves. The Spanish historian Antonio Herrera observed in 1601 that "there are so many Negroes on this island [Hispaniola], as a result of the sugar factories that the land seems an effigy or an image of Ethiopia itself."[8]

However, the most destructive legacy of the Genoese merchant was the introduction of diseases such as smallpox, typhoid, scarlet fever, and tuberculosis to the natives of the West Indies, a people who had not developed immunity to these "Old World" illnesses. During the sixteenth and seventeenth centuries, roughly 90 percent of island Caribs perished as a result of these tragic but unforeseen consequences of European contact. Although some subsequent explorer-entrepreneurs exterminated certain groups of natives quite deliberately, that was not the case with Columbus and his cohorts. In fact, the rapid disappearance of the native tribes of the Caribbean bolstered the argument for importing African labor to work the sugar plantations, just as the Portuguese had done on their colonial island of Madeira.

Nevertheless, history would not be forgiving about the Columbian origins of both native subjugation and black slavery in the New World. But in early sixteenth-century Europe, these aspects of Columbus's voyages were dwarfed by more immediate concerns. Assuming that Pedro Alvares's "discovery" of Brazil in 1500 was not the result of a navigational error, the Portuguese explorer's decision to risk an Atlantic voyage to India is an important aspect of the Columbian legacy. Columbus's attempt at a western route to Asia failed in its original intent but, as one of history's most lucrative failures, it was bound to inspire legions of copycats.

Other powers in Europe, alarmed at recent Iberian successes in overseas trade and colonization, were eager to back expeditions of their own. Some of these sought to discover an alternate route, a *north*west passage, to Asia. Though they were unsuccessful, the quest for this elusive passage resulted in discoveries like the 1497 sighting of modern-day Newfoundland by the British-sponsored "John Cabot" (born Giovanni Caboto in the city-state of Venice) and Frenchman Jacques Cartier's 1534 exploration of modern-day Quebec. This led to British and French explorer-entrepreneurs and merchant companies developing the highly profitable Canadian fur trade.

Conquistadores

In light of the Spanish backing of Columbus's voyages and the fact that his "discovered" territories were now considered possessions of the Crown of Castile, the Columbian phenomenon aroused the greatest interest among ambitious Spaniards. Although the term has a fairly broad meaning, "conquistadores" would be most closely associated with those who would expand Spanish territory from the West Indies to the much larger continental territories.

Many of these were professional soldiers, but the archetypal conquistador, Hernán Cortés, was "an entrepreneur and an opportunist,"[8] as the management expert Richard Luecke described him. Initially, like Columbus, Cortés was eager to delve farther into the New World to obtain as much gold and silver as could be found, finagled through trade, or stolen. But as time wore on, he was compelled to develop other sources of income, sources more reliant on production than plunder. In this manner, he helped pioneer more sustainable forms of entrepreneurship in a rapidly expanding New World economy.

Among the first Spaniards who sought fortune in the islands recently claimed by Columbus, Cortés arrived in the New World in 1504 or 1506. He was only twenty or twenty-two years old, unaccompanied by friends or family, and without any significant capital. He settled in the island of Hispaniola, home to the modern-day states of the Dominican Republic and Haiti. Over the next dozen or so years, following a spell working as a notary, Cortés played a more active, if junior, role in the effort to expand and consolidate the Spanish colonization of the West Indies. He demonstrated his mettle both as a fighter and an administrator by assisting with the conquest of Cuba and serving as a secretary to Diego Velázquez, the governor of that Spanish island territory.

Yet, like Columbus, Cortés harbored his own grand ambitions of vast personal wealth and fame. Reportedly, while still working as a notary in Hispaniola, the young colonial boasted to his friends that "one day he would dine to the sound of trumpets, or else die in the gallows."[9] In 1518, his long-awaited opportunity for glory and riches finally materialized. During the previous year, Francisco Hernández de Córdoba, a Cuban-based Spanish explorer-entrepreneur of some means, lost his life in an ill-fated expedition to the Yucatan peninsula, the easternmost portion of modern-day Mexico.

Figure 6.1
Hernán Cortés (1485–1547). *Source:* Obtained with permission to reuse from Google
Images (wikiwand.com).

Seeking precious metals and possibly indigenous slaves to labor on
his sizable Cuban estate, Córdoba was unprepared for the fierceness
of the Mayan resistance. However, the store of gold trinkets that made
its way back to Cuba was large enough to inspire other adventurers.
Although the second Spanish expedition to the Yucatan, led by Juan de
Grijalva, was completed without incident, it was still a financial disap-
pointment. It was especially disappointing to Velázquez, an investor in
both the Córdoba and Grijalva expeditions. Nonetheless, the results of
peaceful bartering with the Mayans yielded enough gold to suggest that

greater bounties could be found through a more extensive exploration of what is now Mexico.

Velázquez was growing restless, as was Cortés, who had been eyeing the gold trinkets from the failed expeditions with an intoxicating mix of hope and lust. As Cortés would later explain to the Aztecs, "I and my companions suffer from a disease of the heart which can be cured only with gold."[10] With Velázquez's somewhat tentative blessing—the governor and his secretary were at odds—Cortés was appointed to lead the next Mexican expedition. Columbus had an appetite for risk, albeit a calculated one, but Cortés's entire life had been marked by an astonishing recklessness. For example, shortly before leaving Spain as a young man, he sustained a serious injury after leaping from the bedroom balcony of a married woman.

Moreover, Cortés, a profligate spender, had amassed significant debt long before his first expedition. Leveraging his new status of captain-general, Cortés proceeded to borrow eight thousand additional pesos from a group of merchants with high hopes for the upcoming expedition. Before he even set sail, Cortés spent much of that money on personal effects and lavish parties. So when Governor Velázquez changed his mind about approving the expedition, Cortés brazenly "ignored him," David Graeber recounts, and in February 1519, "sailed for the mainland with six hundred men, offering each an equal share in the expedition's profits."[11]

If he dared to return empty-handed, Cortés faced death or ruin at the hands of his many creditors, not to mention the wrath of Governor Velázquez. So upon landing in Mexico, the conquistador issued the order to disembark from the Spanish ships and then burn them. Over the course of the next two years, Cortés would proceed to burn and otherwise destroy much of Mexico, including Tenochtitlán, the city that he described in his own letters as "more beautiful to look at than any in Spain, for it is well proportioned and has many towers."[12]

Indeed, the civilization of the Aztecs, then led by Montezuma, was considerably more advanced than that of the Carib Indians on the islands. In fact, given its long history of enslaving and massacring weaker indigenous civilizations, Montezuma's civilization was in many ways just as ruthless and expansionist as Cortés's. Yet even the Aztecs were ultimately helpless against the superior weaponry of sixteenth-century Europe. And so in 1521, Cortés and his crew, with the enthusiastic support of some of the Aztecs' long-suffering indigenous rivals, destroyed the city and one of the world's most remarkable civilizations. Various remnants of this destruction can still be seen in modern-day Mexico City. Yet despite seizing the largest bounty of treasure in human history, Cortés would remain a debtor for the rest of his life.

Nonetheless, Cortés did help transition the economy of this new vast Spanish colony from theft to more sustainable economic activities—sugar plantations and long-distance trade. However, like many entrepreneurs, he was ill prepared for another transition: the shift from conqueror to day-to-day manager of the enterprise of "New Spain" that he had played a large role in founding. In fact, Luecke cites Cortés as a prime historical example of the ongoing tension between entrepreneurial and managerial roles, remarking, "He did not know how to play the game of organizational politics and did not care to learn. He became obsolete, and his daring spirit made him troublesome." Luecke adds, "Modern business entrepreneurs often find themselves in the same situation when their successful enterprises reach [a certain] stage."[13]

Vasco Balboa and Francisco Pizarro were also great conquistadores of this era. Both conquered vast territories for the Spanish Crown, largely in the pursuit of gold and slaves. Like Cortés, Balboa was inspired by Columbus's example and sought his fortune in the New World. By 1515 he had conquered much of modern-day Costa Rica, Nicaragua, and Panama, becoming the first European to reach the Pacific by traveling west. Roughly a decade and a half later, Pizarro followed a trail of gold to the heart of the Incan Empire, which he proceeded to destroy. He then founded the Spanish province of Peru in its stead, now the independent country of the same name.

Along with the New World gold making its way back to the motherland from various sources, a flood of "raw money" was unleashed into Spain, and ultimately the wider European economy, following the conquest of silver-rich Peru. In time, both the mining industry and general trade of Spain's New World colonies would fall into the hands of private entrepreneurs, and by the late sixteenth century the primary role of the Spanish government in the economic activity of its colonies was the provision of naval galleons that would escort privately owned and operating merchant fleets.

Although a portion of these expeditions' profits would still find their way to the royal treasury, the role of the Spanish Crown had certainly diminished since the Columbian era less than ninety years earlier. By the mid-eighteenth century Spain had lost its dominance as a commercial and military power. Moreover, beset by wars with Britain and Holland, the original New World colonizer could no longer spare its galleons for security escorts to Latin America.

Portugal and Its *Bandeirantes*

Alvares's expedition in 1500 to the South American mainland would have profound consequences, not just for the Portuguese and the many indigenous tribes of the enormous area that would become Brazil, but for millions of black Africans. The Spaniards were the first to transport black slaves to the New World, but Portugal was the first European power to engage in the slave trade on a massive scale. Through various trading stations they owned in West Africa, the Portuguese had developed a more extensive mercantile presence in the region than any other European power of the sixteenth century.

Well positioned to import Africans en masse, and with their Crown in possession of a large new territory that was well suited to sugar plantations, Portuguese merchants profited handsomely not only from the sale of sugar but also the trade of the laborers on which the production of sugar relied. As a contemporaneous observer remarked, "The working of the farms of Brazil depends on blacks and more blacks."[14] In 1550 the new Portuguese colony had five sugar mills or *engenhos*. Some thirty-five years later, there were more than fifty such mills. An enterprising mill owner usually fared very well in this new environment. Gabriel Soares de Sousa, a Portuguese naturalist who had settled in Brazil, observed in 1587: "Many who arrive in this land completely impoverished leave for Portugal wealthy."[15]

Of course, many settlers never returned to Europe. Instead, some of these Brazilian pioneers and their offspring decided to make their fortunes by actively expanding the nascent colony's frontiers. During the seventeenth and eighteenth centuries, these daring adventurers, known as the *bandeirantes*, prevailed over both indigenous tribes and armed Spanish missionaries in the interior and pushed Brazil's boundaries far to the west and south. The fact that Brazil is presently the largest country in Latin America and the fifth largest in the world owes much to these men. However, just like the conquistadores, the primary motivation of the bandeirantes was not patriotism but profit, usually in the form of gold and in some instances, indigenous slaves.

New Holland, Incorporated

The only other European power that managed to establish an official colony in the territory of modern-day Brazil was the Dutch Republic, whose home territory included most of modern-day Holland and a portion of modern-day Flemish-speaking Belgium. In 1630 this ascendant colonial power overwhelmed Portuguese forces in a sizable portion of northeastern Brazil and established "New Holland." Dutch Brazil lasted until the Portuguese reclaimed the area as one of the provisions of a 1661 treaty. Curiously, during that thirty-one-year period, the governing power of the Dutch colony was not a branch of the Dutch Republic but was instead a privately owned mercantile entity known as the Dutch West India Company, headquartered in Mauritsstad, now known as the Brazilian city of Recife.

Founded in 1621 by the Flemish entrepreneur Willem Usselincx, the Dutch West India Company was modeled after the Dutch East India Company that had been established in 1602, and which was itself inspired by the formation of the British East India Company two years earlier. Before 1600, most Asia-bound British maritime ventures were structured as joint-stock companies that would expire upon the return of the fleet and the distribution of principal and, hopefully, profits. The latter, of course, did not always materialize.

Previously, British merchants had formed long-term joint-stock companies for specific lines of trade and regions, such as the Levant Company (1581), mandated with representing the interests of British merchants with trade interests in the Middle East and Turkey. By forming one for Asia that was granted a monopoly by the British Crown, the privately controlled British East India Company streamlined the financing and organization of a permanent trading entity. It was thought that such an entity could better manage the ongoing risks of such expeditions.

Like the British, the seafaring Dutch also had a tradition of temporary passive-equity structures for mercantile expeditions. At the turn of the seventeenth century, with European powers vying for dominance of Asian trade routes, a united front of British merchants and investors, as represented by the British East India Company, posed a threat to competing interests. By 1602, Dutch merchants, investors, and their respective trading organizations had already completed a number of successful spice-trading expeditions in the Far East and were intent on launching more.

So the leaders of the various Dutch trading organizations decided to put their differences aside and pool their resources and knowledge as the British had done. These Dutch businessmen, known as the "Lords Seventeen," formed a team of "the most powerful merchants in Holland."[16] For its part and in anticipation of larger tax revenues, the Dutch Republic government granted a monopoly of Dutch trade to the newly amalgamated company, known in Dutch as the Vereenigde Oost-Indische Compagnie (VOC). It was even given military power and the ability to make treaties. In fact, it was the Lords Seventeen, not the Dutch government, that appointed the VOC's governor-general. That official's decision-making power was ultimately subordinate to the seventeen Dutch merchants who had appointed him.

It is remarkable that all of these powers were in the hands of an entity owned by private shareholders and directed by private merchants. In effect, these entrepreneurs had taken on a measure of strategic power from the government—with the explicit support of that government. Moreover, unlike the Iberian powers and their explorers, who often described their territorial ambitions in religious terms, the Dutch East India Company was unambiguously and unapologetically mercantile. In their book *Indonesia*, historians Donald Fryer and James Jackson wrote that the objective of the VOC was "to maximize profits from trade" by attaining "the most complete monopoly possible of the [Indonesian] archipelago's more lucrative products, especially spices."[17]

In 2010, *Bloomberg Business* published an article revealing that one of the original 1606 share certificates of the Dutch East India Company, the world's first printed share certificates, had just been accidentally unearthed in Holland. The writer of the piece observed that such a document carries enormous historical weight, not to mention an estimated auction value of more than $760,000. After all, aside from the fact that the share may be the world's oldest extant stock certificate, the VOC is "considered to be the first corporation in history that laid the foundations for the Amsterdam exchange, reputedly the oldest in the world."[18]

In its early stages, when insufficient funds were available to pay dividends in full, shareholders of the Dutch East India Company were sometimes paid partly in spices. Nonetheless, considering how successful the VOC was throughout the seventeenth century and much of the eighteenth as well, the holder of that share probably made out extraordinarily well. The VOC established strong business relationships with almost all of the important east Asian trading countries of that era, including China, Japan, Thailand, Formosa (modern-day Taiwan), Annam (modern-day Vietnam), Malacca (a state in modern-day Malaysia), and Bengal (modern-day Bangladesh).

The Dutch East India Company established various trading stations and forts in those countries, many of which were seized in battle from the Portuguese. As Jan Pieterszoon Coen, who served two terms as governor-general of the company in the early seventeenth century, wrote to the Lords Seventeen, "we cannot carry on trade without war, nor war without trade" because "the weapons must be paid for by the profits from the trade."[19] Clearly the VOC did not hesitate to exercise its military power, not only to take control of trading posts but also to conquer sizable territories.

In Asia, its primary conquests took place in Ceylon (modern-day Sri Lanka) and most significantly, in some of the "spice islands" in modern-day Indonesia. In this manner, the Lords Seventeen and other shareholders succeeded in their objective of driving out European competition—particularly Portuguese and British—from important trading routes. The Dutch East India Company thus enjoyed dominance of trade in spices from southeast Asia and the monopolist profits that such dominance facilitated. It was not uncommon for a Dutch spice trade expedition to yield a 400 percent profit. At its late seventeenth-century peak, the VOC employed more than twenty thousand Dutch and was one of the most powerful economic and military powers on Earth.

Certainly, the Dutch East India Company succeeded in its mandate to enrich its owners and help raise Holland to the status of a major European power. However, its legacy, like that of other mercantile colonial projects, is not free of controversy. Describing the VOC's 1621 takeover of the nutmeg-rich Banda Islands, Fryer and Jackson note that the inhabitants of those Indonesian islands were "ruthlessly exterminated" while the spice gardens that the indigenous Bandese had cultivated were "distributed to [Dutch East India] Company servants to work with imported slave labor."[20]

Regarding the latter, like the Portuguese and the Spaniards, a number of Dutch merchants were eager participants in the slave trade, particularly in the emerging Dutch Caribbean. Most of these merchants were Protestant but there was a sizable minority of Dutch Jews in their ranks as well. The Dutch *West* India Company was the vehicle of choice for these traders in sugar and the mostly African labor that produced it. Much of that labor was supplied by the VOC which, en route to Asia, had established trading stations in several points on the western coast of Africa. The Dutch East India Company also established a full-fledged colony farther south, in modern-day South Africa, that it would hold for almost a century and a half. White Afrikaners descend from the Dutch and Flemish settlers who colonized the land under the aegis of the VOC.

Aside from its briefly held territory in northeastern Brazil, the Dutch West India Company colonized the Netherland Antilles, a group of six Caribbean islands, three of which are still part of the greater kingdom of the Netherlands. The Geoctroyeerde Westindische Compagnie (GWIC), and initially the VOC as well, played a prominent role in the European colonization of North America. In 1609 Henry Hudson was hired by the VOC to find a northwest passage to India. The British explorer had previously been in the employ of the Muscovy Company, a joint-stock company formed by London merchants seeking to profit from Russian trade. Like John Cabot and Columbus, Hudson placed his ambition above any particular national loyalties.

Already familiar with North America from his expeditions for the Muscovy Company, Hudson proceeded to gain a foothold for the VOC in North America around the river that still bears his name. By the 1620s the VOC had abandoned hope of reaching Asia through a western route. The Dutch West India Company expanded upon Hudson's work by establishing New Amsterdam on the site that would be rechristened New York City by the British colonists who supplanted the Dutch in 1674. While it lasted, New Amsterdam allowed the GWIC to claim a share of the lucrative fur trade and the fertile farmland in the area. Some Dutch names, like Harlem and Brooklyn, remain as relics of the longtime presence of the GWIC in New York.

Gaul Around the Globe

The European history professor Roland Wenzlhuemer observed that "more often than not the real beneficiaries of colonialism have been private merchant companies, European entrepreneurs, and the members of the local collaborating elites."[21] The Dutch colonial experience is among the most vivid illustrations of Wenzlhuemer's observation. While his comment certainly applies to the French colonial experience too, France was generally less willing than the Dutch Republic to cede colonial powers to private entrepreneurs.

However, Dutch and British colonial entrepreneurial success, along with the higher tax revenues those countries enjoyed as a result, did not go unnoticed in Paris. By the end of the seventeenth century, many French merchant companies had surpassed the Dutch and the Iberians and in terms of foreign territories were second only to the British. Yet like the British, the French began their colonial project gradually and somewhat tentatively. As the French Empire grew, so did the role of France's private entrepreneurs.

After eyeing the Spanish discovery of the New World in the 1520s with a mix of curiosity and envy, the French Crown entered the colonial fray in a rather unorthodox fashion. Instead of partnering with a merchant-explorer, King Francis I assigned a company of Florentine pirates to attack Spanish fleets returning from the New World. In 1522, commenting on the extraordinary haul of Spanish loot that was laid before him, the French monarch despaired, "The (Spanish) Emperor can carry on the war against me by means of the riches he draws from the West Indies alone!"[22]

Twelve years later, Francis I was introduced to Jacques Cartier, an accomplished navigator and explorer who, as a born and bred Frenchman, inspired the trust of his king. By 1534, Cartier had already led trading expeditions for various merchant groups to both South and North America. He welcomed the opportunity to lead a westward expedition commissioned by Francis I. From a sixteenth-century European perspective, the natives encountered by Cartier in modern-day eastern Canada were sufficiently exotic to convince him that he had, in fact, reached the promised land of India.

But like Columbus's failed attempts to reach Asia, Cartier's attempt bore some accidental fruit. The explorer had initiated French contact with a region teeming with fur-bearing animals, a development that would hold great significance for a future generation of French entrepreneurs. France, beset by violent sectarian strife and European wars for the remainder of the sixteenth century, did not return to the Americas until the first decade of the following century. The seventeenth-century settlement of New France in modern-day eastern Canada was largely the handiwork of another French explorer, Samuel de Champlain.

Champlain's colonial project was authorized by the Crown but following the British and Dutch example, was financed initially by a joint-stock company known as the Compagnie du Canada. Alternatively known as the "Compagnie du Conde," the first entity behind the establishment of a permanent French colony in the Americas was granted an eleven-year monopoly on trade across a large region by the French Crown. The Compagnie was established by a group of prominent merchants from the regions of Normandy and Brittany in northern France.

The latter in particular supplied many of the French settlers to modern-day Canada. Drawn by a sense of adventure to the New World's opportunities, ambitious and generally lower-class young Frenchmen arrived to make their fortune in the new settlement. Due to its less established and in some ways less restrictive social environment, New France also attracted some nontraditional entrepreneurs. Among these were French women eager to establish successful fur businesses—with or without husbands.

Following a pattern that would recur elsewhere in the French colonial world, Champlain was forced by various legal and financial complications to work with multiple French merchant companies in order to complete his mission. This somewhat chaotic situation changed in 1627 when Cardinal Richelieu, a personal friend of Champlain and France's second most powerful government official,[23] established the Compagnie des Cent-Associés. As its name suggests, the "Company of One Hundred Associates" was a joint-stock company with one hundred member-investors, of whom Richelieu and Champlain were two.

Later in the century, the North American French presence expanded to Louisiana when the young colonist Robert de La Salle sold his property in modern-day Montreal to self-finance an expedition he believed would eventually take him to Asia. Of course, it didn't, but the French expedition's luck was better than its sense of direction, as yet again the pull of Oriental spices and silk ultimately led to riches of another sort—in this instance, cotton plantations. Unfortunately, to a great extent, the prosperity of French plantation owners in the Gulf of Mexico region would be built on the backs of imported black slaves. So like that of most of the explorer-entrepreneurs, the legacy of La Salle's "discovery" of Louisiana and its subsequent development by other Frenchmen remains highly contentious.

Nonetheless, there is no question that the French foray into the American Southeast exhibited the same adaptability with which many profitable enterprises have been built, past and present. Reid Hoffman, a cofounder of LinkedIn, summarized this principle best: "You jump off a cliff and you assemble an airplane on the way down."[24] In 1731 the land where La Salle's "airplane" had landed became a prized French Crown colony, and it soon attracted a new crop of French entrepreneurs, many of whom would amass fortunes from the sale of cotton and the imported slave labor that harvested it.

For example, Antoine Crozat and his brother Pierre became two of France's wealthiest merchants and financiers due in large part to the import of African slaves to Louisiana. The French also made ample use of black slaves farther south in the Americas, where they had acquired a number of Caribbean and South American territories during the seventeenth and eighteenth centuries, including French Guiana, Martinique, Guadeloupe, St. Pierre and Miquelon, and Saint-Domingue, the western half of an island first colonized by Columbus.

The latter, known today as Haiti, proved to be the most economically productive colony in Franco-America. By the late eighteenth century, Saint-Domingue's coffee, cacao, indigo, cotton, and, above all, sugar, accounted for more than two-thirds of France's overseas trade. The amount of labor required to produce a third of the sugar consumed in Europe was immense. By the end of the century, French slave runners had transported more than nine hundred thousand slaves to Saint-Domingue—the largest slave importation to any Caribbean colony, French or otherwise. As they did in Louisiana, French entrepreneurs in the Caribbean turned to the Slave Coast, the western coast of Africa, where the French had been active since the 1620s.

In the mid-seventeenth century, the "Compagnie des Indes Occidentales" or "French West India Company," ran operations on both sides of the Atlantic, populating French colonies in the Caribbean with human cargo from trading posts and colonies in Senegal, Guinea, and elsewhere on the Slave Coast. This company proved short-lived, as did other French joint-stock companies operating in Africa, including the "Compagnie de Guinee" and the "Compagnie de Senegal." In both Africa *and* the Americas, the French enterprises seemed to lack the staying power of some of their Dutch and British competitors.

Moreover, the African trade in gold, ivory, and slaves became something of a rogues' gallery in which the most opportunistic of Frenchmen and Africans tried to make their fortune. While some did, many more came to ruin. As recounted by the historian C. W. Newbury, the story of de Montaguere in the territory of modern-day Benin is illustrative in this regard:

> At least one of the French directors, d'Oliver de Montaguere, went into partnership with a Bordeaux captain, supplied merchandise on credit, and levied a personal tax on all transactions carried on in the fort. His commercial sleight of hand carried him too far; and when his agents sold better goods to Oyo traders at the Cana market than to King Kpengal of Abomey (who had been fobbed off with inferior articles at the same price), they were seized and murdered and d'Olivier himself expelled.[25]

Perhaps such administrative chaos was one reason why the African-based French trading companies generally did not last beyond a dozen years or so. The most enduring of France's joint-stock colonial companies of this era was a largely Asian enterprise, the Compagnie Française des Indes Orientales or "French East India Company." This French response to the British and Dutch East India Companies focused its activities on southern India, though it also had some involvement in other French colonies, particularly those in Africa that had been mismanaged by other French merchant companies. The French East India Company's operations and finances were often just as unstable as the lesser French companies, but the Crown, in modern parlance, considered the company "too big to fail" and injected considerable capital to keep it afloat.

The French East India Company's primary purpose was to gain direct French access to spices and other Eastern goods. To serve that end, there were times in its 125-year history when the company deemed it necessary to colonize territory on the Indian subcontinent. At its peak in the mid-eighteenth century, it had gained control of more than two hundred square miles of southern India, while its volume of trade, dangerously low at previous periods in its history, had risen to half of that generated by the British East India Company, the largest and most profitable of all colonial joint-stock companies.

"Rule, Britannia!"

At the peak of their empire, the British had jurisdiction over more than one-quarter of the world's territory. As the British prime minister Benjamin Disraeli described it, his was an "empire on which the sun never sets."[26] Like that of their Dutch competitors, the colonial motivation of the British merchant companies was unabashedly entrepreneurial. When describing the state of Victorian England during Winston Churchill's youth, Churchill biographer William Manchester outlined the origins of "Her Majesty's Empire" in starkly commercial terms:

> The conquest of India had begun with a small trading station at Surat, on the west coast. Canada had been an acquisition of the Hudson's Bay Company, a firm just as zealous in its pursuit of profits as the [British] East India Company. Victorian Australia was built on the need for cargoes of gold and wool. And each new territory meant a further boost of England's entrepôt trade, expansion of markets for the coal of Wales, the textiles of Lancashire and Yorkshire, and the steel of Sheffield and Birmingham.[27]

Unlike the French royalty, the monarch of Britain never held a controlling interest in the colonial merchant companies, although there were members of Parliament who, through the company's widely sold shares, held minority interests in the BEIC. The British colonials were generally less interested in religion than their Catholic counterparts, making the British model more comparable to that of the Dutch Republic, the other major Protestant colonial power of the era. Yet, in the organization and sophistication of their merchant companies, the British colonials surpassed *all* others. In so doing, they laid the foundation for modern-day "Anglo-Saxon capitalism," which is characterized by the investment of large financial markets in large-scale entrepreneurship.

Buccaneers of Britain

The British found greater and more enduring success in their colonial enterprise than any other European power. But like the French, their first forays into colonialism were both tentative and predatory. Aside from Cabot's strictly exploratory voyages to the northeastern coast of North America in the immediate aftermath of Columbus's discoveries, the British did little until the latter half of the sixteenth century. In 1562, a group of London merchants salivating at the profits earned by Spanish and Portuguese merchants in the Africa trade joined an investment syndicate formed by England's first slave trader, John Hawkins. The experienced seaman's prominent financial backers included Sir Thomas Lodge, a successful merchant who had become London's mayor.

Despite the Spanish prohibition against unauthorized traders, Hawkins's first voyage, in which slaves procured from the Slave Coast were sold illegally to plantation owners in the Spanish Caribbean, generated windfall profits for his investors. Over the next thirty-three years, Hawkins engaged in further slave trading, as well as piracy and other forms of mischief against Spain and its merchant fleets. Sir Francis Drake, Hawkins's second cousin, joined him on some of these adventures. A hero to Englishmen for being the second maritime adventurer after Magellan to circumnavigate the globe, Drake was known as "El Draque" (the Dragon) to Spaniards unfortunate enough to encounter him on the open seas.

Drake and Hawkins still rank among history's most controversial entrepreneurs. Hawkins, in particular, owns the rather dubious distinction of initiating the British slave trade. Over the course of two centuries and roughly eleven thousand voyages, almost three and a half million black Africans were taken to the Americas by British traders; another four hundred thousand died en route. British merchant companies expanded their presence on the Slave Coast as they accumulated colonies in both the Caribbean and the southeastern region of the modern-day United States. In so doing, Britain's "triangular trade" was born, offering a wide array of profit-making opportunities for enterprising Englishmen, Scots, Welshmen, Ulstermen, and to a lesser degree, Irishmen.

Describing a three-way circuit of commerce, all slave-trading European powers practiced some form of triangular trade during the colonial period. A typical example began with an Africa-bound ship leaving a European port loaded with textiles, guns, or any other kind of manufactured product for which there was great demand in West Africa. Upon reaching its destination on the Slave Coast, the ship traded its manufactured cargo for slaves and then set sail for a slave colony in the Americas. In order to pay for the shipment of slaves, the colonists exchanged the cotton, sugar, and tobacco that their slave-powered plantations produced. These goods, in turn, fetched a high price back in Europe, though in many cases these triangular expeditions generated a large profit at all three transaction points.

The British became so proficient at this triangular trade that in later years, entrepreneurs in the Africa trade based in what were then the New England colonies established a triangular trade of their own. Taking on the traditional European role, these transplanted Brits actually brought their New England–distilled rum all the way to the Slave Coast, brought the newly obtained slaves to the British Caribbean in exchange for molasses, and then took the molasses home to make more rum. Whereas Hawkins mixed his slave trading with piracy, these New Englanders, in the same spirit of irreverent opportunism, combined it with running liquor.

However, the impact of the triangular trade was just as evident on the home islands of the United Kingdom as it was on the sugar plantations of Jamaica and the cotton plantations of Virginia and in the distilleries of New England. Collectively, colonial sugar, cotton, tobacco, and the African slaves who produced those goods formed a ladder of upward mobility for legions of Britons. In light of the socioeconomic class structure that was still a dominant feature of British society, a disproportionate share of the colonial spoils wound up in the hands of the upper classes. Rebecca Fraser writes in *The Story of Britain* that "many respectable English merchant families made their fortunes in this convenient triangular trade."[28]

Through the provision of even small amounts of trade goods or capital to ship captains in exchange for a proportional share of the profits, even common shopkeepers and others in the less "respectable" rungs of the middle class participated in the triangular enterprise. For example, regarding the port city of Bristol, Eric Williams, the late Caribbean historian and former prime minister of Trinidad and Tobago, concluded that as early as 1685, "there was scarcely a shopkeeper in the city who had not a venture on board some ship bound for Virginia or the West Indies."[29]

Company of Colonists

Like those of the Dutch, the wealth and power of the British joint-stock companies were legendary. From its formation in 1600 until 1773, when the House of Commons passed the Regulating Act, the British East India Company operated with astonishing independence. In 1757, when the BEIC conquered the Indian province of Bengal, the company's policy in this colony was determined by votes held at meetings of its shareholders. By then, BEIC shareholders numbered roughly two thousand, the overwhelming majority of whom were *not* British government officials.

In fact, even at its inception in 1600, more than 90 percent of the company's 237 shareholders had invested less than £300. That threshold is roughly equivalent to US$90,000 in 2015—a substantial sum of money but modest enough to allow a wide swath of the British merchant class to participate. For example, the initial subscription included such investments as "Nicholas Barnsley, Grocer, £150," "Ralph Hamer, Merchant Tailor, £200," "Richard Wiseman, Goldsmith, £200," and "Thomas Smithe, Haberdasher, £200."[30]

As Brian Gardner notes in his history of the BEIC, these shareholders were not "princely gentlemen." Rather, they were "ordinary city tradesmen and merchants prepared to take a gamble,"[31] not unlike the millions of ordinary people nowadays who have US$45,000 or more directly or indirectly invested in General Electric, Toyota, Archer Daniels Midland, and other kinds of large-scale enterprises. Indeed, the larger colonial joint-stock companies, particularly as administered by the Dutch and British, foreshadowed both the benefits and pitfalls of the modern system of large-scale entrepreneurship backed by a wide pool of investors.

The directorship of the company was composed chiefly of several prominent merchants, including Sir Thomas Smyth. Smyth, a shrewd English businessman, became the first BEIC governor before putting his hand in the Muscovy (Russian) trade and, perhaps most notably, establishing the London Virginia Company that would later play such a formative role in the British colonization of what is now the American South. In the BEIC directorship, alongside Smyth and other luminaries of British colonial entrepreneurship, was James Lancaster, the seafaring trader and erstwhile pirate who personally led the BEIC's early expeditions in the early 1600s. By casting a fairly wide "net" for Company membership, the entrepreneurs at the helm of the BEIC were able to collectively obtain all of the capital they required at reasonable terms.

Just as successful large-scale enterprises and their lobbyists currently wield considerable political power in many countries, the BEIC's economic leverage usually ensured that its needs were met by the Crown and, in later years, by the House of Commons. Regarding how its future directors set to work establishing the company prior to obtaining the formal approval of Queen Elizabeth I, Gardner states, "The merchants knew that the Queen's assent was something of a formality." Their confidence, borne out by subsequent events, was "partly due to the vast customs dues she [the Queen] would receive if the stories of the riches from direct eastern trade were only half true."[32]

They were *entirely* true. After profits from the first expedition were distributed, the initial 237 shareholders nearly doubled their money. Moreover, the average profit generated by the first twelve expeditions amounted to an astonishing gain of almost 140 percent. These successes enlarged the shareholder pool even further, enabling the directorship of the BEIC to raise the modern equivalent of tens of millions of dollars as needed. Through such ventures as the Hudson's Bay Company and the Royal African Company, trade, settlement, and production enterprises throughout Britain's expanding empire were being financed.

Yet powerful entities largely founded, funded, and governed by profit-seeking merchants and explorers posed complicated questions about their role and influence—as comparable companies do today. The shareholders of the Royal African Company, perhaps the most controversial of these enterprises, were "interested in exports and imports, shipping and slaves, forts and factories, only in so far as they contributed to the making of profits."[33]

Shaped and steered by these profit-driven entities, the British colonial project was often effective in extracting a healthy financial return from a vast range of activities. But to African slaves, North American natives, and domestic manufacturers harmed by the influx of cheaper Indian goods, British imperialism could be a Darwinian experience. Meanwhile, a *Dickensian* experience was imminent as another group of imaginative British entrepreneurs embarked on discoveries of a different kind. These colorful characters, the directing minds behind a global Industrial Revolution, are the focus of the next chapter.

7

Captains of the Revolution

The duty of man is the same in respect to his own nature as in respect to the nature of all other things, namely not to follow it but to amend it.

—JOHN STUART MILL

"Without innovation," the Austrian economist Joseph Schumpeter wrote, "no entrepreneurs."[1] Of course, there are varying levels of innovation involved in different business endeavors. So an enterprise does not need to involve a radically new product or service to qualify as innovative. For example, while they were not in a technology-oriented business, the directors of the European merchant companies discussed in the previous chapter were, nonetheless, habitual innovators. From financing to the exploitation of profit-making opportunities, their creativity was legendary. In fact, considering that the Latin origin of the term "innovate" means "to make new," the establishment of novel trade routes and production centers in once remote corners of the globe certainly qualifies as innovation.

However, prior to the Industrial Revolution, innovation in the form of disciplined scientific inquiry rarely intersected directly with the world of entrepreneurship. The *original* Industrial Revolution, that is, the one that occurred in Britain and peaked during the seventy-year period of 1760–1830, is when those two worlds coalesced in unprecedented ways. The result was a remarkable series of groundbreaking practical innovations that galvanized dozens of industries and created many that had never existed.

A Climate of Curiosity

In the seventeenth century, Francis Bacon's scientific method had, through the work of Isaac Newton, Robert Boyle, and others, placed Britain at the helm of an intellectual renaissance. Alongside Britain stood continental Europe, where scientists like Johannes Kepler and Nicolas Copernicus made seminal contributions of their own to what would be known as the Scientific Revolution. Yet, driven by a combination of innovation and entrepreneurship, the *Industrial* Revolution was, not surprisingly, a specifically British phenomenon.

Certainly, by the early eighteenth century, educated and inquisitive scientific minds could be found throughout western and central Europe. However, the conceptualization of practical ideas and their subsequent development into new products and processes required more than mere brainpower. With respect to twenty-first-century companies, the modern innovation experts Tom Kelley and Jonathan Littman often highlight the importance of "fostering a culture of innovation."[2] In eighteenth-century Britain, such a culture was fostered through the implementation of effective political, legal, and economic policies.

With respect to policy making, it is worth noting that since 1688 the real power in Britain's "monarchy" lay with Parliament. So, unlike the absolute monarchy that still ruled France, for example, policy making in Britain was determined by a body of elected representatives, not the titular king or queen of the realm. The British Parliament was generally eager to promote technology and commerce and in that spirit granted an unusual degree of autonomy to innovators and entrepreneurs. Conversely, in some other European countries, inventors had to submit their ideas for royal approval, and even then, the inventor's ownership of the concept, let alone his right to develop its practical applications into a business, was often not recognized.

The British government, on the other hand, was the first to issue patents to inventors. More generally, due to a relatively stable legal and political system, innovative entrepreneurs in Britain were more likely to be treated fairly than their counterparts on the Continent. Meanwhile, eighteenth-century British *society*, flush with wealth from a growing empire, was crawling with ambitious industrialists seeking new ventures—foreign or domestic—in which to invest their surplus capital. These investors mingled with inventor-entrepreneurs across Britain. Some of these meetings were coordinated in formal settings such as London's Royal Society or

Birmingham's Lunar Society. However, most took place in coffeehouses and other informal settings.

In eighteenth-century Britain, practical scientific advances offered a means of upward mobility for enterprising innovators, many of whom were full-time "artisans" of modest means. "Most of these inventions and improvements," a writer in the *Manchester Mercury* newspaper observed in 1784, "have been struck out by such as are usually denominated the inferior ranks of mankind."[3] Indeed, it was the inventiveness and resourcefulness of the "inferior ranks" of British society that led the way toward the machine age.

Such an open and "classless" environment of innovation was extraordinary in eighteenth-century Europe. Even in seventeenth-century Britain, experimental science was still "imperfectly aligned with rewards," as the historian William Rosen noted, so that it "remained disproportionately the activity of those with outside income."[4] By encouraging and even financing the more practically minded science of millers, weavers, iron-smelters and other hands-on artisans, British ingenuity would not only reshape but also re*create* the industrial landscape of Britain, western Europe, and America.

The Productivity Explosion

Living with the fruits of the Industrial Revolution all around us, it can be difficult to appreciate the enormity of the changes that took place. One of the best illustrations of the dramatic contrast between British life before and after the technological advancements of the late eighteenth century is provided in a book about the Luddites—the textile workers who protested bitterly *against* the Industrial Revolution. For illustrative purposes, the author of *Rebels Against the Future*, Kirkpatrick Sale, describes the dramatic shift in cotton production that occurred in the town of Lancashire, on England's northwestern coast.

In 1780, that is, before the major innovations of the era had been widely implemented, Jones paints the following picture:

> The workshop of the weaver was a rural cottage, from which when he was tired of sedentary labor he could sally forth into his little garden . . . The cotton wool which was to form his weft was picked clean by the fingers of his younger children, and was carded and spun by the older girls assisted by his wife, and the yarn was woven by

himself assisted by his sons . . . One good weaver could keep three active women at work upon the wheel.[5]

Thirty-four years later, cotton production in the same town has metamorphosed from a cottage vocation to a smokestack industry:

> At the side of each factory there is a great chimney which belches forth black smoke and indicates the presence of the powerful steam engines. The smoke from the chimneys forms a great cloud . . . To save wages mule jennies have actually been built so that no less than 600 spindles can be operated by one adult and two children . . . In the large spinning mills machines of different kinds stand in rows like regiments in an army.[6]

Around 1790, the first full-fledged steam-powered textile looms became operative. By 1830, there were more than one hundred thousand such looms in Britain. "By then," Sale writes, "one man could do the work that two or three hundred men had done at the start of the Industrial Revolution."[7] Of course, the Industrial Revolution transformed other areas of production besides the textile industry. To illustrate, between 1700 and 1800, annual British coal production tripled and iron production more than quintupled.

Due to its technological superiority, Britain's productivity had risen much higher than any of its rivals on either side of the Atlantic. So much higher that, despite Britain's political differences with the breakaway colonies that had recently formed the United States, by the end of the eighteenth century an independent America was buying far more product from the land of the "redcoats" than was ever sold to colonial America. Due to its unparalleled productivity and the astonishing innovations that fueled it, Britain would become known as the "workshop of the world." Moreover, like Steve Jobs and Bill Gates in the modern age, some of Britain's greatest innovator-entrepreneurs of the early industrial era would become heroes of both science and business.

Pioneers of Production

Abraham Darby

Technologically and chronologically, the work of Abraham Darby, born in 1677, is a precursor to the Industrial Revolution. However, Darby's life is worthy of discussion, as in several respects he set the "mold" for the British inventor-entrepreneurs who would carry the torch of industrial innovation forward in the decades that followed. As mentioned previously, the directing minds of the British Industrial Revolution hailed, for the most part, from the ranks of the artisans—generally regarded as part of the undistinguished "middling" classes of society.

Another curious commonality of many of these British innovators was their unorthodox religious beliefs. In the parlance of the time, they were "Dissenters." In other words, they subscribed to branches of Protestant Christianity that refused to conform to the teaching and rites of the Church of England. A Quaker and the son of a tenant farmer who also worked as a locksmith, Darby's origins were far removed from the upper-class Anglican stock of the British elite.

If, as the economist Israel Kirzner argues in *Competition and Entrepreneurship*,[8] equilibrium is the enemy of the entrepreneur, it stands to reason that those most willing to disrupt equilibria—social, technological, or otherwise—are those who benefit least from the status quo. So like the entrepreneurial surges of many societies from ancient Rome to twentieth-century America, the British Industrial Revolution was for the most part the handiwork of oddballs and outcasts.

Darby began his career as an apprentice to a Birmingham malt-mill maker until he struck out on his own in 1698. At the time, the process of milling malt (typically sprouted barley) for the purpose of brewing alcoholic beverages involved contraptions made from brass. After six years of making malt mills and various kinds of cookware from brass, Darby became intrigued with the idea of using cast iron instead. This initial curiosity led Darby to embark on a period of experimentation with iron smelting that would have consequences well beyond the Baptist Mills Brass Works established by Darby and four coreligionists who put up seed capital in exchange for a partnership share.

At that time, the challenge in smelting iron was that it relied upon furnaces fueled by charcoal, a derivative of wood, of which Britain had a limited supply. So, having observed the use of the hotter-burning and more abundant metallurgical coal in the smelting of copper, Darby thought of experimenting with that substance, also known as coking coal or "coke," in iron smelting. However, as Darby would soon learn, although his concept was sound, there were a number of technical challenges that needed to be overcome to make coke-powered iron smelting a sustainable process. So he tapped into his natural ingenuity again and with the assistance of one of his junior employees perfected a coke-powered process by smelting the iron in sand. In 1708, Darby was granted a patent on this process and the modern iron industry was born.

The Brass Works was soon sold off. It seems that Darby's original partners were growing increasingly uneasy with the brash inventor's forays into the uncharted waters of iron smelting. An irrepressible entrepreneur, Darby used his share of the sale to commence development on what would soon become the Bristol Iron Works. Strategically located in the West Midlands village of Coalbrookdale, then a rich source of easily accessible coking coal, Darby's new business began with the manufacture of iron pots and various other small utensils and tools. Due to the superior efficiency of coke-powered smelting and Britain's vast deposits of coal, ironware could be produced less expensively than brassware without compromising either sturdiness or form.

However, Darby would win his most lucrative and historically significant contract several years later: in 1712, the Bristol Iron Works was commissioned to build six-foot iron mine-pumping engine cylinders for the "Newcomen engines," the first viable steam-powered water-pumping engines. These engines, in turn, led directly to the work of James Watt, the most iconic inventor-entrepreneur of the Industrial Revolution. Moreover, while forging the initial link between coke and the iron industry increased the demand for coking coal, assisting with the development of more effective water-pumping machines expanded *access* to both kinds of coal.

After all, Thomas Newcomen did not invent the first steam engine, but his engine was the first to effectively decrease the incidence of mine flooding. The latter was one of the great perils of the deeper mining that became increasingly necessary as the supply of surface-level coal diminished. Darby passed away in 1717, by which time he had amassed a considerable fortune. By 1758 Darby and his son and successor Abraham Darby II had completed production of one hundred steam engine cylinders. The Darby legacy would persist, with Abraham Darby III helping to build the world's first iron bridge in 1779. After the death of Darby III, the Bristol Iron Works built several other groundbreaking items, including the world's first locomotive engine.

Thomas Newcomen

Thomas Newcomen was the first in a line of steam engine innovators extending back to ancient Rome whose work actually yielded real benefits in an industrial context. As such, like the work of Darby I, that of Newcomen—particularly the 1712 commercial launch of his engine—remains a fundamental aspect of the Industrial Revolution that he would not live to see. Born in 1664 in Dartmouth, in the southwest of England, to a family of Baptists—another branch of religious Dissenters—Newcomen was a fairly colorful character. Unconventionally, he divided his time between his work as an ironmonger and his passion for Baptist preaching. Perhaps, like Darby, being raised in one of the Nonconformist branches of Protestantism had instilled a willingness to flout convention and consider alternative ideas and approaches.

Certainly that is the attitude with which he addressed the challenges that confronted him as an ironmonger. Especially since his business specialized in iron tools for the burgeoning coal-mining industry, Newcomen spent a considerable amount of time at various mining sites, where he noticed the limited effectiveness of horse-powered water pumps. Aside from the uncertainties of relying upon animals as a source of power, these contraptions could only pump to a depth of ninety feet, meaning that large deposits of coal could not be reached and remained untapped. So beginning in 1701, Newcomen and his assistant John Cawley, a plumber by trade, began experimenting with various designs for an effective steam-powered water pump.

Prior to Newcomen, the most advanced model was at the heart of a 1698 patent in the name of Thomas Savery, an Englishman inspired by the scientific work of seventeenth-century French physicist Denis Papin. Savery's makeshift pump was too limited to be reliably useful, but his patent claims were so broad that Newcomen was unable to obtain a patent without him. So along with Newcomen himself, the 1708 patent for the world's first commercially successful steam engine listed both Cawley and Savery as co-inventors. The product of over a decade of experimental work—mostly by Newcomen and Cawley—the Newcomen engine, running on steam generated from water heated by burning coal, was unveiled in 1712.

Whereas the power of Savery's machine was limited by the extent of steam pressure, the piston in Newcomen's single-cylinder engine was forced up by steam pressure but was forced downward by the more powerful *atmospheric* pressure that bore down to fill the vacuum created by steam condensation. The new engine marked an extraordinary leap forward in functional design and industrial use. One Newcomen engine could pump as much water as twenty horse-powered pumps, removing water *hundreds* of feet deep. Although the Newcomen engine ran on large amounts of coal, since it facilitated access to what seemed to be almost inexhaustible supplies of the mineral, it still managed to become the standard pumping apparatus in mining operations across Britain. By Newcomen's death in 1729, more than one hundred of his engines were in use.

James Watt and Matthew Boulton

James Watt is the first in a series of "superstar" inventor-entrepreneurs that includes such legends as Thomas Edison, Henry Ford, and Steve Jobs. These notables were all celebrated figures of their respective eras, admired not only for their technical ingenuity but also for the fact that, during their lifetimes, large and lucrative markets were found for their breakthroughs. Indeed, they are among the select few who have scaled the heights of public renown as both businesspeople *and* technical geniuses.

Watt, whose name is immortalized as a fundamental unit of energy measurement, still stands as the original in that regard, although there is still some controversy regarding his deserved place in history. Certainly in terms of overall business success and, more specifically, tailoring products for maximal market appeal, much of the credit is owed to his longtime financial backer and business partner, Matthew Boulton, a name remembered by relatively few. Moreover, from a technical perspective, one can certainly argue about which innovator of the era is responsible for the most significant breakthrough. Nevertheless, justly or not, it is a fact that the name of James Watt is the one that has come to represent Britain's Industrial Revolution.

Born in 1736 in the Scottish town of Greenock, near Glasgow, James Watt was raised in a family of "Covenanters." A devout and rebellious group of Scottish Presbyterians who had been subject to religious persecution and even violence during the sectarian turmoil of the previous century, the Covenanters were, like the Quakers and Baptists, a Nonconformist religious sect. Watt's father was a trader in ship equipment who also repaired nautical instruments. During his formative years, James spent many hours in his father's workshop and became quite fascinated with the construction of those instruments and how they were repaired. So when he turned eighteen, Watt started an apprenticeship that took him to Glasgow and later London as a precision engineer.

As an apprentice, Watt demonstrated an exceptional aptitude for designing and building various scientific instruments by hand. Nonetheless, upon completion of his apprenticeship in London, when Watt returned to Glasgow, his training was considered insufficient by the local guild. So he was barred from establishing a proper shop in the city. Forced to seek alternative arrangements, Watt came to an agreement with the University of Glasgow in 1757. In exchange for providing some of his instrument-making and repair services to the school, he would be allowed to run his small shop on the campus. By working at the university, Watt, who never studied formally at an institution of higher learning, gained direct access to the latest technologies and ideas.

Most fortuitously, the scientific faculty with whom he fraternized was fixated on the steam engine and when their miniaturized replica of the Newcomen engine broke down one day, they took it to their young friend's workshop for repair. With a model of Newcomen's 1712 breakthrough sitting on his workbench, Watt was forced to contemplate steam engines for the first time in a career that until then had been dedicated to relatively small scientific instruments. Though impressed with the utility of Newcomen's engine, Watt also noticed its structural inefficiencies. A habitual tinkerer like his father, Watt began to devise fixes for those problems. Over time, these fixes led to a steam engine design that was sufficiently distinct from the Newcomen engine to warrant its own identity—the Watt engine.

For Watt, the most glaring inefficiency of the Newcomen single-cylinder engine was how the engine had to be chilled with cold water and then reheated to activate condensation. Recognizing that this cycle of cooling and reheating wasted much of the steam supply, Watt devised a two-cylinder engine in which energy could be preserved in one cylinder while condensation occurred in the other. However, thus far, Watt's improvements had only taken place on a model or miniaturized scale, and in order to demonstrate the industrial benefits of his ingenuity, the young inventor needed to build a full-scale engine.

The problem was that the construction of such a large machine would require much more money than Watt had at his disposal. In fact, even his small-scale experimentation would not have been possible without a loan from a professor he had befriended. Fortunately, Watt's work aroused the interest of John Roebuck, then a wealthy proprietor of an ironworks near the Scottish city of Edinburgh. Crucially, Roebuck was an innovator in his own right, having conducted a number of important experiments pertaining to sulfuric acid in his earlier years. As such, he possessed the combined business and scientific background to appreciate Watt's invention and its industrial potential.

So in 1768 Roebuck financed the further development of the Watt engine in exchange for two-thirds of Watt's first patent, issued the following year. By then, Watt had left the campus for work as a land surveyor, helping to map out routes for the Scottish portion of Britain's expanding canal system. Much of the conceptual work around the Watt engine been accomplished, but on the commercialization front, matters progressed slowly until the mid-1770s. In 1772, due to his foundering ironworks, Roebuck declared bankruptcy and sold his share of Watt's patent to Matthew Boulton. The son of a small-scale toy manufacturer who had expanded his father's business into more lucrative items, Boulton had met Watt several years earlier through the Lunar Society in Birmingham, England.

The society was a rather informal group that would meet monthly in the Birmingham area. At least intermittently, such notables as Benjamin Franklin and Erasmus Darwin, a noted intellectual of his time and the grandfather of Charles, would attend. "Lord! What inventions," Darwin wrote to Boulton, lamenting his absence at an upcoming meeting of the Lunar Society, "what wit, what rhetoric, metaphysical, mechanical and pyrotechnical, will be on the wing, bandy'd like a shuttlecock fro, one to another of your troop of philosophers!"[9] By 1775, Watt had become Boulton's most important "philosopher" (which, in eighteenth-century Britain, was, in terms of modern usage, analogous to intellectual), having relocated to Birmingham to establish Boulton & Watt, a sizable plant dedicated to the production of Watt steam engines.

The legendary pairing of Watt with Boulton was, in the words of historian Asa Briggs, "a classic partnership of technical inventor and businessman."[10] Within one year of incorporation, Boulton & Watt was already enjoying a brisk business, installing pumping engines at mines in the "tin country" of southwestern England. Yet Boulton, who was always considering larger and more lucrative markets for Watt's inventions, encouraged his partner to modify his engine so that its application could extend beyond water pumping to other important functions. This milestone was attained in 1782, with the advent of Watt's double-acting steam engine. Through a clever configuration of steam pressure release and blockage mechanisms and the attached condenser, Watt employed steam power not only to drive the piston down but to drive it up as well.

Moreover, Watt, through several additional innovations, including one he called "sun-and-planet gearing," was able to convert this up-and-down pattern into rotary motion. Consequently, the Watt engine had now been converted into a more efficient substitute for wheels operated by water or wind.

As such, it was soon found at cotton and paper mills across Britain, revolutionizing productivity wherever it was installed and significantly expanding demand for the products of Boulton & Watt.

Like all great entrepreneurs, the partners were attentive to their customers' needs. For example, some cotton mill operators noticed that when the engine was used to run multiple looms, the speed of the engine would fluctuate, requiring manpower to keep it stabilized. In response to these complaints, Boulton urged his partner to address this issue in the next iteration of the engine. What followed was one of Watt's most brilliant inventions—the "flyball governor," a contraption that leveraged the principle of centrifugal force to regulate the speed of the steam engine automatically.

By 1800 more than five hundred engines manufactured by Boulton & Watt were in active use across Britain, and both men had grown enormously wealthy. In fact, by 1790 Watt was already reported to have earned more than £75,000 for his minority share of the patent revenues. That is truly a staggering sum, equivalent to more than US$700 million today. So, by 1800 it is very likely that Watt and Boulton, both born into what the *Manchester Mercury* described as society's "inferior ranks," each possessed the wealth of a modern-day billionaire. The upward mobility of middle-class colonial traders was significant, but the majestic affluence of a Covenantist instrument maker and the son of a toy maker demonstrated that in the course of revolutionizing industry, Britain's inventor-entrepreneurs had also reshaped their society.

James Hargreaves

By providing an efficient and well-regulated source of automated power, Watt and Boulton are partially responsible for the surge in the productivity of the cotton industry during the second half of the eighteenth century. However, even before Watt filed for his first patent, a transformation of the cotton industry was already under way. Beginning in 1764, a series of innovations were introduced that transformed the process of spinning cotton from a labor-intensive and often ineffective manual undertaking into a mechanized process.

As with the progression of the steam engine from Savery's relatively crude design to the final version of the Watt engine, the mechanization of cotton spinning was similarly iterative. "Innovators," as Kelley and Littman proclaim in their 2005 classic *The Ten Faces of Innovation*, "set out to create, to experiment . . . to build on new ideas."[11] The advancement in cotton-spinning technology during the Industrial Revolution is a strong illustration of this cumulative process of technological experimentation and improvement. Moreover, the contrast in the fortunes of the three leading innovators in that transformation—James Hargreaves, Richard Arkwright, and Samuel Crompton—reveals much about the tenuous link between ingenuity and monetary success.

Born in 1720 on a farm near the northwestern English village of Oswaldtwistle, James Hargreaves's origins were, like most of the other founding fathers of the Industrial Revolution, decidedly undistinguished. Yet despite his poverty and illiteracy, Hargreaves had a knack for boldly original thinking. As an adult, he became a handloom weaver in the nearby village of Stanhill, and as was commonly done, he put his children to work on a spinning wheel, where cotton was spun into yarns. Then he and his wife would weave those cotton yarns into textiles on a hand-powered apparatus. However, frustrated with its limitations, Hargreaves began tinkering with various aspects of the traditional spinning wheel/handloom process.

Eventually, this experimentation led to the introduction of his "stock-card," a wooden bench covered with wires that enabled one person to "card" or untangle much more cotton at one time than had previously been possible. Hargreaves's more famous invention, the spinning jenny, applied the same principle of multiplying productive output to the spinning wheel. Previously, spinning wheels had been set vertically. Instead, Hargreaves set his wheel so that it was horizontally slung, thereby facilitating the spinning of as many as eight vertically set spindles at once. Some thirty years earlier, the English handloom maker John Kay had managed to double productivity with his "flying shuttle" device, but Hargreaves's innovation was on another level entirely.

Since the jenny enhanced productivity so dramatically, its invention in 1764 is considered by some to mark the official beginning of the Industrial Revolution. While Watt lived by his words that "an engineer's life without patent is not worthwhile,"[12] it seems that Hargreaves, brilliant but illiterate, was not sufficiently aware of the importance of patents and failed to apply for one until 1770. News of his invention had spread quickly, inspiring copycat craftsmen throughout northern Britain for several years before Hargreaves's patent had been issued. So, the humble hand weaver would never reap significant financial rewards from his historic innovation.

What he did reap was the fury of the region's hand spinners who, quite presciently, began to feel threatened when Hargreaves began building and selling his invention in the mid-1760s. Tensions boiled over in 1768, when a throng of these proto-Luddites broke into Hargreaves's home and vandalized his workshop. Concerned for the safety of his large family, Hargreaves left Stanhill for the faraway city of Nottingham, in England's East Midlands region. With Nottingham local Thomas James, Hargreaves established a business of a different sort, perhaps to avoid the controversy of the recent past. Instead of selling spinning jennys, they opened a mill that leveraged the efficiencies of that invention to spin yarn for stockings and other hosiery.

Meanwhile, Hargreaves, an irrepressible innovator, kept refining his jenny, and the results were impressive: instead of eight spindles spinning from one frame, later iterations spun as many as one hundred and twenty! By the time of Hargreaves's death in 1778, some twenty thousand spinning jennys were in regular use in Britain's textile industry. Despite the impact of his invention, Hargreaves never enjoyed more than modest business success, and he died with little money to his name. Although his approach was highly entrepreneurial, Hargreaves's lackadaisical patent strategy reveals a man of great inventiveness and ambition hamstrung by a poor grasp of business. In this regard, he was the inverse of Richard Arkwright, a man of extraordinary business savvy who was probably not as technically inventive as Hargreaves.

Richard Arkwright

Like Hargreaves, the next inventor-entrepreneur in the cotton industry trilogy, Richard Arkwright, was born into poverty in northwest England and never attended school. Born in 1732, he was the son of a Preston tailor who had thirteen children and little money to spare on education. However, Arkwright was not burdened with the illiteracy that handicapped his predecessor. One of his cousins taught young Richard to read and write, skills that would prove indispensable later in life.

Arkwright's career path began in typical working-class fashion, progressing from a barber's apprentice to, at some point in the early 1760s, ownership of his own barbershop and wig-making business. Yet even in these modest environs, the young man's enterprising and innovative spirit soon became evident. He experimented with various formulas for wig dyes and, as soon as he found one that was sufficiently waterproof, he proceeded to patent it. Whereas Hargreaves was too slow to protect his intellectual property,

Figure 7.1
Richard Arkwright. *Source:* Obtained with permission to reuse from Google Images (Wikipedia).

Arkwright was well aware, possibly *too* aware, of the force of patent law in monetizing inventions.

Due in large part to his dye invention, sales of Arkwright's wigs took off and he was able to save a substantial sum of money from his first enterprise. However, in due time, Arkwright, whom the historian Shepard Clough described as a man with "a keen eye for opportunities for earning an extra penny,"[13] had that eye set on larger game. At some point in the mid-1760s, a business trip to another region of northwest England brought him into contact with the second John Kay in the history of cotton-spinning industrialization—a watchmaker in the town of Warrington.

Kay, inspired by the popularity of Hargreaves's jenny, had been attempting to build what he called a spinning "frame" with many more spindles that was configured to run on water power. However, as revealed by evidence submitted in later legal proceedings against Arkwright, Kay may have had another source of inspiration—an inventor by the name of Thomas Highs in the nearby town of Leigh who claimed to have hired him to help build a similar machine two years before Arkwright filed a patent for the spinning frame. Highs alleged that Arkwright knowingly conspired with Kay to appropriate Highs's invention. After years of legal battles, an English court annulled Arkwright's patent rights to the spinning frame in 1785.

Despite the controversy surrounding this issue, Arkwright leveraged his temporary legal ownership of the concept with tremendous energy, market savvy, and ingenuity. Having filed his spinning frame patent in 1769, Arkwright now held exclusive rights on building a spinning apparatus that could operate almost one hundred spindles at once. More importantly, unlike the jenny, it involved an array of wheels weighted and positioned in such a way that one wheel would spin faster than the one before and so on. This clever configuration straightened the cotton fibers rapidly before spinning them together into an impressively strong thread. In this manner, aside from multiplying the original jenny's multispindle capacity, the spinning frame was an all-around more effective tool than the jenny for converting raw cotton into thread.

However, Arkwright, having hired Kay and others to build it, soon realized that such a large contraption could not practically be powered by human hand (and foot) power, as originally intended. In fact, even the pull of horses was not sufficiently powerful or steady. This posed a problem, and the solution devised by Arkwright and his engineers is arguably more significant than the intricately designed frame itself. The team decided that the large multispindle device would be powered by a waterwheel, requiring no human or animal effort as it churned out large quantities of spun cotton.

The waterwheel, whereby the flowing water of a river, for example, would rotate a wheel that would, in turn, power some other process, had been utilized in Europe since Roman times. Indeed, long before the 1770s, flour mills, sawmills, and various other entities across Britain had enjoyed the laborsaving benefits of the waterwheel. However, applying the power and speed of the waterwheel to cotton spinning was a truly revolutionary concept, one that Arkwright dubbed the "water frame." By 1771 he had gone into business with two junior partners, the memorably named Jedediah Strutt and Samuel Need. They proceeded to establish Cromford Mill, the world's first water-powered spinning and weaving factory, named after the East Midlands village where it was built.

Cromford Mill was only the first in an empire of large factories that the partnership would build across the Midlands (both East and West), northwest England, and farther north into Scotland. However, it was Arkwright who was the directing mind behind this new factory system that was revolutionizing working life in Britain. In the 1780s, he made eager use of Watt's steam engine, a change that provided more efficient power while freeing him from the geographical constraints of building mills on riverbanks. From a technological perspective, from spinning to carding to the power source itself, Arkwright's mills were the culmination of the British Industrial Revolution.

Moreover, from the concept of highly structured coordinated on-site work involving thousands of people on multiple shifts (versus stay-at-home piecework), Arkwright had designed a system to extract maximal productive capacity from his workers. This new phenomenon of mass production was "comparable in scale and significance," as the British writer Bill McGuire concludes, to "the switch from hunter-gathering to a sedentary, agrarian economy, 8000 years earlier." While Arkwright became so rich that a few years before his passing in 1792, he boasted that his wealth could pay off the national debt, thousands of people were forced to abandon their crafts and their ancestral villages permanently for urban factory work. Although industrialization did raise the overall standard of living, it was still a wrenching transformation for many.

Samuel Crompton

Born in 1753 in the town of Bolton, Samuel Crompton was another great innovator from northwestern England. However, unlike Hargreaves and Arkwright, Crompton was not raised in poverty, and he was able to attend a day school. As well, Crompton was one of the few notable inventor-entrepreneurs of his era who was born into the Church of England. Yet, being the son of a farmer, he was certainly not born into privilege, and after Crompton's father passed away when he was still very young, the inventor's childhood was a difficult one. It seems that his mother, who did an admirable job sustaining her late husband's butter, honey, and elderberry wine business, routinely beat her well-behaved Samuel "not for any fault, but because she *so* loved him."[14]

When he completed his basic schooling, his mother insisted that in order to help support the family, the sixteen-year-old Crompton must stay at home to spin a certain amount of cotton each day. After five years of working with a spinning jenny, the young man was convinced that he could design and construct a better spinning machine. Of course, such a project would involve the purchase of various materials and tools. So, using a violin that he built himself, the musically gifted youth earned money in the evenings by playing with an orchestra. Over the next five years, all of this performance money and much of his spare time would be dedicated to his new machine. "My mind," Crompton wrote of this period in his life, "was in a continual endeavor to realise [*sic*] a more perfect principle of spinning."[15]

In 1779 Crompton had a completed prototype of what was to be known as the "spinning mule." Building upon the best of both Hargreaves's jenny and the spinning frame associated with Arkwright, the primary benefit of the mule was the quality of its thread. Tightly stretched and spun, the thread dispensed by the mule was so fine that it was typically sold for more than double the price of the relatively coarse thread of other machines. Unfortunately, Crompton would see little of the great wealth that his quality-enhancing innovation would yield for so many others.

By his own admission, Crompton was "not calculated to contend with men of the world."[16] So when he discovered that he lacked the funds for a patent, instead of attempting to find a partner who could put up the money, he naively "gave the mule to the public."[17] His gift was made with the understanding that, as fifty-five manufacturers promised him in a letter, they would each pay him a modest one-time sum for use of the mule. Most of them never even did that. Unfortunately, Crompton's small cotton-spinning business only enjoyed moderate success, while dozens of machine manufacturers and large cotton mills were profiting handsomely from his unpatented work.

In 1811 he was awarded a £5,000 grant from Parliament as a relatively modest form of compensation for a great industrial innovator who had been denied his reward. After all, by then, four million spinning mule spindles, mostly in automated steam-powered versions of Crompton's invention, were producing Britain's finest cotton fabric. Always the entrepreneur, he used his grant money to set up several cotton-related businesses. Sadly, none enjoyed much success, and Crompton would struggle financially until his death in 1827.

There is some irony in the fact that the only one of these three cotton-spinning inventor-entrepreneurs to have prospered is Arkwright, a man who patented but may not have actually invented a spinning machine. Although there is a lesson there about the importance of protecting one's ideas, the contrast between the struggling Hargreaves and Crompton and the man who amassed a fortune large enough to pay the national debt has broader implications. In brief, it is another cautionary tale underscoring the fact that a great idea, even in the form of a finished product, does not guarantee a successful enterprise. "Every enterprise," the management expert Tom Peters admonishes, should be "about balancing system/infrastructure . . . and inventing the new."[18] Or, put another way, balancing innovation with *execution*. Arkwright understood that.

Josiah Wedgwood: The Original "Mad Man"

Another pioneer of the Industrial Revolution with an uncanny knack for monetizing innovative ideas was the pottery magnate Josiah Wedgwood. This eighteenth-century British entrepreneur, whose surname is still found on china sets throughout the world, was not only an outstanding product innovator but also one of history's most creative and effective marketers. The popular television series *Mad Men* (2007–2015), about the heady world

Figure 7.2
Josiah Wedgwood. *Source:* Obtained with permission to reuse from Google Images (wedgwoodcapital.org).

of 1960s corporate advertising on New York's Madison Avenue, often high-lighted how advertising executives manipulate product associations to tap into consumers' social aspirations. Wedgwood mastered and in some ways originated this approach two hundred years earlier—in the 1760s.

Born in 1730 in the West Midlands town of Burslem, Wedgwood was raised by proud religious Dissenters. Notably, Josiah's father Thomas hailed from a line of potters that extended back over a century. Nine years later, when Thomas passed away, the family's circumstances forced young Josiah to work at the potter's wheel. He demonstrated talent for the craft, and by 1744 Josiah was already an apprentice to his older brother. Eight years later, eager for more independence, Josiah Wedgwood left the family business and entered into a short-lived partnership with another potter in the region. Shortly thereafter, in 1754, he partnered with Thomas Whieldon, one of the Britain's most respected potters. Working closely with a potter of such high caliber further enhanced Wedgwood's already considerable knowledge of the craft.

Moreover, it was during this partnership that the young potter's inventive flair became apparent. Most significantly, he invented a superior form of green glaze that remained popular until the late nineteenth century. Excited by the unique opportunities presented by his burgeoning ingenuity, after five years with Whieldon, Wedgwood struck out on his own yet again. He soon got to work on producing earthen dinnerware of an exquisite cream color. In 1765 he sold a set of this cream-colored earthenware to Her Majesty, Queen Charlotte. The pottery entrepreneur's unusual creative talents had already borne fruit; now his genius for marketing would soon make Josiah Wedgwood a household name.

Britain's gross domestic product (GDP) doubled during the eighteenth century, and by the early nineteenth century its per capita GDP was substantially higher than that of any country on the Continent. While this growth was certainly not evenly distributed, its impact extended well beyond the British upper crust. Certainly, that era's "ruling elite," as the British historian Paul Langford describes them, "seemed to live in a blaze of conspicuous consumption." Yet as Langford continues, there was "also the more modest but cumulatively more influential rise in middle-class standards of living."[19]

Meanwhile, as reflected in *Pride and Prejudice* and other novels by Jane Austen, eighteenth-century Britain was obsessed with its class system, and many in the newly moneyed middle class were eager to deploy their growing disposable income to appear more "respectable." Having already won the patronage of the queen, not to mention various prominent British nobles, during the early 1760s, Wedgwood knew that he was well positioned to profit from the social aspirations of the swelling middle class. So did Thomas Bentley, the savvy merchant who became Wedgwood's partner from 1768 until Bentley's passing in 1780.

Their first stroke of collective brilliance was branding their new product line Wedgwood & Bentley's "Queen's Ware," targeted squarely at social climbers among the middle class. To reinforce this prestige factor even further, all company invoices proudly proclaimed that Josiah was "Potter to Her Majesty" and mentioned other high-status clients such as the Duke of York. During the nineteenth century, "the desire for a magical transfiguration of the self," the advertising historian Jackson Lear wrote, was "a key element" in that century's "carnivalesque advertising tradition."[20] Wedgwood and Bentley, already selling a kind of self-transfiguration during the *eighteenth* century, were partially responsible for that tradition.

Perhaps this is why the company participated eagerly in the circus-like atmosphere of touring market fairs that, along with more conventional offerings, featured exotic "medical cures" and bizarre entertainers. The tours extended from urban markets in Britain to prosperous continental cities like Lyons and Leipzig, thereby raising Wedgwood & Bentley's international profile. Meanwhile, back in Britain, the partners introduced a boldly novel promotional concept when they opened a large and opulent retail outlet in London's chic West End. This, the world's first showroom store, was credited with a significant expansion of domestic sales.

Among the other innovative marketing tactics pioneered by Wedgwood & Bentley was direct mail, a linchpin of the promotional launch of "Queen's Ware." In fact, the tactic proved so successful that direct mail has since become a staple of advertising, enriching the postal service (and latterly the mental health industry) for well over two hundred years. However, the marketing ingenuity of Wedgwood and his partner is not the main reason why the former is profiled in this chapter. Aside from various glaze and gilt inventions credited to Wedgwood alone, the potter had also reinvented his craft—from a network of cottage businesses to steam-powered industry. Special roads and canals were even built to his potteries in the Stoke-on-Trent region as the government recognized that they comprised one of Britain's great industrial centers.

Wedgwood was also personally responsible for the invention of the pyrometer. A device for measuring temperatures much higher than the "normal" (mercury) thermometer range, the pyrometer had practical implications well beyond the pottery ovens. In recognition of the inventiveness behind this important scientific instrument, in 1783 the Royal Society granted a fellowship to Josiah Wedgwood. When he passed away twelve years later, Wedgwood was memorialized as one of the wealthiest industrialists in Britain. Today the Wedgwood brand endures, more than two hundred and fifty years after its founding.

A Lasting Legacy

The success attained by Wedgwood, Arkwright, Watt, and others of mostly "low birth" was certainly not lost on ambitious Britons. In fact, it spurred a flood of inventor-entrepreneurs, some of whom made notable contributions of their own. In the early nineteenth century, the innovations of Richard Trevithick and George Stephenson gave rise to steam-powered trains, thereby revolutionizing transportation. Similarly, with respect to weaving technology, Edmund Cartwright and others made significant advances during the first half of the nineteenth century. During the same period, J. B. Neilson and Henry Bessemer introduced groundbreaking improvements to the iron and steel industries, respectively.

Collectively, the work of all the British inventor-entrepreneurs of the Industrial Revolution amounted to what a Scottish economist writing in 1839 described as "the most striking example of the dominion obtained by human science over the power of nature."[21] From the use of mineral resources as an almost limitless (albeit not entirely clean) source of power to the mechanization and, to a large degree, automation, of important industries, the inventor-entrepreneurs had bent nature to serve their commercial objectives.

In this manner, some of Britain's "least likely to succeed" in socioeconomic terms had indisputably changed not only their country but, ultimately, the whole world. Several countries in continental Europe, physically close to Britain, would be among the first to be transformed by spreading industrialization. The United States, still both culturally and economically close to its Anglo-Saxon motherland, was also affected relatively early. By 1820, an American Industrial Revolution was under way that would last five decades. This industrialization, coupled with several other factors, would transform the former British colony into a land of wildly varied, creative, and often daring entrepreneurial activity. In this manner, by the late nineteenth century, the locus of entrepreneurship had shifted from Britain to America, the setting of the next chapter.

8

The Land of (Entrepreneurial) Opportunity

The chief business of the American people is business.
—PRESIDENT CALVIN COOLIDGE, 1925

The United States, particularly during the period from the Civil War until the end of the twentieth century, stands as the quintessential entrepreneurial society. Certainly, there have been few nations and epochs so molded by entrepreneurship and its attendant marvels and perils as America was during that time. From John D. Rockefeller to Henry Ford and all the way to late twentieth-century Information Age pioneers like Bill Gates and Steve Jobs, America spawned one iconic and internationally renowned entrepreneur after another. Moreover, there were many other transformational American entrepreneurs during this period, some of whose stories may be less well known but are no less compelling than those of the business legends. Some of these lesser-known entrepreneurs will be spotlighted, alongside some of the legends, in this chapter.

As discussed in chapter 6, even as British colonies, the lands that would break away to become the first thirteen states of the Union were established as entrepreneurial projects by various British merchant companies. Regarding the colonial period, the American business landscape was dominated by slave-dependent planters in the southern colonies and merchants of various sorts—including those who traded in slaves—in the north. Both regions were teeming with eager entrepreneurs, many of whom were natural risk takers, having uprooted themselves from the British Isles in search of both adventure and wealth in the New World. Notably, the disproportionate level of entrepreneurship among immigrants continues to be a distinctive feature of American enterprise.

In the newly independent nation, the enterprising spirit of the former colonists only intensified—an intensification proudly fostered by the young country's political and legal institutions. For example, in 1790, just fourteen years after America's independence and only two years after the ratification of its Constitution, Congress passed a fairly comprehensive patent law to encourage industrial innovation. Clearly enterprise had been an integral element of the American project long before the late nineteenth century, when both the scale and ingenuity of American entrepreneurship would rise above all others.

The Crucible of War

During the first half of the nineteenth century, much of America had adopted the technological and organizational advances of Britain's Industrial Revolution. It was the rapid industrialization of the northern states that helped lay the groundwork for a "battle of the states" in which slavery was at the very least one of several significant points of contention tied in with the wider issue of federalism and states' rights. After all, it was the more agrarian South that had become reliant upon slave labor. Yet despite the carnage of the ensuing war, which would claim some 752,000 lives and destroy billions of dollars of property, the Civil War period of 1861 to 1865 marked an important transition in American entrepreneurship.

The eminent historians Allan Nevins and Henry Steele Commager date the emergence of what can be described as modern America to the war itself. "That conflict," Nevins and Commager explain, "gave an immense stimulus to industry, speeded up the exploitation of natural resources, the development of large-scale manufacturing, the rise of investment banking, the extension of foreign commerce. It enormously accelerated the construction of the railway and telegraph network and ushered in the railroad age." Perhaps most importantly, the Civil War "put a premium upon inventions and labor-saving devices and witnessed the large-scale application of these to agriculture as well as to industry."[1]

The Mass Producers

As in almost every war in recorded history, there were some entrepreneurs who profited handsomely from both sides of the struggle. During the Civil War, the most notorious of these was a Connecticut inventor-entrepreneur in the weapons industry by the name of Samuel Colt. The father of the Colt 45 and many other weapons that bear his name, Colt was the inventor of the revolving multichamber cylinder mechanism, commonly known as the "revolver." Aside from various advances in firearms, Colt was also responsible for the first remotely detonated explosive and even some innovative work in the telegraph industry.

A highly successful gun manufacturer, Samuel Colt is still regarded as a pioneer of an American defense industry that continues to lead the world in both sales and technological sophistication. Yet like many American weaponry entrepreneurs who would follow in his wake, Colt was a contentious figure. By the time of the Civil War, the Connecticut Yankee was already an old hand at selling both sides of a war the means to obliterate each other. Colt, born in 1814, had played this opportunistic role in several mid-nineteenth-century inter-European conflicts. Up until the present day, private arms dealers, American and otherwise, have preserved this controversial approach to war profiteering.

However, the impact of Colt and his Colt Armory extended well beyond the defense industry. Along with the sewing machine maker Isaac Singer and the bicycle maker Colonel Albert Pope, the arms manufacturer was a pioneer of both mass production and the national advertising campaigns required to sell large quantities of competitively priced mass-produced goods.

In 1863, the New York-born Singer and his fellow Yankee Edward Clark, with whom he had already enjoyed considerable success in the large-scale manufacture of sewing machines, formally established the Singer

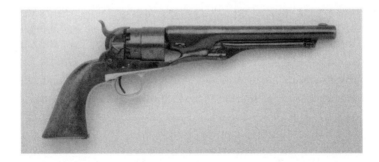

Figure 8.1
Colt Model 1860 Army percussion revolver. *Source:* Obtained with permission to reuse from Google Images (Wikipedia).

Manufacturing Company. By 1870 Singer and Clark's company was producing more than one thousand sewing machines per day, an astonishing feat of mass production for that era and generally credited to Singer's ingenuity. (Incidentally, the great "mass producer" would also be remembered as the man who fathered between twenty-three and twenty-six children—many of them in secret families he had established in various locales.) Both the Singer Manufacturing Company and the Colt Armory reaped enormous gains in efficiency by producing large quantities of components that were almost identical and then having them assembled into finished sewing machines and firearms, respectively. However, because there was still some slight variability in the components of these companies, "fitters" were employed to force components together.

Complete uniformity and, hence, interchangeability of components was only attained later in the century, with the work of the Boston-based bicycle maker Colonel Albert Pope. Having established the Pope Manufacturing Company in 1878, the former Union soldier proved a master of the manufacturing process, with components "machined to two-thousandths of an inch."[2] Such unprecedented fineness of production and component uniformity, whereby any part A would, without any forcing and finessing, fit perfectly with any part B, accelerated and cheapened the assembly process dramatically. Due in part to the colonel's remarkable advances in mass production, by the early 1890s America was seized by a bicycle craze.

The "Robber Baron" Philanthropists

In medieval Germany, the armed noblemen along the Rhine River who would demand tribute from passing ships were known as "robber barons." In nineteenth-century America, the term was used as a colorful slur against wealthy industrialists believed to have engaged in aggressive business tactics. These included the likes of John Astor, fur and opium trader; Cornelius Vanderbilt, shipping magnate; and Jay Gould, railroad speculator. The two most renowned of these men, particularly during the post–Civil War period, were Andrew Carnegie and John D. Rockefeller. Despite being derided as robber barons during their lifetimes, in time both of these industrialists would also be lauded as great philanthropists.

Carnegie, born and raised in Scotland, was certainly not the first in America's celebrated line of legendary immigrant entrepreneurs. John Astor, for example, was born Johann Jakob Astor in what is now Germany and in 1848 died as America's wealthiest man. In a sense, Carnegie carried the torch of "New American" mega-entrepreneurship into the second half of the nineteenth century. Moreover, the Scotsman's transformation from poor immigrant to American tycoon would serve as a model for the many eager immigrant entrepreneurs who streamed into the country during the twentieth century.

Born in 1835 to a handloom weaver, Carnegie would witness the impact of the Industrial Revolution firsthand when its efficiencies rendered his father's trade obsolete and threw his family into severe financial hardship. As it has for many successful entrepreneurs before and since, the pain of childhood poverty would serve as a compelling motivator for Andrew. "It was burnt into my heart then that my father had to beg for work," Carnegie recalled, "and, then and there, came the resolve that I would cure that when I got to be a man."[3] The loss of his father's job to a mechanized operation also inspired a lifelong reverence for technology that would yield substantial competitive advantages for the future steel magnate.

Shortly before Andrew's thirteenth birthday, the impoverished Carnegie family left Scotland and joined a group of relatives who had settled on the outskirts of Pittsburgh, Pennsylvania. Shortly after landing in America, Andrew, who only had five years of schooling in Scotland, was sent to work the furnace of a cotton factory, a terrifying job that gave him nightmares and motivated the youth to seek employment elsewhere. He was soon working in a telegraph office, and six years later Carnegie was hired as the personal telegrapher and secretary of Thomas Scott.

Scott was the superintendent of the Pittsburgh division of the Pennsylvania Railroad Company, among the largest enterprises in nineteenth-century America. By 1859, Carnegie had succeeded Scott in what was a fairly stable and well-paid position. However, it soon became evident that *any* salaried position, no matter how lucrative and prestigious, would not do for the wide-eyed Scottish immigrant. Even while he served as superintendent, Carnegie's independent business activities were extensive and varied, ranging from investments in various railroad parts manufacturers to the sale of American railroad-related securities to foreigners during trips to Europe.

It was during one of these trips that Carnegie, impressed by the emerging British iron and steel industries, foresaw the growing demand for such operations in a rapidly expanding America. So in 1865, Carnegie resigned from the Pennsylvania Railroad Company to manage the Keystone Bridge Company, a Pittsburgh iron bridge–building enterprise that he had invested in several years earlier. In one of his earlier strokes of promotional genius, upon building the 2,200-foot-long Mississippi Bridge, Carnegie demonstrated its sturdiness by inviting the press to watch an elephant make its leisurely way across. However, his most brilliant promotional maneuver occurred in 1873 when Carnegie named his new plant the J. Edgar Thomson Steel Works, after the man who was running the Pennsylvania Railroad Company. Of course, Thomson was running the company to which Carnegie hoped to sell enormous quantities of steel, which is precisely what happened.

The emerging steel magnate had also developed a reputation for thrift due to his disdain for credit and his merciless cost-cutting measures. However, when it came to maintaining a technological edge over his competitors, Carnegie spared no expense. In the 1870s, he built the first American steel mills that used the more efficient steelmaking process developed by Henry Bessemer, an Englishman mentioned in chapter 7. Two decades later, Carnegie's Pittsburgh plants were converted to an open-hearth system. The transformation required an enormous investment, but Carnegie foresaw, correctly, that the resulting efficiencies would make him the world's largest steel producer. Even his more established competitors back in Britain would be left behind, and by 1900 Carnegie's plants produced more steel than all of the British plants combined. Moreover, largely due to the Carnegie Steel Company, from 1865 to 1900 American steel production expanded from nineteen thousand to ten million tons.

In 1900 alone, the steel magnate's personal share of his corporation's profits exceeded $25 million, well over $700 million in 2015 funds. Carnegie, a poor immigrant boy who had risen to the pinnacle of wealth through shrewd and energetic entrepreneurship, is still regarded by some as a timeless embodiment of the American Dream. Yet for some of his employees and for the labor movement in general, the Carnegie Steel Company was an American nightmare. One of its plants in particular, Homestead, was aptly described by a Pittsburgh newspaper as "the scene of a great conflict between capital and labor."[4]

Essentially, Carnegie offered terms that offended the workers, thereby resulting in the Homestead Strike. Worse yet, Henry Clay Frick, the man a vacationing Carnegie entrusted to handle the dispute, brought in men who killed ten workers in the ensuing melee. The steel magnate's disastrously hardheaded handling of labor grievances at Homestead would scar his reputation permanently, and many of those who once admired Carnegie as a hero of American ingenuity now saw him as the quintessential robber baron.

Moreover, the strike was only the most renowned of several incidents in which Carnegie and his associates were accused of callousness. These accusations troubled the conscience of a man torn between personal ambition and the notion that entrepreneurship and its resulting wealth should benefit the masses. Revealingly, in his *Gospel of Wealth*, when reflecting on the benefits of philanthropy for the giver, Carnegie mused that such generosity provides a "refuge from self-questioning."[5]

In 1901, the Carnegie Steel Corporation was sold to the United States Steel Corporation, an entity controlled by the financier J. P. Morgan. Andrew Carnegie pocketed an astonishing $250 million from the sale—more than $7 billion in current funds—and devoted the remainder of his life to philanthropy. He certainly adhered to his "gospel of wealth," spending almost his entire fortune on a wide variety of philanthropic projects, including more than three thousand libraries around the world. Like Carnegie, John D. Rockefeller would also dedicate his retirement years to philanthropic projects. There were several factors, including Rockefeller's deep Baptist faith, behind this generosity. Nonetheless, there is no question that, like his Scottish acquaintance and erstwhile rival, the elder Rockefeller was eager to shed his robber baron image.

Like Carnegie's, the early life of John Davison Rockefeller was exceptionally challenging, albeit for different reasons. For one, Rockefeller was far removed from Carnegie's immigrant experience. The Rockefellers descended from Johann Peter Rockenfeller (the surname was altered slightly in America), who left Germany in 1723 to settle in what was then the northern colony of New Jersey. John was born 116 years later in Richford, a small town in south-central New York State. Yet despite the fact that both sides of his family had relatively deep roots in America, Rockefeller's early life was marked by the same economic insecurity that had plagued the Carnegie family.

The source of the Rockefeller household's misfortune was its head, William Rockefeller Sr. "Big Bill" was a lifelong womanizer who dabbled in the lumber industry before becoming a full-time huckster. His financial situation was unstable and, worse yet, his many scandals humiliated his family, particularly his brooding eldest son John. These disgraces, which included an 1848 indictment for rape, were compounded further by Bill's frequent and often extended absences from home. Most notably, in 1856, while still married to John's mother, he adopted an alias and married another woman in Canada. However, by then, John had already become what Rockefeller biographer Ron Chernow described as the "stand-in" for his father, and the teenager "kept a tight rein on the family budget and learned to appraise the world shrewdly."[6]

Due to the difficult circumstances endured by their families, both Rockefeller and Carnegie were compelled to assume significant financial responsibilities as youths: experiences that are common to *many* successful entrepreneurs. However, unlike Carnegie, Rockefeller completed school and did not linger long in a salaried position before becoming an entrepreneur. At the age of eighteen, Rockefeller formed a partnership with his neighbor in Cleveland, Ohio—the last of several locales to which Big Bill had moved the family over the years. Clark & Rockefeller became a successful "commission house" that bought and sold various bulk goods.

However, like Carnegie, Rockefeller always had an eye out for bigger game, and by 1863, having tired of dealing in bulk goods, the twenty-four-year-old entrepreneur went all in for oil. He recognized that, especially in the oil fields of the neighboring state of Pennsylvania, there was more oil being extracted from the pits than current refining capacity could handle. Consequently, if Rockefeller could establish a refinery that delivered a high-quality product, he knew that there would be ample opportunity for large-scale expansion. Moreover, as oil use later expanded from lamp fuel to powering various cycling vehicles and then automobiles, Rockefeller and his son and successor John D. Rockefeller Jr. were well-positioned to reap the rewards.

He became a partner in Andrews, Clark & Company, a refinery that, after Rockefeller bought out Clark and his brothers, became Andrews & Rockefeller. This would be the first of a long string of buyouts and other, more controversial, maneuvers that would cement Rockefeller's dominance of his industry. In 1870 he and several partners established Standard Oil. Within two years, this Rockefeller-led company, still based in Cleveland, had gained control of almost every refinery in the city.

For those competing refineries he was unable to purchase or effectively control through some sort of "partnership," Rockefeller would devise clever schemes that squeezed the holdouts until they relented. For example, by leveraging the size of his growing empire of refineries, Rockefeller was able to negotiate a significant *hidden* rebate from the Pennsylvania Railroad Company and others. In this way, while it seemed that Standard Oil was paying the very same rate as competitor X, with the hidden rebates, Standard was actually paying considerably less, thereby putting X at a significant competitive disadvantage. In time, frequent use of such heavy-handed tactics would tarnish the prominent oil magnate's reputation.

Among the all-time masters of large-scale entrepreneurship, Rockefeller continually leveraged the size of his business to expand it further. The chairman of Standard Oil was also savvy enough to collaborate with the dominant entities of complementary industries, especially transportation, for his company's benefit. Aside from the Pennsylvania Railroad, these included the Erie Railroad (controlled by Jay Gould), and the Empire and Star freight lines. Conversely, the smaller railroads and refineries excluded from the Rockefeller cabal generally operated "from day to day without cohesion or long-range planning," as the business historian Albert Z. Carr characterized it. "On the principle that power tends toward those who seek it," Carr continues, "the advantage was all with Rockefeller and his associates."[7]

Although he was not an inventor in the technical sense, as an avid opportunist, Rockefeller was open to novel methods of all sorts that might advance the interests of Standard Oil. For example, with respect to corporate structure, Standard, first incorporated as an Ohio company, became the country's first business trust; then, to evade recently enacted U.S. antitrust laws, it morphed into one of America's first holding companies. In fact, the antitrust laws of 1890 were aimed squarely at the monopolistic practices of Rockefeller and Gould and their cronies. The clamor for such laws reflected the widening gulf between the interests of large-scale enterprises and those of smaller American enterprises threatened by the new behemoths. In subsequent decades, this divergence would be the source of frustration for some smaller entrepreneurs and opportunity for others.

Rockefeller, the wealthiest American in recorded history, with a total fortune equivalent to almost $400 billion in 2015 funds, came to epitomize both the power and the pitfalls of large-scale industry. Before Hollywood and professional sports took hold of the national imagination, the great entrepreneurs were America's foremost celebrities. There were some in the press who cited both Rockefeller's monopolist practices and Carnegie's labor practices as cautionary tales about industrial power concentrated in the hands of robber barons. Meanwhile, others marveled at the astonishing wealth of these self-made entrepreneurs and, in later years, their generosity. Regarding the latter, Rockefeller dedicated the last four decades of his ninety-seven-year life to philanthropy that still supports many prestigious educational, medical, and scientific institutions.

Miracles of Light and Sound: American Inventor-Entrepreneurship

There were only 276 inventions filed with the U.S. Patent Office during the 1790–1799 period. One hundred years later, during the decade of the 1890s, the same office processed the filings of an astonishing 235,000 new inventions. As highlighted earlier, late nineteenth-century America provided a legal system that was generally sympathetic to inventors, especially inventor-entrepreneurs. This supportive infrastructure benefited some highly inventive and ambitious minds and fostered an American echo of the British inventor-entrepreneurship of the Industrial Revolution.

In fact, one of the two most famous American inventor-entrepreneurs of the late nineteenth century was Alexander Graham Bell, an American citizen born and raised in Britain. Bell invented the telephone while alternating between an American residence in Boston and a Canadian one in Brantford, Ontario. That is why Britain, Canada, and the United States have all laid some claim to the man behind one of the world's most extraordinary inventions. Yet Bell, like the best of his native land's inventor-entrepreneurs, also managed to prosper from his ingenuity, earning tens of millions of dollars in current funds. Along with an attorney, a financier, and his renowned assistant Thomas Watson, Bell established the Bell Telephone Company. Both AT&T ("Ma Bell") and Bell Canada began as subsidiaries of that company.

However, the most famous inventor of that time and of *all* time was not Bell but Thomas Edison. Almost inhumanly prolific, the midwesterner authored 1,328 patents. More importantly, the *impact* of his labyrinth of intellectual property was staggering. Along with what Edison described as the "soft radiance"[8] of electric light, he also invented phonographs and moving pictures. In fact, at least from a technical perspective, it was Edison who laid the foundation for an American entertainment industry that would mesmerize the world during the next century. Aside from protecting his intellectual property, the inventor was savvy enough to establish the Edison Electric Light Company and then pocket the equivalent of more than $50 million in current funds from selling it to J. P. Morgan.

An Unlikely Entrepreneur: Andrew Beard

Although some of the American entrepreneurs highlighted in this chapter thus far were immigrants, all were white and, more specifically, of the white Protestant stock that dominated American entrepreneurship well into the twentieth century. As Max Weber details in *The Protestant Ethic*, hard work and individualism are important aspects of Protestantism. So America's Protestant roots help account for the unusual vigor of American enterprise, a vigor that would be adopted by many Catholics and Jews, whose numbers were swelling from the 1880–1924 Great Wave of immigration. However, during this period, non-Protestants were deliberately kept on the periphery of American industry. In later years, some of the more ambitious of these outsiders responded by developing businesses, even industries, of their own.

Yet especially during the late nineteenth century and early twentieth centuries, the discrimination endured by immigrant Catholics and Jews paled in comparison to the legally sanctioned second-class citizenship of African Americans. In the immediate aftermath of slavery, the efforts of Reconstruction largely failed to guarantee basic rights to black southerners. During the era of Jim Crow that followed, laws were passed that disenfranchised many African Americans and largely kept them trapped in subsistence-level domestic and agricultural employment. That is why black entrepreneurial success stories from this era are so remarkable. The life of Andrew Beard, a black slave who became a notable inventor-entrepreneur, is perhaps the most significant of these Cinderella stories.

For nineteenth-century America, it would be difficult to imagine socioeconomic circumstances more disadvantaged than those of Beard's early life. Born near Birmingham, Alabama, in 1849, the young Andrew knew nothing but slavery until 1864 when Congress, following President Lincoln's lead, abolished the institution. In an early indication of the young man's extraordinary initiative, during his first year of freedom, Beard married his sweetheart and set up a small homestead of his own on the rural outskirts of Birmingham.

A natural innovator, Beard was continually experimenting with tool modifications and new processes to enhance the productivity of his farm. He patented the first of these, a more efficient plow, in 1881, and proceeded to sell the patent for $4,000—more than $100,000 in current funds. Six years later, Beard patented yet another ingenious plow design, which he managed to sell for around $150,000 in current funds. A true inventor-entrepreneur, Beard parlayed the early fruits of his inventiveness into a series of successful real estate speculations. He also filed a patent for a more efficient flour mill and ran such a mill on his property for several years.

Before turning forty, Beard had distinguished himself as both a serial inventor and a self-made entrepreneur, accomplishments of which anyone of any race would have been proud. However, for a young African American man to attain these lofty goals in the immediate aftermath of slavery was truly astonishing. Pressing on, in 1892 the forty-three-year-old inventor filed a patent pertaining to an enhancement of the steam-powered rotary engine. Shortly thereafter, for reasons that are not entirely clear, Beard went to work in the railroad industry.

During the 1890s, as the railroads expanded their reach through the newer territories of the West, lines were also being added in the east, including Alabama and other southeastern states. Beard was employed in the railroad yards where, among other tasks, he was responsible for linking railway cars together. In a procedure known as "car coupling," Beard had to drop a metal pin that would link two moving cars together at the very moment they were about to make contact. Of course, timing such a movement accurately could be a perilous procedure, and a career in car coupling often ended with the railway worker being crushed between two cars. Of those who survived such an accident, many, like Andrew Beard, lost a limb in the process.

Endowed with the opportunistic attitude of most successful entrepreneurs, instead of grieving over the loss of his leg and, consequently, his job, Beard resolved to invent an automatic coupler that would help prevent such accidents. In 1897, a patent was issued for Beard's "jenny coupler," a clever contraption that linked cars together automatically. There were a number of other automatic coupler patents that had been issued previously, but Beard's design was especially strong and his patent sold to a New York City firm for the equivalent of almost $1.5 million in current funds. Little is known about the remainder of Beard's life, but as a creatively and financially successful black inventor-entrepreneur during some of the bleakest years of the African American experience, he had already secured his place in history.

Henry Ford: Twentieth-Century Titan

During the mid-1890s, as Andrew Beard was experimenting with railcar couplers in Alabama, a young midwesterner was conducting some transportation experiments of his own as he built his first gasoline-powered "quadricycle." While Henry Ford was not the first to build, let alone invent, what would become known as the automobile, he would be the first to mass-produce the new wonder vehicle successfully. In Ford's own words, he set out to "democratize the automobile" by manufacturing and pricing it to accommodate the needs of the middle class. In the process, he revolutionized everyday life throughout the world. Consequently, Ford came to personify the ingenuity, energy, and *power* of early twentieth-century entrepreneurship in America, the young country whose industrial output had recently surpassed Great Britain's.

The grandson of Irish Protestant immigrants, Ford, born in 1863, was raised on his family's large farm near Dearborn, Michigan. Even as a young boy, Henry was a habitual, even *obsessive*, tinkerer. This tendency was so pronounced that his siblings would hide their toys when Henry came around, knowing that he would promptly disassemble their playthings and attempt to build something new. As Ford grew up, along with his mechanical inclinations, his disdain for farm work became disappointingly evident to his father. Clocks, trains, and practically every other machine that existed in the Dearborn area were a source of continual fascination for the boy.

By the age of sixteen, finished with school and eager to realize his mechanical ambitions, Ford relocated to Detroit to work as a machinist. After working in such a capacity for several employers in Detroit and then doing a stint in Dearborn as a steam engine repairman for Westinghouse, Ford, now a husband and father, moved his family back to Detroit in 1891 for a new opportunity: Ford had been hired at the local branch of the Edison Illuminating Company. Established by Thomas Edison eleven years earlier, his new employer operated electricity-generating stations in several large urban markets. Two years later, Ford was promoted to chief engineer and was on standby at all hours to address potential electrical service interruptions. Consequently, he did not need to put in regular office hours on the company's premises.

For an inventive young man who had built his own tractor back in Dearborn just a few years earlier, the promotion was an ideal scenario. After all, Ford was being paid handsomely to maintain a flexible work schedule that allowed him to spend long stretches of time in his home workshop. The results speak for themselves. By the end of the year, Ford had completed work on a functional gasoline-powered engine; in 1896, he had completed work on his first Quadricycle; and several car designs later, he launched his first company in 1899. The Henry Ford Company, which became the Cadillac Motor Car Company after its founder left in 1902, focused primarily on racing cars.

Captivated by the vision of building a more practical car for the masses, the budding entrepreneur established the Ford Motor Company in 1903. A testament to its founder's extraordinary resourcefulness, the automaker that now employs a global workforce of almost two hundred thousand began with a total capital investment of less than $1 million in current funds. The new company found eager buyers for its vehicles, although the Model A initially took twelve hours to manufacture. In October of 1908, the first of the more than 16 million Model Ts that would be sold over the next eighteen years rolled off the Ford assembly lines. The latter had been reengineered successfully, inspired by the efficiency of the *dis*assembly line of Chicago meatpackers, and the democratization of the automobile had arrived.

In his autobiography *My Life and Work*, Ford laid out his idealistic vision behind building a "business that wants to serve 95 per cent of the community."[9] This vision was the inspiration behind the unparalleled production speed that facilitated the affordable pricing for which Ford vehicles became known. As well, the company shrewdly leveraged the "everyman" appeal of the Model T in its advertising materials. "It's the one reliable car that does not require a $10,000 income to buy," a promotional booklet distributed in Ford dealerships read, "a $5,000 bank account to run and a college course in engineering to keep in order."[10]

Unlike some entrepreneurs of his era or, for that matter, our own, Ford possessed an intuitive grasp of enlightened self-interest. For example, troubled at the high turnover rate at his assembly line, Ford, against some of his associates' advice, acceded to his vice president's suggestion to raise the daily wage to five dollars per day. Aside from solving the turnover problem, the increased salary, almost three times the standard rate for assembly work, made loyal Ford customers of many employees. Of course, he was also known to harbor certain views that many would regard as less enlightened, such as his strident anti-Semitism.

Ford's innovative approach to product assembly, promotions, and labor relations would pay enormous dividends, and by 1921 the Model T had captured 60 percent of the new car market. "Legendary entrepreneurs like Henry Ford, Dave Packard, and Bill Gates," Jack and Suzy Welch observed, "are undeniably examples of the excitement and glory of starting something new from scratch and watching it grow to astonishing proportions."[11] In time, more vigorous competitors, particularly General Motors, would diminish those proportions somewhat. Nonetheless, long after the passing of its founder, the Ford Motor Company continues to innovate and enjoy periods of great success. In 1947, when Henry Ford died from a brain hemorrhage, his net worth in current terms exceeded $190 billion.

Al Capone: Underworld Entrepreneur

Another internationally renowned, albeit less revered, American entrepreneur passed away in 1947. However, aside from the years of their deaths and the possession of extraordinary business skills, Henry Ford and Al Capone had little in common. The son of immigrant Italians who had arrived in New York just six years before his birth in 1899, Alphonse Capone spent his early childhood in a run-down Brooklyn tenement. In 1910 the Capone family moved to a better neighborhood in the same borough. By all accounts, Al's father, a barber, and his pious mother, a seamstress, were both upstanding citizens in every respect. From an early age, it was evident that little Alphonse was not.

The short but bulky kid joined up with the toughest juvenile gangs, including one run by Johnny Torrio, the man who would later become his mentor in crime. Meanwhile, Al was having a difficult time at the Catholic school to which his parents sent him. His last day there was particularly trying, ending with a caning administered by his principal. It seems that earlier in the day, the temperamental student had assaulted one of his teachers. After the caning, he decided to quit school. Capone hadn't completed the sixth grade.

Despite his academic delinquency, as a teenager he made several attempts to live what gangsters of the era called "the straight life." Capone found employment as a cloth cutter in a bookbinding company and in other low-paying but respectable jobs. The serious trouble began when Capone decided to supplement his income with part-time work as a bouncer at the Harvard Inn, a Coney Island nightclub that, despite its amusingly pretentious name, was run by a mobster. Frankie Yale, the establishment's owner, was a powerful gangster-entrepreneur from whom the tough-minded bouncer would learn a lot.

Moreover, it was at the Harvard Inn where an eighteen-year-old Capone, having dishonored a young woman with a crude compliment, sustained a knife injury on the face from her outraged brother. Soon thereafter he would be known as "Scarface." By the time of Capone's knife injury, his old friend Torrio had been recruited by James Colosimo to help run the extensive network of nightclubs, brothels, and gambling dens that "Big Jim" owned in Chicago. Business in the Windy City was brisk and Torrio, needing a lieutenant, recruited Capone in 1919.

The timing of Scarface's overnight promotion to the executive suite of Chicago's nightclub and brothel operations was auspicious: between 1921 and 1928, Americans' per capita income grew by almost 40 percent to $716, then the highest in the world. With unprecedented sums of disposable money in their pockets, aside from Model Ts and other vehicles, Americans purchased washing machines, radios, gramophones, and electric refrigerators, thereby laying the foundation for modern consumerism. Particularly in urban centers like Chicago, they also spent plenty of money on the less virtuous products and services that Capone and friends provided.

Foremost among these was alcohol. The National Prohibition Act, passed in 1919, went into effect in 1920. The illicit trade in alcohol was tailor-made for the likes of Colosimo, a man who had built a business empire largely around the outlawed businesses of prostitution and gambling. Colosimo, Torrio, and others were well schooled in the peculiar mix of bribery, intimidation, and violence that such fringe enterprises entailed. Yet Colosimo was reluctant to become a bootlegger. Salivating over getting in on a new "racket" at the ground level, a frustrated Torrio proceeded to murder his boss with the help of both Capone and Yale.

Figure 8.2
Al Capone. *Source:* Obtained with permission to reuse from Google Images (fbi.gov).

Five years later, when Torrio retired, Capone would take his place as the kingpin. By then Torrio's protégé had proven his mettle and was already running much of the operation himself, finding creative ways of obtaining product from Canadian shipments (ostensibly sent to Cuba to bypass Canadian customs on the lookout for American-bound alcohol) and an assortment of domestic "wildcat" breweries. When it came to supplying a market, Scarface, like Rockefeller, was a gifted monopolist. To this end, Capone, a man who had given up on "going straight" long ago, was free to use a wider range of persuasion techniques than the CEO of Standard Oil.

For example, if a speakeasy chose not to purchase Capone's booze, its owner would be threatened, and if he or she still would not relent, the establishment would be bombed. Then Scarface would offer to loan money for the repairs: the Capone carrot and stick. Of course, there were other Chicago-area gangsters of various ethnicities, Polish, Irish, Jewish, German, and others, who engaged in similar activities. However, gangsters like Bugs Moran (the man whose underlings were executed in Capone's Saint Valentine's Day Massacre) and Hymie Weiss never attained the same notoriety because, unlike Capone, they never succeeded in monopolizing the bootlegging business.

Scarface also possessed a rare entrepreneurial adaptability, likely a product of the street smarts honed during his youth. For example, when a new mayor of Chicago decided to enforce Prohibition more strictly, Capone relocated to the suburb of Cicero and effectively colonized it. In short order, he established the town's first betting parlor and converted Cicero into the hub of his interstate bootlegging network. At its peak, Capone's enterprise of vice took in the modern equivalent of $1.6 billion annually and employed four hundred workers, many of them white collar.

Instead of roughing someone up in an alleyway, most of the kingpin's working hours were spent sitting at a desk in a well-appointed office, taking phone calls from suppliers and distributors, conferring with his deputies, and strategizing expansion opportunities. "I make my money by supplying a public demand . . . Everybody calls me a racketeer. I call myself a businessman," Capone once explained, "When I sell liquor, it's bootlegging. When my patrons serve it on a silver tray on Lake Shore Drive [a fashionable section of the Chicago waterfront], it's hospitality."[12]

There's no question that Capone, like most of his rivals, was a cold-blooded murderer. However, that does not negate the fact that he was also a talented underworld entrepreneur who, like those of later decades who smuggled illicit drugs into America and elsewhere, recognized an unmet consumer demand and profited from it. Nonetheless, in time, Capone's criminality, along with his reckless lifestyle, led to his ruin. He would serve nine years of his eleven-year prison sentence for tax evasion in Alcatraz. Capone was allowed out early due to evident deterioration from syphilis, a condition the married father of one had contracted from a prostitute at one of his own brothels. He passed away several years after his release, at the age of forty-eight.

The Great Depression: Starting Up During a Downturn

In 1922, several years before he became president, Secretary of Commerce Herbert Hoover wrote *American Individualism*, a book extolling the virtues of America's individualistic political and economic system. "We build our society," Hoover wrote, "on the attainment of the individual."[13] However, in the midst of the economic carnage of the following decade, the era of the Great Depression, such individualism became less popular. So aside from the diminished opportunity that resulted from the anemic economy of the 1930s, from the entrepreneurial perspective, a pernicious attitudinal shift was taking place in American society. In such an environment, ambitious American entrepreneurs were more likely to be regarded skeptically, even disapprovingly, by the public, the press, and even the government.

Nonetheless, there were those who, among the rubble of a ruined economy, recognized the seeds of opportunity. For example, Charles Darrow, who lost his job selling heaters in the aftermath of the 1929 stock market crash, helped make other economically distressed Americans *feel* rich by playing his game of real estate acquisition. In 1935 the Philadelphia resident filed a patent for Monopoly, and within a year Parker Brothers was selling twenty thousand copies of Darrow's game every week.

Similarly, in 1931, Drs. Don Baxter and Ralph Falk began mass-producing intravenous medical treatments, only available previously at large research hospitals. The two Iowan biotech entrepreneurs shrewdly took advantage of Depression-era conditions. For example, they converted an automobile showroom, vacated due to the downturn, into their low-rent laboratory. Today, Don Baxter International sells $15 billion of medical products annually and employs more than sixty thousand people around the world.

Even before America's official entry into World War II, the conflict had helped lift the country out of economic inertia by stimulating production of weapons and supplies for a besieged Britain and a U.S. military that was all but certain to be drawn into the war in the near future. The war itself brought America back to full employment and rising wages. Moreover, when the veterans returned, the generous benefits of the G.I. Bill were an impetus behind the large families of the baby boom and the vast expansion of housing to accommodate them. In the years following the war, America, long the world's preeminent industrial power, was now the wealthiest civilization in recorded history. With disposable income at an all-time high, a wider variety of opportunities emerged—including some from unlikely sources.

Atlantic Records: Mining for Black Gold

In 1944, shortly before the end of the war, the Turkish ambassador to the United States passed away in Washington, D.C. Upon his death, Munir Ertegun's wife and daughter decided to move back to Turkey. However, his two sons Nesuhi and Ahmet decided to stay in America. Since their family had relocated to the American capital nine years earlier, the Ertegun brothers had developed a fascination, even an obsession, with African American culture. What captivated them the most was black music, which at that time consisted primarily of jazz and, increasingly, blues and related forms of music.

In fact, by the time of his father's passing, a twenty-seven-year-old Nesuhi was already out in Los Angeles running a record store that specialized in such music. Meanwhile, Ahmet, only twenty-one, was studying philosophy at Georgetown University but spending much of his time learning about the music business at record stores in D.C.'s large black community. Both young men were eager to pursue their passion for this exotic music, but born into the Turkish aristocracy and accustomed to luxury, they had to find a way to make it *pay*. By the end of the war, Ahmet, a gifted entrepreneur, was confident that it would.

"Black people had work. Women had work. Everybody had work and people had money," Ahmet observed, speaking of the immediate postwar period in America, "And there was a sudden boom for records and there wasn't enough supply of records and there weren't enough pressing plants."[14] By 1947 Ahmet was ready to launch a record company. With a substantial investment from the Erteguns' family dentist, all Ahmet needed was a partner. The dentist provided that as well, in the form of a young man who had trained under him only to return to New York City and give up dentistry for music talent scouting.

In October of 1947, Ertegun and Herb Abramson launched Atlantic Records and initially ran it out of a Manhattan hotel for more than a year before settling into office space on Fifty-Fourth Street. Atlantic enjoyed considerable success during its early years, due in part to the reverence its founders shared for their predominantly black artists, a reverence that translated into paying them the same royalty rates as the major labels. After 1953, when Abramson was, effectively, replaced by Jerry Wexler, that culture would continue. Ben E. King, a singer in The Drifters, and later, on his own, the voice of "Stand by Me," was an Atlantic artist from South Carolina. "I am from an era and a place where people would say, 'Hey, you don't talk until you're talked to.' And then I was brought to New York where people [Ertegun and Wexler] asked me for advice!"[15]

Many of those behind the "race music" labels of this post-jazz era were, like Abramson, Wexler, and the Bihari brothers of Modern and Meteor Records, the sons of Jewish immigrants or, in the case of Leonard and Phil Chess of Chess and Checkers Records, Jewish immigrants themselves. There were also a number of celebrated executives of Italian background, such as Tommy LiPuma, not to mention, of course, the Turkish Muslim immigrants Ahmet and his brother Nesuhi, who would join Atlantic in 1955.

Motown Records, founded by the black entrepreneur Berry Gordy Jr., would not be established until 1959. So during this period of the late 1940s and the early 1950s, recording and distributing black music was to a large degree the work of these very ethnic Caucasians. Perhaps it took a certain sense of otherness from being Jewish, Italian, and/or an immigrant to build a business around a culture that was still considered alien by the American mainstream. After all, only a few years earlier, while whites of all sorts served side by side in the U.S. military of World War II, black soldiers were still kept isolated in their own units.

Neal Gabler's *An Empire of Their Own* describes the immigrant origins of many of the entrepreneurs who established Hollywood during the early decades of the twentieth century. Describing Carl Laemmle, an immigrant from Germany and the founding father of Universal Studios, Gabler states that "one of the reasons Jews like Laemmle were able to gain a foothold" was that "big money, gentile money, viewed the movies suspiciously—economically, as a fad; morally, as potential embarrassments."[16] Post-jazz black music, particularly blues, soul, and the other precursors to rock 'n' roll, was viewed in a similarly derisive light by mainstream America during the early years of Atlantic. Yet it was that disdain that left the door open to outsiders with an entrepreneurial bent, people like Ahmet and Jerry, the son of a window cleaner.

Including such luminaries as Ray Charles, Aretha Franklin, Otis Redding, The Coasters, The Drifters, Sam & Dave, and many others, the Atlantic roster reads like a who's who of the soul music of that era. Under Nesuhi's direction, the label also picked up a strong stable of jazz artists including Charles Mingus and the Modern Jazz Quartet. In later years, Atlantic would also sign some notable rock acts, many of which, like the British bands Cream and Led Zeppelin, were deeply influenced by black music.

In 1967, a year of monster hits for Aretha Franklin, Cream, and other Atlantic artists, Wexler believed that it was an opportune time to cash out. The Erteguns were less enthusiastic but eventually relented. So in October of that year, Atlantic was sold to Warner Brothers Records for the equivalent of roughly $120 million in current funds. The fact that Warner was willing to pay that kind of money was proof that the entrepreneurs behind Atlantic had found and developed a significant opportunity to which the major labels had been blind. Jerry continued working at the company until 1975, and Ahmet would remain for several decades longer. Both partners passed away in the 2000s.

Other People's Money: The Investor-Entrepreneurs

The Warner-Atlantic deal was hardly unusual for the second half of the 1960s. There was a merger wave under way not only in entertainment but across many industries. From initial public offerings (IPOs) to the prospect of being acquired by a larger entity for a big payout, the vibrancy of American finance not only facilitated large-scale enterprise but, by making it possible for the principals of a start-up like Atlantic to make such a lucrative exit, stimulated entrepreneurship on all levels.

Although Warner Brothers Music was still privately held, the overall merger wave was prompted, in part, by the high stock prices of the late

1960s. Following a crash in 1966, the market hit some new highs over several years, until the recession of 1973 to 1975. The relatively high market capitalizations of the late 1960s provided expanding companies with ample ammunition for hunting attractive acquisition targets. Other stakeholders who benefited from those high prices were investors who had purchased the same companies at much lower valuations earlier in the decade. One of these individuals was Warren Buffett.

Known today as America's second wealthiest individual, Buffett was just starting to garner national attention in the late 1960s with the astounding returns of his investment partnership. With the help of his vice chairman Charlie Munger, the Omaha native has since expanded his operations into a $300 billion publicly traded entity known as Berkshire Hathaway (the name of a textile mill that Buffett bought out in 1964). Berkshire, an enterprise of enterprises, boasts full ownership of such marquee brands as GEICO and Dairy Queen and significant minority positions in such companies as Coca-Cola and IBM.

In 1974, another notable investor-entrepreneur, John Bogle, established the Vanguard Group. A mutual fund company that specializes in index funds, Vanguard has since become a major provider of exchange-traded funds as well. The Pennsylvania-based company manages $3 trillion in assets and is the largest mutual fund company in America. Like Buffett's family, Bogle's was also hit hard by the Depression, and both investment masters adhere to prudent investing principles. Buffett and Bogle, along with dozens of other prominent American investor-entrepreneurs, built lasting enterprises that, through expansion and innovation, have permanently altered the money management landscape in America and beyond.

It was also in the 1970s when chinks in the armor of America's long-standing industrial dominance became apparent. During much of that decade, the country was beset by inflation, energy crises, and relatively high unemployment. Meanwhile, efficient foreign competitors, particularly those from Japan, were making domestic inroads into cars and consumer electronics, industries that to a great extent were invented in America. There was an element of copycat in those imports although the superior efficiencies attained by some foreign competitors were certainly innovative. Along with abundant physical and human resources, it had been America's ingenuity, powered by entrepreneurial energy, that had given birth to those industries. In the 1970s a much-needed new industry was emerging from "out of left field," the West Coast.

A Tale of Two Dropouts: Steve Jobs, Bill Gates, and the PC Revolution

Although the region would not be known as Silicon Valley until the early 1970s, California's Santa Clara Valley had already been a hotbed of entrepreneurial activity for several decades prior. Much of the credit is owed to Frederick Terman, the Stanford engineering professor who, as far back as the late 1920s, lobbied for government-funded projects in which university faculty and students collaborated with industry. Moreover, Terman actively encouraged his students to convert their ideas into businesses. In this manner, he converted Stanford into a giant start-up incubator. His two most famous engineering students were Bill Hewlett and Dave Packard, who would found Hewlett Packard in 1939. In later decades, other notable Stanford start-ups included Sun (Stanford University Network) Microsystems and Cisco Systems.

However, the University of California–Berkeley scholar AnnaLee Saxenian attributes the entrepreneurial dynamism of the valley to employment mobility[17]. Therefore, it can be traced even further back than Terman—to 1872, when the twenty-two-year-old state of California enacted its first civil code. Within the code was a curious provision safeguarding the right of Californians to change employers as they saw fit. In practice, that meant that employees could not be compelled to sign noncompete agreements. In the valley, the significance of this provision became most apparent in the 1950s, when eight engineers defected from Shockley Semiconductor in Mountain View to form Fairchild Semiconductor in nearby San Jose. In 1968, two of those engineers, Gordon Moore and Robert Noyce, would branch off yet again to establish another legendary valley company, Intel, where they were later joined by Andrew Grove.

Intel's launch of its first microprocessor and its successful IPO, both in 1971, foreshadowed a promising decade for Silicon Valley. The following year marked the launch of Sunnyvale's Atari, Inc. Atari's product was a consumer electronics hit, but the functionality of its devices was limited to video games. In 1974 Steve Jobs worked there for several months as a video game designer. Shortly thereafter, alongside Steve Wozniak (Woz), Jobs's high school chum and a UC Berkeley–trained engineer, Jobs pursued a vision for a personal *computer* (PC) with a much broader range of functionality than Atari's products.

The product of a romance between a Syrian foreign student and his German American girlfriend, Steve Jobs was immediately given up for adoption upon his birth in 1950. To the great chagrin of Steve's biological mother, neither Paul nor Clara Jobs had completed high school. So, Mr. and Mrs. Jobs had to sign a pledge that they would send the boy to college. When the time came, Steve was sent to Reed College, an expensive private liberal arts institution in Oregon. Yet as Jobs rather boldly stated in his 2005 commencement address to the graduates of Stanford University, "After six months, I couldn't see the value in it." He continued, "I had no idea what I wanted to do with my life and no idea how college was going to help me figure it out . . . So I decided to drop out and trust that it would all work out ok."[18]

In stark contrast to Jobs, by the time Bill Gates dropped out of college toward the end of 1975, not only was he not wondering what to do with his life, but the twenty-year-old Harvard dropout was already doing it. Gates, along with his longtime friend Paul Allen, had recently won a significant contract providing software to MITS, one of the first microcomputer companies. In April of 1975, several months before Gates completed his fifth and what would turn out to be his final semester at Harvard, the two Seattleites founded Microsoft.

Especially for a young country, and more specifically the Pacific Northwest—one of America's younger regions—Gates's lineage was distinguished, even patrician. William Gates III is the great-grandson of J. W. Maxwell, a midwesterner who had established First National Bank, and the son of William Henry Gates II, who was among Seattle's most prominent attorneys (now retired). Sent to the exclusive Lakeside School, Bill had distinguished himself as an excellent student, and when the school became one of the first to gain access to a mainframe connection, a thirteen-year-old Gates and his fifteen-year-old school chum Paul Allen got hooked on writing code.

Bill's background and early life were a world away from Steve's, but both of these entrepreneurs had placed themselves at the vanguard of the personal computer revolution at the same critical period. Apple, Inc., was founded in April of 1976, just one year after the establishment of Microsoft. Hand-built by Woz in the Jobs family's Cupertino garage, the Apple I found a limited but enthusiastic audience. The Apple II, with a more powerful circuit board, care of Woz, and a more appealing all-in-one product, replete with a keyboard and a case, care of Jobs, was a massive success. IBM and the other traditional "mainframe" computer manufacturers were on notice that a revolution was under way.

By 1980 IBM was eager to compete in the burgeoning PC market. Microsoft, which had supplied its software successfully to hardware manufacturers in the late 1970s, was tapped to provide an operating system. Microsoft in turn decided to purchase the rights to such a system from a local company, Seattle Computer Products (SCP). A classic illustration of Gates's shrewd negotiating skill, while Gates managed to obtain DOS from SCP for a total expense of only $75,000, when IBM asked to purchase the operating system from Microsoft, Gates refused. Instead, he compelled IBM to pay a licensing fee for each installation of DOS on every IBM PC. Moreover, Microsoft proceeded to sell software to the many knockoff PC manufacturers that were entering the market. By 1983 every third PC in the world was running Microsoft software.

In October of that year, Gates and Jobs shared a stage at an Apple conference held in Hawaii that featured promotions for the company's upcoming Macintosh computer, slated for release in January of 1984, and running on Microsoft software. "To create a new standard," Gates proclaimed, "takes something that's really new and captures people's imagination. And the Macintosh . . . is the only one that meets that standard."[19] Four years later, when Gates's company (Allen had left in 1982) released Windows 2.0, Microsoft was accused of copying Macintosh's attractive graphical user interface (GUI). In later years, the company would be challenged, both rhetorically and legally and from various corners, on grounds of anticompetitive practices—denunciations that Gates would vigorously deny.

As for Jobs, in the long term, the Mac would prove to be Apple's signature product, at least until the introduction of the iPhone in 2007. Nonetheless, the mid-1980s was a troubled time at the company, where former Pepsi CEO John Sculley, along with the Apple board, ousted Jobs from his own company in 1985. Jobs had proven himself a master of marketing, distribution, and consumer product design. Concurrently, his often-prickly management style generated resentment that would worsen when some Apple products, such as the first run of Macs, sold poorly. Although the firing was a terrible emotional blow, Jobs took the opportunity to become involved with other ventures. The animation studio Pixar, which Jobs helped develop for over twenty years, was the most significant of these. It was Pixar—not Apple—that made him a billionaire.

Gates, on the other hand, had been a billionaire since 1986, and by 2006, when Jobs sold Pixar to Disney for $7.6 billion, Gates had long been the wealthiest person in the world, with a net worth of over $50 billion. The year 2006 was significant for Gates as well, being the one in which he decided to transition out of day-to-day management of Microsoft. In close collaboration with his wife Melinda, his friend Warren Buffett, and renowned philanthropists like the Irish rock star Bono, Gates has since devoted much of his time and some $30 billion of his wealth to philanthropic projects, including those designed to promote entrepreneurship in agriculture, the life sciences, and other areas that can impact the lives of the world's ill and impoverished.

In 1997, Jobs was back at the helm of Apple, a company that was on the verge of collapse before he returned. Over the next decade, a series of extraordinary innovations would emerge from a reinvigorated Apple. These included the iMac, iTunes, the iPod, and the iPhone. "Life can be much broader," Jobs once told a television interviewer, "once you discover one simple fact: Everything around you that you call life was made up by people that were no smarter than you and you can change it, you can influence it, you can build your own things that other people can use."[20] Certainly, the daring entrepreneur who transformed computers, animation, music, and telecommunications lived by those words until his untimely death in 2011.

Both Jobs's and Gates's companies were fundamental to the PC revolution of the late twentieth century. By the time the Internet became widely available in the mid-1990s, PCs, the nodes of this network, were ubiquitous around the world, as was the Windows operating system. These commonalities, in turn, amplified the impact of the World Wide Web and made collaboration with people across the world just as quick and seamless as collaboration with people across the hall. As such, the work of Jobs, Gates, and the entrepreneurs behind Netscape and other late twentieth-century American companies helped lay the groundwork for the more globalized business world of the twenty-first century. Entrepreneurship has internationalized significantly in recent years and as the next chapter will discuss, has even expanded beyond our planet.

9

Flattening the World and Colonizing Space

Be conscious of the global elements in your dreams.
When starting local, dream of taking it global sooner.
—ISRAELMORE AYIVOR, GHANAIAN ENTREPRENEUR,
2014

At a speaking engagement held at Williams College one year after the April 2005 publication of the first edition of *The World Is Flat*, its author, the longtime *New York Times* foreign affairs correspondent Thomas Friedman, explained how a 2004 trip to India had inspired the book: "Somewhere between the Indian entrepreneur who offered to do my tax returns from Bangalore and the Indian entrepreneur who wanted to write my new software from Bangalore," Friedman declared, "and the Indian entrepreneur who wanted to read my X-rays from Bangalore and the Indian entrepreneur who wanted trace my lost luggage on Delta Airlines from Bangalore, I got this really sick feeling that something really big had happened in this globalization story and I had completely missed it."[1]

I had a similar encounter in the summer of 2004, the same year of Friedman's fateful trip to India. At the time, I was considering setting up a consulting practice in Silicon Valley, and I went to see some office rental units in the San Jose area. One of these was a space being subleased by an entrepreneur from India. During the course of my visit he offered to handle "payroll or any HR [human resources] services you might need." These services, he explained to me, were being provided by his staff of human resources professionals based in India and he was already serving a number of midsized Silicon Valley companies, all of which had seen "significant increases in their EBITDA [an important measure of earnings]" from outsourcing their human resources functions to his lower-cost Indian employees.

Having completed a technology degree a few years earlier, I was well aware of the outsourcing of software production to India, Russia, and other relatively lower-cost Asian and Eastern European countries. Moreover, partly because I had recently met a former assembly worker in the Silicon Valley area whose job had been shipped to China, I was also well aware of the increasing rate of manufacturing offshoring and its impact on the United States.

However, the revelation that even functions like human resources were being sent overseas made it clear that this newly connected world had become a gateway of opportunity for entrepreneurs, especially foreign ones, and a source of growing vulnerability for Western workers. In Friedman's terms, the global business world had been flattened. That is, a playing field that had once been a fairly exclusive club of Americans, Western Europeans, Canadians, Australians, and since the 1970s, Japanese, Taiwanese, and Hong Kong residents as well, had now been opened to *all*.

Building with BRICs

In 1980 the Chinese Communist Party was only in its third year of implementing a set of economic reforms designed to encourage private enterprise and attract foreign investment. India's trajectory of development was considerably slower. Allied with the former Soviet Union for much of its history since attaining independence from Britain in 1947, India was nonetheless a democracy, albeit one with much of its economy controlled by the state. It was not until 1991 that the Indian government began to implement a reform program designed to liberalize a stagnant economy.

In 1980 China and India collectively constituted less than 5 percent of global economic output. Thirty-five years later, that proportion has leaped to over 23 percent. So while Naomi Klein and other antiglobalization activists have highlighted the deteriorating labor and environmental conditions in some regions of China and India, there is no question that, at least from the perspective of growth, the free-market reforms undertaken by those two countries in recent decades have been successful. To varying degrees, similar reforms have been adopted in Brazil, Russia, and South Africa—the three other countries represented by BRICS, an expanded variant of the BRIC acronym coined in 2001 by the economic analyst Jim O'Neill.

Of course, these economic reforms, coupled as they often were with such political developments as the demise of the Soviet Union, were accelerated enormously by the technological leveling process initiated by American entrepreneurs. Yet once the technological infrastructure was in place, foreign entrepreneurs, recognizing the enormity of the opportunity, proceeded to accelerate the flattening. So the growth of the BRICS, and more broadly globalization itself, is a phenomenon rooted largely in the efforts of entrepreneurs from all corners of the globe. Collectively, the BRICS now comprise more than 30 percent of the world economy, and China, now the world's largest economy by some measures, accounts for more than half of the BRICS' economic output.

However, in recent years, the pace of BRICS growth has begun to slow from the brisk double-digit rates of the 2000s. For example, in January of 2015 General Motors president Dan Ammann told his investors that the Chinese market, to which GM has dedicated significant resources, "is maturing rapidly."[2] Economies that are generally growing faster than the BRICS include the MINT countries of Mexico, Indonesia, Nigeria, and Turkey, and the RISE countries of Rwanda, Ivory Coast, Sierra Leone, and Ethiopia. Notably, Mexico is home to Carlos Slim, an entrepreneur with large holdings across multiple industries and countries who has topped the Forbes 400 list several times over the past decade. Meanwhile, the RISE group represents some of the most rapidly expanding economies of sub-Saharan Africa, the world's fastest-growing region.

Thus far, our current century has seen the locus of both economic growth and purchasing power shifting steadily from the United States and Western Europe to Asia, first and foremost, followed by Latin America, Africa, and the Eastern European and central Asian countries of the former Soviet Union and its former satellite states in central Europe. Particularly since much of the economic growth in these regions has been spurred by private enterprise, some of the world's most exciting entrepreneurial developments are taking place in countries that businesspeople generally paid little attention to during the previous century. To bring this transformational shift to life, this chapter will explore a compelling entrepreneurial story from each of the four emerging economic regions.

China's BYD: A Battery-Powered Dream

The entrepreneur known today as China's wealthiest person, Wang Chuanfu, was born in 1967 in the eastern Chinese province of Anhui. His parents were farmers of limited means and education, and both would pass away while Wang was still a schoolboy. An outstanding student, Chuanfu was accepted into China's prestigious Central-South Industrial University, from which he graduated in 1987 with a degree in metallurgical science and engineering. Three years later, Chuanfu graduated with a master's degree in the same field from the Shougang Metallurgical Research Institute in Beijing. Upon graduation, he took a job at the institute under the title "deputy supervisor," leading research projects pertaining to metallurgical engineering.

In the mid-1990s, as mobile phones made their first appearance in China, Chuanfu was shocked by their hefty price tag, especially relative to the incomes of all but the wealthiest Chinese at that time. Upon investigating the matter, he discovered that the prohibitive pricing was due primarily to the high cost of the phones' batteries. The man who Berkshire Hathaway vice chairman Charlie Munger would later describe as "a combination of Thomas Edison and Jack Welch"[3] sensed an opportunity. Chuanfu recognized that sound engineering, coupled with low-cost Chinese labor, could produce such batteries much less expensively, thereby putting mobile phones within reach of a much wider swath of the Chinese public.

So, with his friend Xia Zuoquan, he established a new company in 1995 and christened it BYD, an acronym for the English phrase "Build Your Dream." The name would prove to be an apt one, given the cumulative

Figure 9.1
BYD E6. *Source:* Obtained with permission to reuse from Google Images (Wikipedia).

nature of the company's technical and financial accomplishments. Chuanfu obtained seed capital, the equivalent of roughly US$500,000 in current funds, in the form of loans from relatives. Perhaps counterintuitively, BYD gained efficiencies by replacing the expensive automated factory, standard among Asian battery manufacturers, with a lower-tech assembly method involving only one robot and six hundred people.

Through this initiative, along with a series of other innovative cost-cutting and production optimization measures, BYD met its goal of manufacturing a high-quality mobile phone battery that was roughly 40 percent less expensive than the competition's. Based in the southern city of Shenzen, a renowned industrial center, BYD became the world's largest manufacturer of rechargeable batteries for mobile phones. BYD leveraged its success in handset batteries to win contracts manufacturing entire handsets for Nokia, the Finnish telecommunications giant.

By 2003 the company had laid claim to almost half of the global mobile phone battery market, and Chuanfu was setting his sights on bigger game—the automobile market. To that end, BYD, having mastered the art of efficient manufacturing, built a large new assembly plant for cars. Each year the company sells more than half a million of its gas-powered and hybrid compact and subcompact vehicles in China alone. The hybrid cars, along with BYD's all-electric vehicles, are both powered by the company's high-quality but relatively low-cost automotive batteries.

Betting on the lucrative potential of these innovative green technologies, in 2008 Berkshire Hathaway purchased a 10 percent share in BYD for US$232 million. Considering that Warren Buffett is almost as famous in China as he is in America, the Berkshire investment was both a credibility and valuation booster for a company that had only been in the automotive business for five years. Moreover, it catapulted Chuanfu, only 42 at the time, to the coveted position of China's wealthiest person. Presently, the total net worth of BYD's founder is estimated at more than US$5 billion. Remarkably, in an ostensibly Communist country, the son of poor farmers climbed up the ladder of entrepreneurship to multibillionaire status.

In recent years, the company has migrated from its lithium-ion batteries to a 100 percent recyclable iron phosphate (Fe) battery. Aside from being environmentally friendly and fire-safe, the Fe battery offers a much longer cycle, thereby enabling drivers to travel for longer distances without recharging. For several years the company's all-electric vehicle line was more of an engineering success than a financial one. However, after disappointing sales of its all-electric sedans, Chuanfu and his team have had some success selling their all-electric buses, often through various levels of the Chinese government.

While China is no longer strictly Communist in its approach to entrepreneurship and private property, in many industries the government still wields tremendous power and is the final arbiter of many business matters. Like many successful modern Chinese entrepreneurs, Chuanfu has ingratiated himself with the right authorities for the benefit of his company. In 2014, with respect to BYD's close coordination with the country's ruling Chinese Communist Party (CCP), a somewhat provocative Chinese reporter asked Chuanfu if his company "has bound itself to the government?"

The entrepreneur's response was revealing both for its nimbleness and its deferential tone toward the government. "The new leadership [of the CCP]," Chuanfu clarified, "has put new-energy development high on its agenda. Pressure over air pollution and local governments' targets to improve people's livelihoods' require a solution. Under such circumstances," Chuanfu continued, "BYD proposed a plan to adopt electric buses for public transportation to reduce auto emissions and air pollution. It coincided with the government's desires."[4] The company has since established green energy partnerships with various entities, both private and public, outside China—from the City of London (UK) to the 2015 Special Olympics in Long Beach, California.

With smartphone demand at record levels in China, BYD's mobile-phone battery business continues to prosper. Moreover, sales of the company's gas-powered vehicles, particularly its new S6 and S7 sport utility vehicles, continue to be brisk. However, longer term, Chuanfu and many of his company's investors are most excited about sales of all-electric vehicles in an economically vibrant but increasingly polluted country of 1.36 billion people. In 2014 sales of such cars tripled in China, albeit to a still modest 75,000 units. Certainly, under Chuanfu's direction, BYD has positioned itself to profit handsomely from the larger-scale growth in green transportation that is anticipated for the world's most populous nation. Similarly, MercadoLibre positioned itself to profit from rapid growth of the countries of Latin America in the world's second most important emerging continent, South America.

Argentina's MercadoLibre: Setting Latin America Free

During the nineteenth century, almost all countries in Latin America gained full independence from Spain and Portugal. However, during the twentieth century, particularly after World War II, foreign interventions beset the region again. As the Cold War raged between the Soviet Union and the United States, Latin America became an important theater of proxy conflicts, with each superpower funding and in some cases arming opposing political parties or paramilitary powers in various Central and South American nations. These Cold War interventions, coupled with significant internal issues pertaining to poor administration, corruption, and socioeconomic divisions, coalesced to generate an atmosphere of political and economic instability that affected much of Latin America until the late twentieth century.

At least with respect to business, the environment has changed dramatically in recent years, with some of the region's largest economies not only encouraging but actively *incentivizing* entrepreneurship. Chile, now Latin America's sixth-largest economy and the region's leader in terms of per capita GDP, is particularly notable in this regard. In 2010 the Chilean government launched Start-Up Chile, an entrepreneurship incentive program that seeds select entrepreneurs from all over the world with a one-year visa and US$40,000 to develop their enterprises in Chile.[5]

Aside from Chile, reforms designed to encourage entrepreneurship have been implemented in such countries as Mexico, Peru, and Panama. This last, the scene of economic collapse and violent conflict in the 1980s, is now considered to be among the most entrepreneur-friendly nations in the world. As early as 2004 it was already evident to Thomas Becker, an economic development academic specializing in Latin America, that "as financial objectives displace political objectives" in the region, "the role of the state is becoming more cooperative, rather than confrontational, toward private enterprise."[6] Appropriately enough for a region in which some large economies are experimenting with what some refer to as free-market reforms, our featured enterprise for the region is known as MercadoLibre ("free market").

An ancient Roman playwright once observed that "fortune favors the bold," and it seems that many successful entrepreneurs live by those words. Bold was the word that came to mind when I learned of how an enterprising young Argentinian raised the all-important seed capital for MercadoLibre. In 1999 twenty-eight-year-old Marcos Galperin was completing his MBA at Stanford. After the Dallas-based private-equity partner John Muse wrapped up his guest lecture, Galperin offered to drive him to the airport. Along the way, the Argentinian technology enthusiast sold Muse on his vision of an eBay-like auction platform for Latin America. By the time they reached the airport, MercadoLibre had a commitment of seed capital from Hicks, Muse, Tate, & Furst. By May of 2000, the company had raised more than US$50 million from the likes of JPMorgan, Goldman Sachs, General Electric, and Spain's Banco Santander.

Even before they completed the MBA program, Marcos, his cousin Marcelo Galperin, and their fellow Argentinian Hernan Kazah were hard at work on their new business, recruiting Stanford classmates from the countries in which they intended to launch. Initially MercadoLibre was planned for Argentina and Mexico and MercadoLivre, a Portuguese version, for Brazil, Latin America's largest economy. In short order, the business would expand to Venezuela, Colombia, Uruguay, Chile, and Spain. With the exception of Spain, the Buenos Aires–headquartered company still operates in all of those countries and has since expanded successfully to Peru, Ecuador, Costa Rica, the Dominican Republic, Panama, and Portugal.

"Latins are very used to bargaining," Galperin told the American technology periodical *CIO* in 2001, "and they don't throw away used stuff." That's why an online auction platform was "a fantastic model for these countries."[7] Certainly, consumers in the region have plenty to sell and continue to be drawn to a site that describes itself as the place "where you buy and sell anything." When I told my "Latin" wife that I was spotlighting MercadoLivre (as it is spelled in Portuguese) in this chapter, she pointed out several items she had purchased through the site and told me more about how it works and how popular it is in her native Brazil.

In time, MercadoLibre found that its fixed-price option selling was far more popular than its auction platform. The winner of multiple entrepreneurship awards, Galperin was nimble enough to retool the business's focus accordingly, telling the not-for-profit entrepreneurial education organization Endeavor that his company "quickly converted to an e-commerce platform as users showed a preference for a 'fixed-price' model."[8] Those selling their products or services on Latin America's leading e-commerce site pay a "publication fee" that is calculated according to how visible their advertisement is, and MercadoLibre usually collects a commission upon processing a transaction as well.

Always on the lookout for additional sources of income, the company also built its own payment system, MercadoPago, and its own shipping system, MercadoEnvios. With annual revenue now approaching US$600 million and almost 110 million registered users, the company's vision has to a great degree been realized. Yet Marcos Galperin, whose personal net worth now exceeds US$400 million, is not one to rest on his laurels. After all, impressive as they are, MercadoLibre's annual revenue figures pale in comparison with those of the Silicon Valley e-commerce giants who inspired its Stanford-educated founders.

However, the company has considerably more room to grow than companies serving more technologically mature markets: The Internet and, more specifically, e-commerce adoption, is still growing rapidly in Latin America, a region where only 2 percent of the population had Internet access when MercadoLibre was founded in 1999. Meanwhile, the competitive position of the company, the number one e-commerce site in every Latin American country, has never been stronger: eBay has a large stake in MercadoLibre and is prohibited from competing in the region, and Galperin's company has already bought out many of its local competitors. So, it is an excellent time for MercadoLibre to, as the Argentinian entrepreneur likes to say, "think big and execute."9 Funke Opeke, the Nigerian entrepreneur who brought broadband Internet to West Africa, would agree.

Nigeria's MainOne Cable: Infrastructure for a New Economy

The twentieth century was both triumphant and troubled for sub-Saharan Africa. With the notable exceptions of Liberia, independent since 1847, and Ethiopia, which had expelled Mussolini in 1941, black Africa had to wait until the second half of the twentieth century for its freedom. World War II had bled Britain, France, and other colonizers of the human and financial resources required to sustain their hold on African territories, and, by the mid-1950s the dominoes began to fall: From the period between Ghana's independence in 1957 and Zimbabwe's in 1980, all former European colonies in the region had gained their autonomy. Since 1994, when Nelson Mandela was elected to power in South Africa, the entirety of black Africa has been under self-rule.

In some instances, the transition from colonial vassal state to sovereign nation was fairly smooth. For example, I know someone who worked in Ghana in the mid-1960s for several months and remembers the country as safe and stable. Yet in other liberated countries, such as the former Belgian colony of Rwanda, the power vacuum left by the flight of the colonial power was one of the factors that allowed long-simmering ethnic tensions to erupt into civil war. Of course, such conflicts hamper economic development, which in turn greatly diminishes entrepreneurial opportunities.

Corruption and stark class divisions have also complicated entrepreneurship, and more generally social mobility, in some parts of the region.

Yet, like in Latin America, which was beset by similar problems during the previous century, the business climate has improved markedly in Africa. For example, Rwanda, one of the world's most troubled countries in the 1990s, is now the world's twelfth fastest-growing economy. In fact, according to the World Bank, sub-Saharan Africa is presently home to six of the world's twelve fastest-growing economies. Ethiopia, famine-stricken in the 1980s, now holds the top spot in that growth list, with an economy growing at an annual rate of 9.5 percent—almost triple the global average. Especially as the pace of expansion is slowing in maturing economies like China, the tremendous growth opportunities in Africa are attracting attention from entrepreneurs and investors alike.

"Yes, we have all these problems, but Africa is a very big place," the Sudanese-born billionaire Mohamed Ibrahim told an American interviewer in 2009. "There are 53 countries," the African telecommunications entrepreneur and anti-corruption activist continued, "and maybe there are severe problems in four or five countries . . . In business, when there is a gap between reality and perception, there is good business to be made."[10] In recent years, enterprising Africans have taken advantage of that gap to position themselves for long-term gain in the world's fastest growing region. Among the most impactful of these new African entrepreneurs is Nigeria's Funke Opeke.

Born and raised in Ibadan, Nigeria, as a child Opeke got her best grades in math and science classes. So when she finished high school, the young woman enrolled in an electrical engineering program at Nigeria's Obafemi Awolowo University. Opeke graduated from Obafemi in 1981 and was accepted into the electrical engineering master's program at Columbia University. Upon completing her master's degree, Opeke spent the next twenty-one years working in the American telecommunications and Internet industries, culminating in an executive position at Verizon. In 2005 the telecom veteran returned to her native country, where she was recruited by Nitel, the country's now defunct state-run telecommunications provider, to serve as chief technology officer.

This position was frustrating for several reasons, and in 2006 Opeke, along with other members of the management team, resigned. However, her ill-fated tenure at Nitel provided the initial inspiration for MainOne, the project Opeke began planning in 2007. With respect to the constraints faced by Nitel and other companies seeking to build a telecommunications and Internet industry in Nigeria, she was convinced that unless the inadequacy of the basic infrastructure was addressed, not only the country but the wider West African region would continue to lag far behind much of the world. More specifically, Opeke "recognized that the absence of submarine cables was the weakest link in the chain,"[11] as she explained to the British periodical *Total Telecom* in 2012.

So she set for herself the Herculean task of establishing an underwater fiber-optic cable connection between Europe and Africa. Composed of silica glass fibers, such cable transmits data through light signals. As such transmission occurs at exceptionally high speeds, it enables generally continuous and rapid Internet service. To offer such service to West Africa, in 2008 Opeke established MainOne Cable and set about raising the requisite US$240 million in both equity and debt. The primary expense, of course, involved the laying of almost four thousand and five hundred miles of cable from Portugal across the Mediterranean and then across several countries to landing stations in Nigeria and Ghana. By the end of 2010, thanks to MainOne, West Africa had its first broadband connection.

As is often not the case, the engineer has proven to be a savvy entrepreneur. Opeke's company is meeting all of its financial obligations to shareholders and debt holders alike as it expands its client base of more than one hundred West African resellers who purchase wholesale broadband access from MainOne. The company also provides data services to the growing number of foreign entities that do business and/or governmental work in West Africa.

Although Opeke serves her shareholders well, her entrepreneurialism is also motivated by genuine concern for the economic health of her country and her region. "What's really fulfilling," she told a Nigerian newspaper in 2014, "is when I see companies like Konga.com and Jumia.com, and educational institutions with access to the Internet, working. Clearly, we have made a difference."[12] With a similar mix of persistence, business savvy, and technical knowledge, Sergei Galitsky, the man behind "the Wal-Mart of Russia," made a difference of his own.

Russia's Magnit: Traditional Retail with an Innovative Twist

In 1922, after a lengthy and bloody civil war, the Communist Reds prevailed against the monarchist Whites. From then until the late 1980s, when Soviet president Gorbachev's glasnost (openness) and perestroika (restructuring) reforms began to take effect, Russian entrepreneurship became a contradictory term. Certainly the Soviet era was a time of considerable Russian innovation in the context of government-funded science, engineering, and weaponry programs. Yet *entrepreneurial* innovation was anathema to the Soviet philosophy, and aside from a thriving black market of contraband goods and some "entrepreneurial" favor selling by unscrupulous bureaucrats, private enterprise had been squelched in Soviet Russia.

Post-Soviet Russia's transition from a command economy to something akin to a free market was a wrenching one. Tariffs were lowered, labor laws were loosened, and foreign investment was encouraged. However, the privatization of some industries, such as Russia's vast oil production and refining operations, proceeded so quickly that the vacuum of authority left by government was often seized by private monopolists. So to some extent the economy had morphed from totalitarianism to an oligopolistic system that also was not entirely conducive to bottom-up entrepreneurship. More ominously, the often haphazard way in which the country's transition was executed allowed some to profit from the chaos through criminality.

Viktor Bout, otherwise known as "the sanctions buster" or "the merchant of death," is a striking example of the criminal form of entrepreneurship that proliferated in Russia during the immediate aftermath of the Soviet collapse. Bout had served in the Soviet army for several years before he proceeded to build an international arms-dealing enterprise that leveraged some of the contacts and knowledge he had gained in the army. From the 1990s until his capture in 2010, Bout sold an astonishing range of weaponry—from AK-47s to attack helicopters—to participants in brutal conflicts raging in central Asia, Africa, and even Latin America. As the Russians were no longer Communist, Bout and others could, in the words of his biographers, "sell to anyone because there were no longer ideological enemies, only potential clients."[13]

However, with the old ideological constraints removed, it was not only Russia's oil and military hardware that could be sold to any willing buyer but its considerable scientific and engineering talents as well. Shortly after the Iron Curtain came down, the whole former Soviet bloc—from central Europe to central Asia—was brought even closer to the first world with the mass adoption of the World Wide Web. So it was an auspicious time for software entrepreneurs in the region, as both the political and logistical barriers that had once locked them out of the West were now dismantled. Like their counterparts in India, tech entrepreneurs in Russia, Ukraine, Bulgaria, and elsewhere in the region hired local software wizards and bid success-fully for lucrative Western coding and design projects.

Forty-eight-year-old Sergey Galitsky hails from the same generation as those software entrepreneurs, but he has leveraged his country's excep-tional programming talent in a different way: One of the world's largest retail chains, Magnit, benefits from one of the world's most sophisticated enterprise resource planning systems, the entirety of which was developed by the company's in-house programming team. The system helps ensure timely restocking of inventory so that just the right type and quantity of fresh goods can be found on the shelves of each and every Magnit store. Such precision helps ensure high customer satisfaction while minimizing the incidence of spoiled and otherwise unsold inventory.

A Russian citizen of Armenian ancestry, Galitsky (né Arutyunian) was born and raised in the southern Russian city of Sochi and completed a bachelor's degree at Russia's Kuban State University. In 1994 he founded Tander, a wholesale cosmetics and household cleaning products distributor, in the nearby city of Krasnodar. By 1998 Galitsky's distribution business had extended to retail, and the Magnit retail chain was born. Today, the com-pany boasts more than ten thousand outlets—convenience stores, super-markets, department stores, and cosmetics stores—across Russia. Notably, the total number of Wal-Mart stores around the world is eleven thousand, and it seems that Galitsky has drawn some inspiration from the success of the Arkansas-based retail giant: Magnit's motto, "Always Low Prices," seems to derive from Wal-Mart's "Everyday Low Prices."

Aside from its technological edge, Magnit has also benefited from a savvy expansion strategy. While his competitors were battling it out in Russia's larger cities, Galitsky shrewdly expanded across the smaller and less competitive population centers, keeping Magnit below the radar of his largest competitors. Then, once the company had attained sufficient finan-cial strength, Magnit ventured into the more competitive markets. As well, Galitsky adopted an innovative approach to sourcing produce by building a large Magnit-owned greenhouse complex in 2010. Since 2011 the complex has supplied the chain with high quality tomatoes and cucumbers.

The company's workforce has grown to 260,000, making Magnit an important employer in an economy that has been among the hardest hit by the recent downturn in oil prices. Listed on the London Stock Exchange, the company's market capitalization exceeds US$18.5 billion. Not surpris-ingly, Magnit's founder has become the fifteenth wealthiest individual in Russia, with an estimated net worth of US$8.3 billion. With a fortune built on technology, agriculture, sound strategy, and other elements that Russians hold in high regard, Galitsky has become an important role model for aspiring entrepreneurs in the region.

"It's no wonder that ordinary people," an American business writer in Eastern Europe observed, "even in Hungary, which has done far better at transitioning than most other former communist countries, can't imagine a life of wealth without assuming that it was created through unethical use of power or criminal activity."[14] Craig Hall wrote those words in 2001. However, thanks to Galitsky and other innovative entrepreneurs across the former Soviet bloc, that perception has changed since then, and especially the younger people of the region have embraced entrepreneurship: A 2013 study published by the American periodical *Entrepreneur* awarded Moscow, the former Soviet capital, with the number fourteen position in the world's "Top 20 Startup Ecosystems."[15]

From Anywhere to Everywhere: The New Global Playing Field

Whereas the flat-world stories of the century's opening years focused primarily on entrepreneurs of former second and third world nations selling their products and services to the first world, midway into the second decade of the century, the world of global entrepreneurship has become considerably more varied and multidirectional. Certainly the Indian entrepreneurs selling back-end office services to Western companies still exist. However, the BRICS and some other emerging economies have matured considerably since then. Some of these countries have large middle classes of their own, and the wage differential is not as dramatic as it used to be. So the tables have turned somewhat, making these countries' consumers and businesses attractive targets for innovative entrepreneurs in the developed world.

For example, in the course of my consulting work, just in the past two years I have encountered a California business that specializes in placing the children of wealthy Chinese industrialists in the best primary schools on America's West Coast, a Canadian start-up that sells proprietary point-of-care diagnostic products to remote communities in the Brazilian Amazon, and a Texas-based oil industry consultancy that serves clients in sub-Saharan Africa. So in many respects, the whole world is becoming an accessible supplier *and* market to any willing entrepreneur, regardless of which country or even which continent that man or woman calls home.

Ready to Launch: Entrepreneurship
and the Coming Space Age

In 1994 the American Society of Civil Engineers convened with business-people in Albuquerque, New Mexico, to discuss the technical and financial feasibility of space tourism. More specifically, they discussed such hypo-thetical phenomena as passenger space shuttles and space hotels. Although the technical hurdles were significant, the attendees concluded that none of them was insurmountable. In their view, what was insurmountable were the financial hurdles, namely, how to charge the extraordinary sums that would be required to make space tourism profitable.

However, today the consensus of that conference seems remarkably shortsighted: From 2001 until 2009, Virginia-based Space Adventures charged seven ultrarich adventurers between US$20 million and US$25 million per spaceflight aboard *Soyuz* rockets manned and operated by the Russian Space Agency. Moreover, serial entrepreneur Elon Musk's SpaceX, already profitable, has several dozen flights scheduled—reservations for which the California-based company has been paid more than US$5 billion. Clearly, even at this nascent and exorbitantly priced stage of space tourism, there is high demand for such voyages. Moreover, from Silicon Valley venture capi-talists to angel investors like Microsoft cofounder Paul Allen and Google cofounder Larry Page, there are large and prominent sources of capital eager to invest in humanity's "final frontier."

The New Mexico attendees correctly predicted that the engineering problems posed by such an objective could be overcome. Nonetheless, the technical challenges are formidable. For example, to reach orbit, spacecraft must attain a speed of at least 17,650 miles per hour. To put that figure in perspective, the velocity of the world's fastest manned aircraft is less than a third of that speed. So transforming such travel into a form of transpor-tation that is comfortable, let alone affordable, for a market that extends beyond the Forbes 400, is no mean feat.

However, by funding the extensive research and development efforts that make the ongoing technical improvements possible, entrepreneurs like Britain's Richard Branson and America's Eric C. Anderson have helped fill a vacuum left by the wavering public sector commitment to space exploration. For example, in the 1990s the space program that had attained legendary sta-tus during the Soviet era was so poorly funded by the Russian government that for several years it was left to a group of mostly American entrepreneurs to come up with profitable uses of the cosmonaut training center and the country's *Soyuz* rockets. However, in 2005 Russia reengaged in its space program, which is currently a high priority for the Putin government.

More recently, the U.S. government has partially *dis*engaged from its space program, a move that has yielded challenges, along with enormous opportunities, for American space entrepreneurs. In this regard, the astronomy professor and author Chris Impey recently noted a "striking parallel" between the flurry of entrepreneurialism that brought the Internet to the masses and enhanced its functionality in the 1990s and the private investment and initiative that is currently advancing the space tourism phenomenon. "Both were incubated by the military-industrial complex," Impey writes, "and both have gained striking new capabilities courtesy of the involvement of entrepreneurs from the private sector, whose investment potentially dwarfs that of the government."[16]

Space Adventures

An MIT-trained aeronautical engineer, Harvard-trained MD, and lifelong entrepreneur, Peter Diamandis typifies the kind of adventurous polymath who seems to be prevalent in this new industry. In 1992 the thirty-one-year-old New Yorker established the Zero G (as in zero gravity) Corporation, selling the experience of spaceflight-like weightlessness. The experience is generated by a U-shaped air flight that simulates the feeling of free fall that occurs in space. Zero G continues to provide this space travel simulation service for roughly US$5,000 a flight and made headlines in 2007 when it took Stephen Hawking up in the air for several such trips.

In 1997, along with aerospace engineer Eric C. Anderson and Mike McDowell, an adventure travel entrepreneur who had been running a successful business taking adventure travelers to the North and South Poles, Diamandis cofounded Space Adventures. Noting the inactivity at the former Soviet cosmonaut training center in the late 1990s, the Virginia-based company entered into an agreement with Star City that granted Space Adventures access to the Russian facility, its simulator capsules, space suits, and so forth. Before 2001 the business model of the world's first space tourism company consisted of US$10,000 space training weekends held at Star City.

On April 28, 2001, Space Adventures, in collaboration with the Russian Space Agency, launched California-based investment magnate Dennis Tito into eight days of space orbit for a cool US$20 million. As mentioned earlier, other diamond-studded clients followed, such as Guy Laliberte, the French-Canadian founder of Cirque du Soleil, who paid US$25 million for the experience in 2009. Although Space Adventures, leveraging the hardware and talents of the Russian space program, has not contributed to the technical advancement of space tourism as much as the other enterprises profiled here, the company was the first to commercialize space travel successfully. Technical advancement would be left to others, like the former Rolls-Royce and British Aircraft Corporation engineers at Reaction Engines.

Reaction Engines

Reaction Engines is among the most advanced space travel entities in the world. For example, in January of 2014 the British company entered into a joint research and development agreement with the U.S. Air Force pertaining to Reaction Engines' hypersonic engine. Chief engineer Alan Bond is the inventor of the SABRE engine, a breakthrough described by the company as "a rocket engine designed to power aircraft directly into space (single-stage to orbit) to allow reliable, responsive and cost effective space access."[17] Regarding space access, the long-term vision of Reaction Engines extends well beyond rockets to its Skylon space plane.

The latter, designed but still under construction, is unpiloted and, unlike most space rockets, reusable. However, the most impressive aspect of the SABRE-powered Skylon is how it has been designed to launch into Earth orbit from any ordinary airport runway. Considering that the space tourism industry has already invested hundreds of millions of dollars in prospective spaceports, if the Skylon functions as promised, it could prove to be an enormous disruptor. Of course, it would also provide Reaction Engines with an impressive competitive advantage, as their spacecraft would be far more versatile and useful than vessels that require specially fitted spaceports. While Reaction Engines figures out better ways of getting to space, a Las Vegas hotel entrepreneur is already making plans for where people will stay when they get there.

Bigelow Aerospace

"One small step for space, a giant leap for private enterprise"[18] is how CNBC recently described the Bigelow Expandable Activity Module, an "expandable living area for outer space"[19] that is slated for launch on a SpaceX rocket. It will be the company's third module in orbit. Bigelow Aerospace is being paid US$18 million by NASA for the module, designed as a long-term human habitat that fits into a rocket but, once deployed in orbit, expands to the size of a standard travel trailer. Clearly, while most other space tourism entrepreneurs have been focused on the means of transport to space, Bigelow Airspace founder Robert Bigelow has been devoting his time and almost US$300 million of his money on where space tourists and perhaps, in later decades, space *residents*, will stay once they reach orbit.

For almost two decades before he founded Budget Suites in 1988, Robert Bigelow enjoyed considerable success building both residential and commercial real estate in and around his native Las Vegas. Of course, Budget Suites proved to be an enormous success on a regional (Southwest) level and by 1999 had enhanced his already substantial fortune considerably. Fifty-five years old at the time and motivated in part by a lifelong interest in UFOs, the successful builder set his sights on outer space, and Bigelow Aerospace was born.

Just as he has done with many of the terrestrial structures that he has built in his forty-five years in the real estate business, Bigelow strives for a balance of function and comfort in the habitats that his company builds for outer space. He plans on sending more of his modules into orbit with SpaceX rockets and/or Russian Dnepr rockets (formerly stocked by the Soviet army as intercontinental ballistic missiles). Moreover, longer term, the entrepreneur sees other opportunities besides tourism in space real estate. For example, he intends to provide habitats for the surface of the moon to be rented or sold to mining companies and scientific research entities. Those who scoff at Bigelow's extraterrestrial ambitions need only look at his previous enterprises to see what he is capable of. The same principle applies to Elon Musk, a serial entrepreneur with his eyes set on the stars.

SpaceX

Born and raised in South Africa, in 1988 Elon Musk left his home country to work and then study in Canada, his mother's native country. Elon was eager to spend some time there, but his journey to Canada was also motivated by his aversion to the Apartheid-era South African military. "Serving in the South African army suppressing black people," he told PBS in 2007, "just didn't seem like a really good way to spend time."[20] After a year of odd jobs and two years at Queen's University in Kingston, Ontario, Musk won a scholarship to the University of Pennsylvania in Philadelphia. At UPenn, he would complete a bachelor's degree in economics and then another bachelor's degree in physics.

In 1995 Musk moved out to Silicon Valley, where he had been accepted by Stanford University for graduate work in physics. Endowed with an uncanny knack for smelling opportunity in the air, Musk arrived at Stanford just weeks after Netscape's successful IPO. Immediately, he knew that it was an opportune time to start an Internet business of his own. He had very little money to his name and, aside from performing odd computer jobs for classmates at Queen's, not much of a business track record either. So it was certainly a bold move to leave Stanford after only two days in the graduate program to start a business. Nonetheless, that is exactly what he did, establishing Zip2 with his brother Kimbal.

Musk's first company carved out a lucrative online niche for itself by hosting and developing consumer business directories integrated with maps and reviews, an astonishingly farsighted concept for 1995. Moreover, especially during the company's initial stages, much of the coding was written by Elon himself. The Musk brothers' long-term vision was vindicated in 1999, when Zip2 was sold to Compaq/Alta Vista/CMGi for US$307 million. Most of that money went to the venture capitalists who had provided expansion capital in 1996, but Kimbal walked away with a personal fortune of US$15 million and Elon with US$22 million.

Elon wasted little time plowing most of that money back in to an even more ambitious venture, PayPal, originally known as X.com. In October of 2002, when the revolutionary online payment system that he had developed with several other Internet visionaries was sold to eBay for US$1.5 billion, Musk walked away with another US$165 million. Once again, the restless entrepreneur took most of that money, US$100 million of it, and invested it into his *next* idea, Space Exploration Technologies or SpaceX. Although Musk's versatile post-PayPal career also encompasses solar energy provider Solar City and the electric-powered car company Tesla, since he personally founded SpaceX in June of 2002, its success has been a consistently high priority for him.

Unlike some of SpaceX's American competitors that work with Russian-made rockets and/or parts, the Los Angeles–area company's vessels are designed and manufactured exclusively in the United States. Moreover, despite relatively high American labor costs, through the use of reusable rockets and efficient product engineering methods that Musk, a natural pollinator, adopted from the software industry, SpaceX is confident that the price of its space voyages will eventually be as low as one-tenth that of competing providers. In 2008 the company's first rocket, a Falcon 1, went into orbit. Since then SpaceX has signed two agreements with NASA, including a US$2.6 billion contract to transport NASA employees to and from the International Space Station (ISS). The company has already made several successful unmanned cargo transport trips to the ISS on NASA's behalf.

SpaceX also developed the Dragon, designed to accommodate seven passengers comfortably, and the Falcon 9. Standing almost 225 feet tall and 12 feet wide, the 1.1-million-pound Falcon 9 rocket is powered by nine engines. An even more impressive rocket, the Falcon Heavy is planned after the Falcon 9, and beyond that there are plans for another spaceship that can, in the words of SpaceX Chief Operating Officer Gwynne Shotwell, "take a busload of people to Mars."[21] SpaceX has had its share of setbacks, such as a post-liftoff explosion of one of its unmanned ISS-bound Falcon 9 rockets in June of 2015. Nonetheless, like any other enterprise with Musk at its helm, it is not advisable to bet against its success. Another famously versatile entrepreneur, Richard Branson, is also making his mark in this field.

Virgin Galactic/The Spaceship Company

"The World's First Commercial Spaceline," Virgin Galactic was founded by Sir Richard Branson, the British entrepreneur behind Virgin Records and the Virgin Atlantic airline. However, until 2012, when Virgin bought out Burt Rutan's stake in the Spaceship Company (TSC), most of Virgin Galactic's technological infrastructure was provided by engineers from Rutan's Scaled Composites, with Virgin acting primarily as the finance and marketing entity. Although the seventy-two-year-old Rutan has recently retired from the space business, both he and Branson have played critical roles in the development of Virgin Galactic.

Like Musk, Branson entered the space industry after successful forays into other industries, most notably, music—both recording and retail—and air travel. As well, the two entrepreneurs are both highly creative but they also have the commitment to execution that is essential to converting an idea into a viable business. In the 1970s, Branson's Virgin Records signed, recorded, and successfully promoted such acclaimed British artists as Mike Oldfield, the Sex Pistols, and Culture Club/Boy George. In the 1980s,

Branson shifted some of his focus to the transportation industry. Today, both Virgin Trains and Virgin Atlantic remain highly profitable entities for the British mega-entrepreneur, whose net worth is estimated at slightly less than US$5 billion.

As Branson told a British reporter at the opening of Virgin Galactic in 2004, space tourism is "a business that has no limits."[22] Burt Rutan, based in the California desert town of Mojave, certainly agreed. Having worked for several public- and private-sector entities since earning his aeronautical engineering degree in 1965, he established the Rutan Aircraft Factory (1974) in Mojave, a town ideally suited to testing planes. By the late 1970s his innovatively designed planes were in high demand. In 1982 he established Scaled Composites, a successful aerospace engineering company that began design of its first spaceship in 2003. Backed by Paul Allen, SpaceShipOne became the first private-sector aircraft to complete a supersonic flight.

SpaceShipTwo was also built by Scaled but was developed under the auspices of TSC, a partnership Rutan formed with Branson in 2005. One of the most prolific dealmakers alive, aside from enlisting technical help and testing space from Rutan and Scaled, Branson proceeded to raise US$280 million from an Abu Dhabi sovereign wealth fund and a commitment from the government of New Mexico to build a spaceport in that state. Spaceport America has since been built, costing that state more than US$200 million. However, many in the state see the investment as a bet on the long-term dividends that will accrue from what is hoped to become a bustling spaceport.

Although Branson had bought Rutan out by 2014, when a manned SpaceShipTwo vehicle failed and killed one of its two pilots, it was a setback for both Virgin Galactic and Northrop Grumman–owned Scaled Composites. Crucially, the National Transportation Safety Board (NTSB) found that the accident was not caused by any structural flaws in the spacecraft's design or any faulty assembly in its construction. However, the NTSB condemned what it saw as Scaled's "failure to consider and protect against the possibility that a single human error could result in a catastrophic hazard to the SpaceShipTwo vehicle."[23]

On a more positive note, the NTSB found that the new fuel type that was being tested on the ill-fated flight did not play a part in the accident. Virgin emphasized this point, stating that due to the polyamide-based fuel, the rocket motor ran "smoother and with less vibration than during any previous powered flight."[24] Moreover, with his characteristic optimism,

Branson stated that in the wake of the NTSB report, Virgin Galactic "can now focus fully on the future with a clean bill of health and a strengthened resolve to achieve its goals."[25] While it could be several years before Galactic's vessels will be making regular use of Spaceport America, Branson's company may still prove itself to be "The World's First Commercial Spaceline." Meanwhile, Jeff Bezos, the founder of Amazon.com, is emerging as one of Branson's most formidable competitors.

Blue Origin

"Earth," the Blue Origin website announces, "in all its beauty, is just our starting place. We are of blue origin, and here is where it begins."[26] The brainchild of Jeff Bezos, the world's fifteenth-wealthiest individual, the company has made considerable progress in the development of its spacecraft. Although Bezos is still very much engaged with Amazon, Blue Origin, a technology-driven company but far removed from the world of e-commerce, certainly marks a divergence in his interests. However, the New Mexico–born entrepreneur has a knack for shifting gears successfully.

In 1994 a thirty-year-old Bezos was earning excellent money as the vice president of Manhattan investment management firm D. E. Shaw. As he learned more about the accelerating development of the commercial Internet, utilizing what he calls his "regret minimization" technique, he determined that quitting his high-paying job to become an Internet entrepreneur was a risk worth taking. Twenty-one years and US$50 billion (Bezos's estimated personal fortune) later, his decision-making process seems pretty sound.

It was a similar regret minimization decision-making process that inspired Bezos in September of 2000. Almost two years before the founding of Space X, Bezos founded a space tourism company of his own. As with his first company, the executive and engineering offices of Blue Origin are in the Seattle area, and in 2004 Bezos purchased 165,000 acres in west Texas as testing grounds for the vessels the company would soon build. Named after Alan B. Shepard, America's first astronaut, Blue Origins' spacecraft is known as the *New Shepard*. In April of 2015, *New Shepard* reached a height of 307,000 feet on its first test flight. Further test flights, a rocket that runs on nontoxic liquefied gas, and even an online spaceflight reservation system are all slated to follow.

Remarkably, the colonization of other planets is being planned quite openly and deliberately by these new space entrepreneurs. While Robert Bigelow is designing human habitats for the moon, the name and concept of Bezos's Blue Origin revolves around planet colonization, and it is clear that at least one of the other space entrepreneurs also has designs on other planets. "I am increasingly concerned about SpaceX going public," Musk wrote in a 2013 e-mail to the entire SpaceX staff, "before the Mars transport system is in place."[27]

Conclusion

Especially when it is guided by that rare combination of imagination, energy, and shrewdness, the entrepreneurial impulse can be the forerunner of momentous transformation, an instigator of significant changes that extend well beyond the realm of industry. As tantalizing as space tourism seems from a modern-day perspective, many of the entrepreneurs highlighted in the earlier chapters of this book were involved in enterprises that, for their respective eras, were just as radically innovative and transformational as the work of Musk, Bezos, and company.

The entrepreneurs behind the PC Revolution, the Industrial Revolution, the conquest of the New World, the marvels of Song dynasty China, the pollinations of the Islamic Empire, the commercial colonialism of the Phoenicians, and the urbanization of Mesopotamia all served as catalysts of momentous and largely irreversible developments in human history. Yet for most of these enterprising individuals, altering the course of human history did not rank high, if at all, on their list of motivations.

Nevertheless, while most entrepreneurs have been compelled by a Darwinian drive for financial gain and greater social status, there are others who have professed more altruistic motivations. With varying degrees of sincerity, these more idealistic men and women have cited such ideals as religion, the spread of "civilization," the democratization of the automobile, and bringing the world together through technology as inspirations for their respective enterprises. However, even history's genuinely idealistic entrepreneurs have been aware that these loftier goals are contingent upon the more basic matter of profitability.

In this vein, Anita Roddick, the founder of natural cosmetics giant the Body Shop, once declared, "Nobody talks about entrepreneurship as survival, but that's exactly what it is."[1] Yet even in those instances in which survival is an entrepreneur's sole motivation, it is evident that the process of creating a new money-making organism, as it were, and tending to its establishment and growth can lead to broader and often unanticipated consequences for society.

Certainly, there have been many entrepreneurs—from the tea traders of Tang dynasty China to the bootleggers of Prohibition-era Chicago—whose overriding ambition was simply the survival and expansion of their respective enterprises. Yet in the service of that goal, they engaged in the disruption that Schumpeter referred to as "creative destruction." In other words, they exercised their entrepreneurial creativity to supplant the old with the new by, for example, replacing unwieldy metal coinage with light paper money.

Moreover, it is evident that many of these disruptive enterprises have not necessarily been wildly innovative in terms of technology, although many have, particularly in recent centuries. Rather, the innovation may lie in how a product or service is created, distributed, promoted, or delivered. The ingenuity of Sergei Galitsky's Magnit, for example, lies not so much in the products it provides to the Russian market but in its sophisticated information systems and the superior efficiency with which its products are sourced, stocked, and shelved. Similarly, much of the novelty surrounding the work of ancient Mesopotamia's merchant-entrepreneurs pertained to distribution, transportation, and finance.

The broader impact of such entrepreneurial initiatives, even when developed by those with no grander ambition than the attainment of another "shekel of private silver," has often been a matter of contention. The resulting disruptions—from the commercial colonization pioneered by the Phoenician maritime-entrepreneurs to the "flattening" of the world pioneered by American dot-com entrepreneurs—continue to inspire passionate moral arguments both for and against the profit-driven creativity of entrepreneurship.

Yet, for better or worse, entrepreneurship stands alongside the other perennial elements of the human condition as one of history's prime movers. It has not only helped shape the kingdoms, empires, and civilizations of our world but, in many instances, it was entrepreneurship that provided the initial impetus behind their creation. Today, it continues to do so, as the emerging space entrepreneurs steer humanity toward new worlds beyond our "blue origin". In this manner, the transformational impact of entrepreneurship will persist—as undeniably profound and inescapably controversial as ever.

NOTES

Introduction

1. Peter Drucker, *Innovation and Entrepreneurship* (New York: Harper & Row, 1985), 27.

2. William Baumol, *Entrepreneurship, Management, and the Structure of Payoffs* (Cambridge, MA: MIT Press, 1993).

1. "One Shekel of Your Private Silver"

1. Kenn Hildebrand, "History Lesson," letter to the editor, *Entrepreneur*, November 2014, 14.

2. *Encyclopedia of Prehistory*, vol. 8, *South and Southwest Asia*, ed. Peter N. Peregrine and Melvin Embe (Berlin: Springer Science & Business Media), 329.

3. *The Epic of Gilgamesh*, tablet I.

4. Leo Oppenheim, *Ancient Mesopotamia* (Chicago: University of Chicago Press, 1964), 110–111.

5. Ibid., 87.

6. Samuel Kramer, *Cradle of Civilization* (New York: Time-Life, 1978), 85.

7. Peter Drucker, *Innovation and Entrepreneurship* (New York: Harper & Row, 1985), 27.

8. Kramer, *Cradle of Civilization*, 101.

9. Isaiah 23:3 (King James Version).

10. Jacquetta Hawkes, *The First Great Civilizations* (New York: Knopf, 1973), 134.

11. Leo Oppenheim, *Letters from Mesopotamia* (Chicago: University of Chicago Press, 1967), 74.

12. David Graeber, *Debt: The First 5,000 Years* (Brooklyn: Melville House, 2011), 215.

13. Hawkes, *The First Great Civilizations*, 182.

14. Oppenheim, *Letters from Mesopotamia*, 74.

15. *The Code of Hammurabi*, trans. L. W. King (New York: Exodus, 1915), no. 102.

16. Drucker, *Innovation and Entrepreneurship*, 27.

17. Troy Adkins, "Why Forward Contracts Are the Foundation of All Derivatives", Investopedia.com, October 23, 2013, http://www.investopedia.com/articles/active-trading/102313/why-forward-contracts-are-foundation-all-derivatives.asp.

18. Peter Cohan, "Big Risk: $1.2 Quadrillion Derivatives Market Dwarfs World GDP", *Daily Finance*, June 9, 2010.

19. International Monetary Fund, "World Economic Output: Legacies, Clouds, Uncertainties" (Washington, DC, October 2014), www.imf.org/external/pubs/ft/weo/2014/02/pdf/text.pdf.

20. Mark Skousen, "Beyond GDP: Get Ready for a New Way to Measure the Economy," *Forbes*, November 29, 2013.

21. Oppenheim, *Letters from Mesopotamia*, 42.

22. Ibid., 74.

23. Stephen Bertman, *Handbook to Life in Ancient Mesopotamia* (Oxford: Oxford University Press, 2005), 256.

24. Oswald Ashton Wentworth Dilke, *Mathematics and Measurement* (London: British Museum Publications, 1987), 46.

25. Cf. ze'pu, CAD; LAR II, 176.

26. Nahum 3:16 (New International Version).

27. Woolley, *Excavations at Ur* (London: Benn, 1963), 113.

28. Kristina A. Vogt, ed., *Forests and Society: Sustainability and Life Cycles of Forests in Human Landscapes* (Cambridge, MA: CAB International, 2007), 7–8.

2. The Pirates of Phoenicia

1. Gerhard Herm, *The Phoenicians: The Purple Empire of the Ancient World* (New York: Morrow, 1975), 69.

2. 1 Kings 10:22 (King James Version).

3. Herm, *The Phoenicians*, 94.

4. Ibid., 192.

5. Aldo Massa, *The Phoenicians*, trans. David Macrae (Geneva: Minerva, 1977), 34.

6. Donald Harden, *The Phoenicians: Ancient Peoples and Places* (New York: Frederick A. Praeger, 1962), 158.

7. Alexandre Dumas, *The Count of Monte Cristo* (London: Chapman & Hall, 1846), 222.

8. Thomas F. X. Nobel, Barry Strauss, Duane Osheim, Kristen B. Neuschel, Elinor A. Accampo, David D. Roberts, William B. Cohen, *Western Civilization: Beyond Boundaries,* Sixth Edition (Boston: Wadsworth/Cengage Learning, 2010), 31.

9. Diodorus Siculus, *Library of History,* trans. C. H. Oldfather, Loeb Classical Library Edition (Cambridge, MA: Harvard University Press, 1939), 38.3.

10. William Beloe, trans., *Herodotus,* vol. 1 (London: Henry Colburn and Richard Bentley, 1830), 242–243.

11. George Rawlinson, *Ancient History* (London: C. W. Deacon, 1887), 301.

12. Harden, *The Phoenicians,* 173.

13. Ibid., 164.

14. William Davis, *The Innovators: The Essential Guide to Business Thinkers, Achievers, and Entrepreneurs* (London: Ebury, 1987), 6.

15. Chronicles 2:14 (American Standard Version).

16. Pliny (the Elder), *Pliny's Natural History,* Vol. 36 (London: Club Press, 1848), 192–193.

17. Ruth Goode, *People of the First Cities* (New York: Macmillan, 1977), 91–92.

18. Thomas C. Frohlich, Alexander E. M. Hess, and Vince Calio, "9 most counterfeited products in the USA," *USA Today,* March 29, 2014.

19. Marcus Tullius Cicero, *The Republic of Cicero* (New York: Carvill, 1829), 2.9.

20. *The Works of Herodotus* (Bybliotech, 2012), 1, http://bybliotech.org/the-complete-herodotus-the-histories.

21. Homer, *The Odyssey* (Boston: Osgood, 1872), 23.

22. Ibid.

23. Ezekiel 28:17 (New American Standard Version).

24. Ezekiel 27:13 (New American Standard Version).

25. Isaiah 23:8 (Jewish Study Bible Version).

26. Herm, *The Phoenicians,* 146.

27. Massa, *The Phoenicians,* 83.

28. Ibid., 84.

29. Herm, *The Phoenicians,* 160.

3. The Reluctant Romans

1. Michael Grant, *A Social History of Greece and Rome* (New York: Scribner, 1992), 50.

2. Ibid.

3. Juvenal, *The Sixteen Satires,* trans. Philip Green (London: Penguin, 1967), 3.29–33.

4. Marcus Tullius Cicero, *De Officiis,* trans. Walter Miller, Loeb Classical Library 30 (Cambridge, MA: Harvard University Press, 1913), 2.25.

5. Ibid., xlii.

6. Ibid., xlii–xliii.

7. Grant, *A Social History*, 77.

8. Livy, *Livy in Fourteen Volumes: Books III and IV*, ed. E. Capps, T.E. Page, and W.H.D. Rouse, trans. B.O. Foster, Loeb Classical Library 114 (Cambridge, MA: Harvard University Press, 1919), 4:2:257.

9. Thomas J. Stanley and William D. Danko, *The Millionaire Next Door* (New York: Pocket, 1998), 3.

10. Ibid., 227.

11. Edward Gibbon, *The Decline and Fall of the Roman Empire*, Vol. I, Modern Library Edition (New York: HarperCollins, 1995), 1.

12. Ibid.

13. H. J. Haskell, *The New Deal in Old Rome: How Government in the Ancient World Tried to Deal with Modern Problems* (New York: Alfred A. Knopf, 1947), 79–80.

14. Cited in Haskell, *The New Deal in Old Rome*, 80.

15. Naphtali Lewis and Meyer Reinhold, eds., *Roman Civilization: Selected Readings, Vol. I: The Republic and the Augustan Age*, Third Edition (New York: Columbia University Press, 1990), 246.

16. Michael Grant, *The World of Rome* (Cleveland: World, 1960), 115.

17. R. H. Barrow, *Slavery in the Roman Empire* (New York: Barnes & Noble, 1928), 100.

18. Ibid., 106.

19. Juvenal, 1.104–105.

20. Jack Welch and Suzy Welch (New York: HarperBusiness, 2005), *Winning*, 206–207.

21. Horace, *The Complete Works of Horace: Interlinear Translation* (New York: David McKay Company, Inc., 1952), Epode 4.

22. Christoph Hocker, *Ancient Rome: An Illustrated Historical Overview* (Barron's Educational Series, 1997), 40–41.

23. Richard Alston, *Aspects of Roman History AD 14–117* (New York: Routledge, 1998), 87.

24. Plutarch, *Fall of the Roman Republic*, Third Edition, trans. Rex Warner (New York: Penguin, 2005), "Comparison of Nicias and Crassus," 55.

25. Stephen Bertman, *The Genesis of Science: The Story of Greek Imagination* (New York: Prometheus, 2010), 91.

26. Ibid., 92.

27. Cited in Jean-Philippe Levy, *The Economic Life of the Ancient World* (Chicago: University of Chicago Press, 1967), 92.

4. An Enterprising Faith

1. Abdul Malik Mujahid, *Golden Stories of Sayyida Khadijah: Mother of the Believers* (Riyadh: Darussalam, 2012), 85.

2. Lesley Hazelton, *The First Muslim: The Story of Muhammad* (New York: Riverhead, 2013), 44.

3. Washington Irving, *Mahomet and His Successors* (New York: Co-operative Publication Society, 1849), 37.

4. Craig Hall and Tom Daschle, *The Responsible Entrepreneur: How to Make Money and Make a Difference* (Wayne, NJ: Career Press, 2001), 24.

5. Irving, *Mahomet and His Successors*, 43.

6. Indus Entrepreneurs, *Essentials of Entrepreneurship: What It Takes to Create Successful Enterprises* (Hoboken, NJ: Wiley, 2003), 128.

7. Alex L. Goldfayn, *Evangelist Marketing: What Apple, Amazon, and Netflix Understand About Their Customers (That Your Company Probably Doesn't)* (Dallas: BenBella, 2011); Tom Cox, *The Product Evangelist Primer: How to Build Relationships with Customers, Investors and Co-workers Through Authenticity and Passion* (Amazon Digital Services, 2014).

8. Diane Morgan, *Essential Islam: A Comprehensive Guide to Belief and Practice* (Santa Barbara, CA: Praeger, 2010), p. 32

9. *Encyclopedia Britannica*, online edition, "The Hadith."

10. Matthew 19:24, King James Version.

11. Bernard Lewis, *The Arabs in History* (Oxford: Oxford University Press, 1993), 26.

12. Frank E. Vogel and Samuel L. Hayes, *Islamic Law and Finance: Religion, Risk, and Return*, Arab & Islamic Laws Series (The Hague, Netherlands: Kluwer Law International, 1998), 60.

13. Marilyn Tower Oliver, *The Importance of Muhammad* (Farmington Hills, MI: Lucent, 2003), 59.

14. Robert Payne, *The History of Islam* (Barnes & Noble Books, 1959), 52.

15. Josef W. Meri, ed., *Medieval Islamic Civilization: An Encyclopedia* (New York: Routledge, 2006), 497.

16. Robin W. Winks, *A History of Civilization: Prehistory to the Present* (Englewood Cliffs, NJ: Prentice Hall, 1996), 131.

17. Gibbon, *Decline and Fall*, vol. 6, 438.

18. Payne, *The History of Islam*, 101.

19. Bernard Lewis, *Race and Slavery in the Middle East* (Oxford: Oxford University Press, 1992), 41.

20. Patrick Hanlon, "California Dreamin': The New State of Innovation," *Forbes*, September 12, 2013.

21. Winks, *A History of Civilization*, 132.

22. 'Abd al-Malik ibn Muḥammad Tha'ālibī, *The Laṭā 'if al-ma'ārif of Tha'ālibi: The Book of Curious and Entertaining Information*, trans. Clifford Edmund Bosworth (Edinburgh: Edinburgh University Press, 1968), 120.

23. Lewis, *The Arabs in History*, 94.

24. Thomas Tryon, *The Good House-Wife Made a Doctor* (1692), http://quod.lib.umich.edu/e/eebo/A63795.0001.001?view=toc.

25. Eric Goldschein, "11 Incredible Facts About the Global Coffee Industry," *Business Insider*, November 14, 2011.

26. Lewis, *The Arabs in History*, 138.

5. Flying Money and Capitalist Monks

1. Marco Polo, *The Travels of Marco Polo*, trans. Sir Henry Yule and Henri Cordier (Chicago: Courier, 1993), 186.

2. Roger V. Des Forges and John S. Major, *The Asian World, 600–1500* (New York: Oxford University Press, 2005), 35.

3. Charles O. Hucker, *China's Imperial Past: An Introduction to Chinese History and Culture* (Stanford: Stanford University Press, 1975), 174.

4. Chen Yuan, *A Study of the Israelite Religion of Kaifeng* (Shanghai: Commercial Press, 1920), 29.

5. Jacques Gernet, *A History of Chinese Civilization* (Cambridge: Cambridge University Press, 1982), 264.

6. Mark Edward Lewis, *China's Cosmopolitan Empire: The Tang Dynasty* (Cambridge, MA: Harvard University Press, 2009), 130.

7. Ann Paludan, *Chronicle of the Chinese Emperors: The Reign-by-Reign Record of the Rulers of Imperial China* (London: Thames & Hudson, 1998), 120.

8. Lewis, *China's Cosmopolitan Empire*, 278.

9. Peter F. Drucker, *The Essential Drucker* (New York: HarperBusiness, 2001), 323.

10. Kevin Reilly, *The Human Journey: A Concise Introduction to World History* (Lanham, MD: Rowman & Littlefield, 2012), 147.

11. David Wolman, *The End of Money: Counterfeiters, Preachers, Techies, Dreamers—and the Coming Cashless Society* (Boston: Da Capo, 2012), 1.

12. Lu Yu, "The Merchant's Joy," 1187, compiled in *The Shorter Columbia Anthology of Traditional Chinese Literature*, ed. Victor H. Mair (New York: Columbia University Press, 2000), 59.

13. Polo, *Travels*, 201.

14. Arthur Cotterrell, *The Imperial Capitals of China: A Dynastic History of the Celestial Empire* (Woodstock, NY: Overlook, 2007), 196.

15. Yoshinobu Shiba, *Commerce and Society in Sung China*, trans. Mark Elvin, Michigan Abstracts of Chinese and Japanese Works on Chinese History 2 (Ann Arbor: University of Michigan Center for Chinese Studies, 1969), 39.

16. Ichisada Miyazaki, "Society, Ethnicity and Civilization: The Rustic Principle in the East" (Tokyo: Heibonsha, 1989), 63.

17. Yeshuixun, quoted in Ichisada Miyazaki, *The Orient: Early Modern Period* (Osaka: Kyōiku Taimususha, 1950), 71.

18. Zhu Xi, quoted in Craig A. Lockard, *Societies, Networks, and Transitions: A Global History* (Boston: Wadsworth, 2009), 282.

19. Dorothy Perkins, *Encyclopedia of China: History and Culture* (New York: Routledge, 1998), 440.

20. Wu Tzu-mu, "Dreaming of Splendors in the Midst of Deprivation," quoted in Yoshinobu Shiba, *Commerce and Society*, 20.

21. Li Yuan Pi, "Guide to County Magistrates," quoted in Yoshinobu Shiba, *Commerce and Society*, 172.

22. Lewis, *China's Cosmopolitan Empire*, 97.

23. Witold Rodzinski, *The Walled Kingdom: A History of China from Antiquity to the Present* (New York: The Free Press, 1984), 103.

24. Ou-yang Hsiu, "The Continuation of the Comprehensive Mirror," quoted in Yoshinobu Shiba, *Commerce and Society*, 195.

25. Yoshinobu Shiba, *Commerce and Society*, 188.

26. Kaisaburo Hino and Yasushi Kusano, "Ho-pen in the Tang–Song Period," *Journal of Oriental Research*, June 1958, 57.

27. Kaisaburo Hino and Yasushi Kusano, "Ho-pen in the Tang–Song Period," 59.

28. Shepard B. Clough, *European Economic History: The Economic Development of Western Civilization* (New York: McGraw-Hill, 1968), 161.

29. Hugh B. O'Neill, *Companion to Chinese History* (New York: Facts on File, 1987), 303.

30. *What Life Was Like in the Land of the Dragon* (New York: Time-Life, 1998), 123.

6. Western Europe and a "New World" of Profit

1. Edwin S. Hunt and James Murray, *A History of Business in Medieval Europe, 1200–1550* (Cambridge: Cambridge University Press, 1999), 102.

2. R. Emmett Taylor, *No Royal Road: Luca Pacioli and His Times* (Chapel Hill: University of North Carolina Press, 1942), 397.

3. Emma Carlson Berne, *Christopher Columbus: The Voyage That Changed the World* (New York: Sterling, 2008), 29.

4. Steven G. Anderson, *New Strategies for Social Innovation: Market-based Approaches for Assisting the Poor* (New York: Columbia University Press, 2014), 145.

5. Christopher Columbus, *Journal of Christopher Columbus (During His First Voyage, 1492–93) and Documents Relating to the Voyages of John Cabot and Gaspar Corte Real*, Trans. Clements R. Markham (Cambridge: Cambridge University Press, 2010), 73.

6. Francisco López de Gómara. *Cortés, the Life of the Conqueror* (Berkeley: University of California Press, 1965). By 1552, Columbus's "discovery of the Indies," in the words of Spanish historian Francisco López de Gómara, was hailed as "the greatest event since the creation of the world." Quoted in M. Carmen Gomez-Galisteo, *Early Visions and Representations of America: Alvar Nunez Cabeza de Vaca's Naufragios and William Bradford's Of Plymouth Plantation* (New York: Bloomsbury, 2013), 1.

7. Ian Chaston, *Entrepreneurship and Innovation During Austerity: Surviving Beyond the Great Recession* (Basingstoke, UK: Palgrave Macmillan, 2013), 46.

8. J. H. Elliott, *Spain and Its World, 1500–1700* (New Haven, CT: Yale University Press, 1989), 34.

9. Richard A. Luecke, *Scuttle Your Ships Before Advancing: And Other Lessons from History on Leadership and Change for Today's Managers* (New York: Oxford University Press, 1994).

10. López de Gómara, *Cortes: The Life of the Conqueror*, 58.

11. David Graeber, *Debt: The First 5,000 Years* (New York: Melville House Publishing, 2014), 316.

12. Hernán Cortés, *Hernán Cortés: Letters from Mexico*, trans. and ed. Anthony Pagden (New Haven, CT: Yale University Press, 2001), 35.

13. Luecke, *Scuttle Your Ships*, 29.

14. Dauril Alden, *Colonial Roots of Modern Brazil* (Oakland: University of California Press, 1973), 171.

15. Ibid., 21.

16. Joel Schapira, David Schapira, and Karl Schapira, *The Book of Coffee and Tea*, Second Revised Edition (New York: St. Martin's, 1996), 161.

17. Donald W. Fryer and James C. Jackson, *Indonesia*, Nations of the Modern World Series (London: Benn/Westview, 1998), 37.

18. Jeroen Molenaar, "Antique Share, Worth as Much as $764,000, Found by Student," *Bloomberg Business*, September 10, 2010.

19. Ian Burnet, *Spice Islands: The History, Romance and Adventure of the Spice Trade Over 2000 Years* (Kenthurst, NSW, Australia: Rosenberg, 2013).

20. Fryer and Jackson, *Indonesia*, 39.

21. Roland J. Wenzlhuemer, "Colonialism: History," in *Encyclopedia of the Developing World*, ed. Thomas M. Leonard (New York: Routledge, 2006), 362.

22. Eric Williams, *From Columbus to Castro: The History of the Caribbean 1492–1969* (New York: Vintage, 1984), 72.

23. Immortalized in Alexandre Dumas's *The Three Musketeers*.

24. Quoted in Ronen Gafni and Simcha Gluck, *The New Entrepreneurz: Changing the Way You Play Life* (Hoboken, NJ: Wiley, 2014), 141.

25. C. W. Newbury, *The Western Slave Coast and Its Rulers* (Oxford: Clarendon Press, 1961), 25.

26. Walter Sydney Sichel, *Disraeli: A Study in Personality and Ideas* (London: Methuen, 1904), 54.

27. William Manchester, *The Last Lion: Winston Spencer Churchill: Visions of Glory, 1874–1932* (Boston: Little, Brown, 1983), 48.

28. Rebecca Fraser, *The Story of Britain: From the Romans to the Present: A Narrative History* (New York: Norton, 2003), 326.

29. Williams, *From Columbus to Castro*, 144.

30. Brian Gardner, *The East India Company* (New York: Barnes & Noble, 1971), 23.

31. Ibid.

32. Ibid., 19.

33. K. G. Davies, *Royal African Company* (New York: Atheneum, 1970), 346.

7. Captains of the Revolution

1. Joseph Alois Schumpeter, *Business Cycles: A Theoretical, Historical, and Statistical Analysis of the Capitalist Process* (Philadelphia: Porcupine Press, 1939).

2. Tom Kelley and Jonathan Littman, *The Ten Faces of Innovation* (New York: Currency Doubleday, 2005), 4.

3. *Manchester Mercury*, January 6, 1784.

4. William Rosen, *The Most Powerful Idea in the World* (New York: Random House, 2010), 71.

5. Kirkpatrick Sale, *Rebels Against the Future* (Boston: Addison-Wesley, 1995), 25.

6. Ibid.

7. Ibid., 30.

8. Israel M. Kirzner, *Competition and Entrepreneurship* (Chicago: University of Chicago Press, 1973), 47.

9. Erasmus Darwin to Matthew Boulton, April 5, 1778, MS 3782/13/53/87 (Library of Birmingham, Birmingham, UK).

10. Asa Briggs, *The Age of Improvement* (Boston: Addison-Wesley, 1959), 25.

11. Kelley and Littman, *The Ten Faces of Innovation*, 6.

12. Rosen, *Most Powerful Idea*, 234.

13. Shepard Bancroft Clough, *European Economic History: The Economic Development of Western Civilization* (New York: McGraw-Hill, 1968), 280.

14. Robert Chambers, ed., *The Book of Days: A Miscellany of Popular Antiquities*, (London: W. & R. Chambers, 1832), 648.

15. Ibid., 649.

16. Ibid., 650.

17. Ibid., 649.

18. Tom Peters, *The Circle of Innovation* (New York: Knopf, 1997), 118.

19. Paul Langford, *Eighteenth Century Britain: A Very Short Introduction* (Oxford: Oxford University Press, 1984), 40.

20. Jackson Lear, *Fables of Abundance: A Cultural History of Advertising in America* (New York: Basic, 1994), 43.

21. John Ramsay McCulloch, *A Statistical Account of the British Empire*, vol. 1 (London: Charles Knight, 1839), 648.

8. The Land of (Entrepreneurial) Opportunity

1. Allan Nevins and Henry Steele Commager, *A Short History of the United States* (New York: Knopf, 1976), 269.

2. Stephen B. Goddard, *Colonel Albert Pope and His American Dream Machines: The Life and Times of a Bicycle Tycoon Turned Automotive Pioneer* (Jefferson, NC: McFarland, 2008), 86.

3. James Mackay, *Little Boss: A Life of Andrew Carnegie* (Edinburgh: Mainstream, 2012), 9.

4. David Nasaw, *Andrew Carnegie* (New York: Penguin, 2006), 413.

5. Andrew Carnegie, *The Gospel of Wealth, and Other Timely Essays* (New York: Century, 1901), 68.

6. Ron Chernow, *Titan: The Life of John D. Rockefeller, Sr.* (New York: Random House, 1998), 32.

7. Albert Z. Carr, *John D. Rockefeller's Secret Weapon* (New York: McGraw-Hill, 1962), 23.

8. Neil Baldwin, *Edison: Inventing the Century* (Chicago: University of Chicago Press, 2001), 137.

9. Henry Ford and Samuel Crowther, *My Life and Work* (Garden City, NY: Doubleday, Page, 1922), 49.

10. *Automobile Quarterly* 10, no. 4, 1972, 384.

11. Jack Welch and Suzy Welch, *Winning* (New York: HarperBusiness), 216.

12. Fletcher Dobyns, *The Amazing Story of Repeal: An Exposé of the Power of Propaganda* (Chicago: Willett, Clark, 1940), 255.

13. Herbert Hoover, *American Individualism* (Garden City, NY: Doubleday, Page, 1922), 9.

14. Robert Greenfield, *The Last Sultan: The Life and Times of Ahmet Ertegun* (New York: Simon & Schuster, 2011), 37.

15. Dorothy Wade and Justine Picardie, *Music Man: Ahmet Ertegun, Atlantic Records, and the Triumph of Rock 'n' Roll* (New York: Norton, 1990), 39.

16. Neal Gabler, *An Empire of Their Own* (New York: Crown, 1988), 53.

17. AnnaLee Saxenian, Regional Advantage: Culture and Competition in Silicon Valley and Route 128, (Cambridge, MA: Harvard University Press, 1994), 61.

18. Steve Jobs, "You've Got to Find What You Love, Jobs Says," *Stanford Report*, June 14, 2005.

19. Walter Isaacson, *Steve Jobs* (New York: Simon & Schuster, 2011), 160.

20. Steve Jobs, interview with the Santa Clara Valley Historical Association, 1994.

9. Flattening the World and Colonizing Space

1. Thomas Friedman, "The World Is Flat: Some Second Thoughts" (lecture, Williams College, Williamstown, MA, April 10, 2006).

2. Mark Magnier, Lingling Wei, and Peter Evans, "China Confronts 'New Normal' of Slower Growth," *Wall Street Journal*, January 20, 2015.

3. Malcolm Moore, "Warren Buffett's Support Helps Make Wang Chuanfu China's Richest Man," *Daily Telegraph*, September 28, 2009.

4. Hu Shuli and Li Xuena, "New-Energy Car Market Is Open Road, BYD CEO Wang Chuanfu Says," *Caixin*, September 16, 2014.

5. Gideon Long, "Latin America Catches Entrepreneurial Fever," BBC, January 9, 2014.

6. Thomas H. Becker, *Doing Business in the New Latin America: A Guide to Cultures, Practices, and Opportunities* (Westport, CT: Praeger, 2004), 101.

7. Lauren Gibbons Paul, "The IPO Dash," *CIO*, February 15, 2001, 161.

8. "Endeavor Entrepreneur Marcos Galperin on MercadoLibre (World Economic Forum Report)" (Endeavor Global, Inc., May 25, 2011). http://www.endeavor.org /entrepreneurs/mercadolibre-wef-report/.

9. Ibid.

10. Vijay Mahajan, *Africa Rising: How 900 Million African Consumers Offer More Than You Think* (Philadelphia: Wharton School Publishing, 2009), 21.

11. Isabelle Paradis, "Interview: Funke Opeke—CEO Main One Cable," *Total Telecom*, October 2012.

12. Benjamin Omoike, "Raising $240M for MainOne was nightmarish," *Newswatch Times*, June 15, 2014.

13. Douglas Farah and Stephen Braun, *Merchant of Death: Money, Guns, Planes, and the Man Who Makes War Possible* (Hoboken, NJ: Wiley, 2007), 8.

14. Craig Hall, *The Responsible Entrepreneur: How to Make Money and Make a Difference* (Wayne, NJ: Career Press, 2011), 83.

15. Kathleen Davis, "A Startup World: The Top 20 Entrepreneurial Hot Spots Around the Globe," *Entrepreneur*, August 14, 2013.

16. Chris Impey, *Beyond: Our Future in Space* (New York: Norton, 2015), 76.

17. "SABRE: How It Works," Reaction Engines, accessed on August 13, 2015, www. reactionengines.co.uk/sabre_howworks.html.

18. Jane Wells, "One giant leap for . . . private, inflatable space housing," CNBC, March 13, 2015.

19. Ibid.

20. "Wired Science: Interview with Elon Musk," PBS, 2007.

21. Ashlee Vance, *Elon Musk, Tesla, SpaceX, and the Quest for a Fantastic Future* (New York: HarperCollins, 2015), 135.

22. "Branson Reaches for the Stars," *The Guardian*, September 27, 2004.

23. Guy Norris Orlando, "Lessons Learned: SpaceShip Two's Accident Findings to Benefit Safety of 'Fledgling' Commercial Space Industry," *Aviation Week & Space Technology*, August 3–16, 2015, 29.

24. Ibid., 30.

25. Ibid.

26. Index page, Blue Origin, accessed on August 13, 2015 https://www.blueorigin.com/.

27. Vance, *Elon Musk, Tesla*, app. 3, 189.

Conclusion

1. Anna Grandori and Laura Gaillard Giordani, *Organizing Entrepreneurship* (New York: Routledge, 2011), 48.

ACKNOWLEDGMENTS

First of all, I would like to thank my wife Miriam, my daughter Laura, my parents Peter and Sarah, and my brother Amos for their warmth and encouragement over the course of this project. Secondly, I extend my heartfelt gratitude to Myles Thompson, the publisher of Columbia University Press (CUP), for granting me the opportunity to work with such an esteemed publishing house. I am also grateful to Stephen Wesley, CUP's associate editor, for his excellent editorial assistance. I would also like to thank Cathy Felgar, Ben Kolstad, Julia Kushnirsky, and all other staff at Columbia and its affiliates who were involved with this project.

Mindy Flanagan, coordinator of the University of California, San Diego's Business Internships for International Students program, deserves considerable credit for facilitating the internships of Jane Chang, Richa Kurana, Ignacio Serra, Koki Tsutsumi, and Shiraho Yanagi. The aforementioned students assisted with some of the wide array of research tasks entailed by a project of this scope. Ms. Yanagi, who not only assisted with research but also helped translate some pertinent Japanese historical writings that had never been translated into English before, deserves special acknowledgment in this regard. As well, thanks to Yayi Hsu for assisting with the promotion of the project.

I also owe a debt of gratitude to the helpful librarians at the Central Library in downtown San Diego, the Copley Library at the University of San Diego, the Rudolph East Asian Library at the University of California, Los Angeles, and the Perry-Castañeda Library at the University of Texas, Austin. I would also like to thank the legendary investor, entrepreneur, and author John Bogle for taking the time to peruse earlier drafts of this work and offer his feedback and enthusiasm.

Other family members that I would like to acknowledge include my mother-in-law Anna, Uncle Bob and Aunt Monica, Aunt Eliane, my sisters-in-law Megan and Regina, my brother-in-law Sergio, Jane, Mauricio, Bruna, Isabella, Mark and Jennifer, Susan and Les, Dafna, Paul and Cathy, Marco and Corinne, Laure and George, Adrien, Genevieve, Anthony, Phillipe, the Ledermans, Kings, Cherniaks, Fullers, Albert and Patricia Kadosh, Miriam's extended family, and others.

Last, but certainly not least, I would like to thank my friends and colleagues: Robert Bell, Simon Eisner, Jeremy Tiefenbrun, Nicky Allison, Russ Weinzimmer, Ieden and Harlen Wall, Nisha Sawhney, Tom and Audra Flaherty, Eric Cohen, Joseph Calandro, Cheri Hill, Hannah Bui, Ron Hall, Asten Izumi, Ryan Caudill, Nathan Stinson, Jerry Ryan, Mark Oliver Yu, Oren Paz, Alejandro Martinez, Dean Linden, Uriel Cohen, Thomas Napier, Jon Davis, Heath, and Lori.

INDEX